BRITAIN'S *100* BEST RAILWAY STATIONS

BRITAIN'S *100* BEST RAILWAY STATIONS

SIMON JENKINS

VIKING
an imprint of
PENGUIN BOOKS

VIKING

UK | USA | Canada | Ireland | Australia
India | New Zealand | South Africa

Viking is part of the Penguin Random House group of companies whose
addresses can be found at global.penguinrandomhouse.com.

First published 2017
001

Copyright © Simon Jenkins, 2017
The moral right of the author has been asserted

Grateful acknowledgement is made for the extract from 'Middlesex' from
Collected Poems, by John Betjeman © 1955, 1958, 1962, 1964, 1968, 1970, 1979,
1981, 1982, 2001. Reproduced by permission of John Murray, an imprint
of Hodder and Stoughton Ltd

Set in 11.5/15 Hoefler Txt by Jouve
Printed in Italy by Printer Trento S.r.l.

A CIP catalogue record for this book is available from the British Library

ISBN: 978–0–241–97898–6

www.greenpenguin.co.uk

Penguin Random House is committed to a
sustainable future for our business, our readers
and our planet. This book is made from Forest
Stewardship Council® certified paper.

To Dashiell

CONTENTS

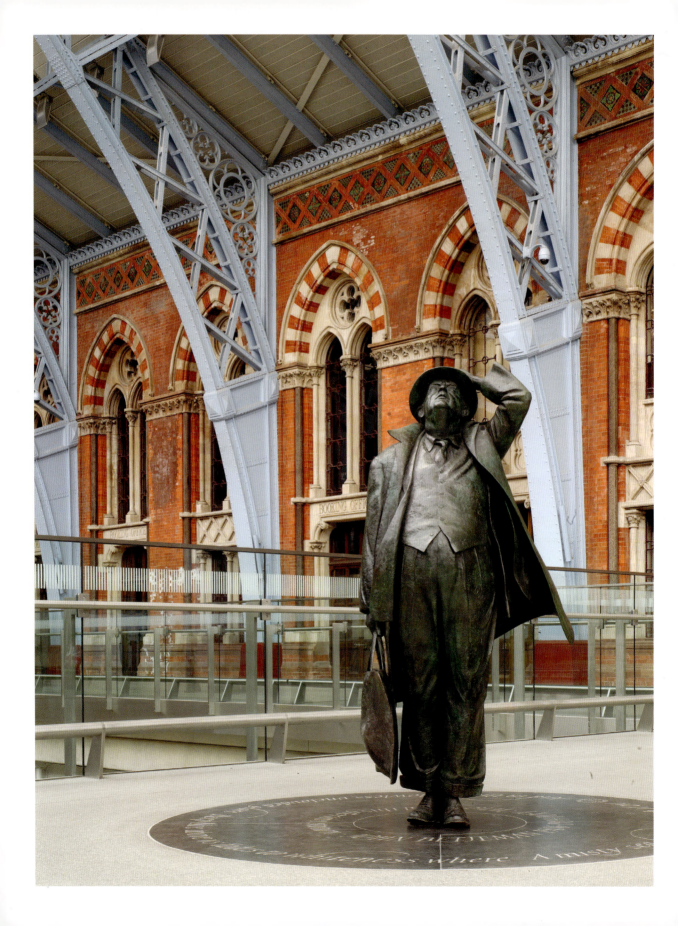

INTRODUCTION:

THE GREAT JOURNEY

Arrivals and Departures

The camera sweeps over a desert of glass roofing, curving into the distance under a smog-laden sky. Slowly it focuses on a figure moving purposefully along a catwalk. He reaches a wall of chimneys, behind which is hidden a row of beehives. Gingerly he removes a shelf of bees and the camera peers inside at the swarm. The bees start to fade. They mutate into humans, hundreds of them, seething far below his feet.

Thus opens John Schlesinger's documentary *Terminus*, filmed at Waterloo station in 1961. But his humans are never a swarm. To the director's lens, each becomes an individual. We see a tramp searching a bin for rubbish. An executive walks to find his chauffeured car. Prisoners are marshalled aboard a carriage. A small boy's face crumples into tears as he realises he has lost his mother. A young woman awaits a lover with flowers, and we watch her growing despair as he fails to arrive. The flowers are left under a seat.

Schlesinger sees Waterloo as theatre. People rush, people work, people wait. Every face conveys emotion. Britons are normally restrained in public. But a station is a place of permitted extroversion, for displays of elation and dismay, greeting and parting, all united in submission to the discipline of time, to the gods of the clock. And Schlesinger embraces characters no longer present today, a cavalcade of towering, roaring, clanking warhorses, straining at every pipe and piston: the steam engines.

For much of the last century, such stations seemed, like the railways of which they were part, in long-term decline. At the time when Schlesinger was filming, steam railways were a mode of transport fast giving way to roads, cars and planes. Stations were their fading presence in the community. Almost all were Victorian buildings and, as such, represented all that the 20th century was expected to leave behind. They were scruffy, below-stairs Cinderellas. No one invited them to the transport ball.

As we shall see, that is no longer the case. The railway fought back. By the start of the 21st century, a revival was in full swing, with passenger numbers passing their post-war peak. Clean electricity was supplanting oil as the engine's energy source. A Channel Tunnel had been built. For the first time since the Victorian age, there was talk of new rail corridors, both north–south and east–west. As the railway acquired a new significance, so did its stations. They were its public face, scrubbed of soot and dereliction, no longer demolished but restored and admired. A station building was recognised as architecture in own right, sometimes vernacular, sometimes grand.

I see the station as did Schlesinger, not just as a building but as a social phenomenon, a place where people perform the timeless rituals, not just of travelling, but of congregating, working, playing, greeting and parting. A station is a public stage of human contact, ever more prominent in what is called the age of hypermobility. It is once again at the heart of British life.

Early days

Britain's railways were born in virtually their present form over an astonishingly short period of time, from the mid-1830s to the mid-1840s. Their immediate precursors were the tramways of the 18th century, when mine and quarry wagons were drawn by horses along wooden and then iron guide tracks. Early attempts at steam traction, such as Richard Trevithick's 1807 engine in Merthyr Tydfil, had foundered on rail fractures. Even when George Stephenson initiated the first steam-hauled wagons between Stockton and Darlington in 1825, his engine, *Locomotion*, was used only for freight. Passenger carriages were gingerly drawn by horses. The innovation was at first viewed sceptically. The Duke of Wellington declared, 'I see no reason to suppose that these machines will ever force themselves into general use.'

The first regular steam passenger railway was the Liverpool to Manchester line in 1830, again initiated by George Stephenson. Here it used a new engine, *Rocket*, built by George's son, Robert, winner of the dramatic Rainhill trials held outside Liverpool the year before. *Rocket* was an instant success. Where Trevithick's engine had been too heavy for its rails, Stephenson's power–weight ratio was satisfactory. The technology was in place for a revolution. For all the credit given to the Victorians for creating the railway revolution, it was strictly a Georgian one.

Two years later, in 1832, Britain experienced a political upheaval following the Great Reform Act. It delivered a new parliament whose mercantilist members adopted railways as a symbol of their modernity and radicalism. In just two years, it approved 380 miles of track, including Robert Stephenson's London & Birmingham company and Isambard Kingdom Brunel's Great Western. By 1836, rail fever had taken hold and 1,500 miles of track were approved.

Overnight, these railways supplanted the improved turnpike roads and canals of the 18th century's industrial revolution. The latter had facilitated an explosion in manufacturing and trade, but the railway was on a different scale. It was a leap in the dark, requiring unprecedented sums of investment, with potentially vast returns. New lines were not planned by any agency of government. Parliament left them to entrepreneurs, wherever they thought money was to be made. MPs merely sped them on their way by granting the new companies extraordinary compulsory purchase powers for their lines of route – powers unheard of on the Continent. It was the moment in British economic history when capital usurped property as the engine of growth. An Englishman's home was no longer his invulnerable castle.

The first railway lines were designed simply to cross countryside at speed and minimum cost. Construction was mostly a matter of bridges, tunnels and viaducts. The first proper stations were shelters, with sheds for engines and warehouses for goods. Station buildings for passengers were not high priorities. Tickets were often sold at wayside inns, as on stage coaches. Steps up to 'carriages' assisted 'boarding' and 'alighting' – railway terms borrowed, ever since, from the coach trade.

The earliest building to claim railway use is a simple brick shed honoured with a small plaque in Stockton, but Britain's oldest proper station, dating from 1830, is Manchester's Liverpool Road. (The title of the world's oldest station is claimed, by a matter of weeks, for Mount Clare in Baltimore, USA.) It stands today, an unobtrusive and dignified Georgian townhouse, with its track concealed on a viaduct behind. First-class passengers entered through the front door, with a smart ticket desk and waiting-room. Second-class passengers entered by a side door. Some trains even offered flat trucks on to which gentry could load their personal carriages, with their horses carried in separate wagons. The Duke of Portland was said never to have left his carriage from door to door.

The first railway bubble burst in 1837, the year of Queen Victoria's accession. Speculative money vanished. For five years, the supply of

J.H.Nixon, del.

THE BIRMIN

The East end of the Tunnel, from

HAM RAILWAY.
Primrose Hill, taken October, 1837.

J. Cleghorn, sc.

By rail to the capital: Primrose Hill tunnel

new railway bills dried as investors waited to see what would happen. But the seeds had been sown. Surveyors, engineers and navvies fanned out across the land to get the approved lines built and running. An entirely new industry sprang into being, virtually overnight.

The men who led this first railway boom were unconventional outsiders, money-men, speculators, agents and contractors. Four were dominant. George Stephenson was a Northumbrian engineer whose faith in the new form of traction was total and hugely influential. Almost every company sought his advice. Although he died in 1848, he was justly known as 'father of the railways'. His brilliant son, Robert, became chief engineer of the London & Birmingham in 1833 at the age of twenty-nine, on a salary of £1,500 a year (roughly £150,000 today). He went on to work on no fewer than sixty railways, including in Latin America, and was involved in building roughly a third of Britain's early network. From humble beginnings, Robert Stephenson became a Tory MP and a member of the Athenaeum Club, and dined with the Queen.

Isambard Kingdom Brunel was the son of a French immigrant engineer, talented and headstrong (see pp. 140–41). He was engineer to the new Great Western Railway at the age of twenty-six and turned it into a one-man powerhouse of railways and ship-building. His errors were costly, like his atmospheric railway (see p. 145) and his choice of a wide-gauge track. But his energy and work rate were prodigious. Like Robert Stephenson, with whom he was friends, he burned out in his mid-fifties and died the same year, 1859.

Fourth of the quartet was an entrepreneur, a brash Yorkshire draper turned railway promoter, George Hudson. Dubbed the 'Railway King', Hudson turned his attention to railways in 1834 having met George Stephenson, and shot to prominence, not so much by building as by merging with or gobbling up rivals. Within a decade, from bases first in York and then in Derby, he gained effective control of half the new railway network, north to Carlisle, east to Ipswich and south to Bristol. Hudson became immensely rich, was elected MP for Sunderland and lived in a Knightsbridge mansion, now the French embassy. His fall into bankruptcy, fraud and imprisonment in 1849 was sensational. Eventually, his debts were met by a coal-mine owner; ironically, his son was killed by a train.

The first railway building boom, instigated by the 1837 bubble, peaked in 1840–41. By then, London was linked to Birmingham, Birmingham to Manchester and Manchester to Liverpool. Yorkshire was crossing the Pennines to Lancashire. London was going to Bristol. Trains ran south from the capital to Brighton and Southampton. In the process, the first tranche of investment was consumed and the railway seemed to pause for breath. The routes approved in 1835–6 had proved mostly profitable, with some paying shareholders what were considered huge dividends of 10–12 per cent. Soon the industry was again straining at the leash, as if readying itself for a new burst of expansion.

The Mania

At the start of 1843, money suddenly surged back into railway shares, leading to a stock market boom on a scale not seen since the South Sea Bubble of 1720. It was spurred on its way by William Gladstone's 1844 bill instituting the joint stock company, which allowed companies to be formed by shareholders without needing a full act of parliament as previously. They did, however, need an act to compel landowners to surrender rights of way. This was followed by the introduction of limited liability, liberating company directors from ruin if they went bankrupt. These reforms galvanised British capitalism and were a crucial boost to rail investment.

Wherever rich men gathered together, they plotted a railway. In the newly reformed parliament, lobbyists for the 'railway interest' roamed the corridors, their pockets lined with cash, and bulldozed all opposition. Compulsory purchase over-rode the once powerful landed interest. Aristocratic estates lived in terror of seeing surveyors on the horizon. A writer to *Fraser's Magazine* told of 'young men with theodolites and chains marching about fields; long white sticks with bits of paper attached were carried ruthlessly through fields, gardens, and sometimes even through houses.' Only in Russia was railway building more tyrannical. When the Tsar was consulted on a route from St Petersburg to Moscow, he laid his sword on the map, drew a line between them and declared, '*Voilà, votre chemin de fer!*'

The Mania had an electrifying impact on society. A Victorian historian, John Francis, recorded that 'the most cautious of men . . . heard the cry at every dinner, uttered by solemn, solid men, upon the glories of the rail; they read of princes mounting tenders, of peers as provisional committeemen, of marquesses trundling wheelbarrows and of privy councillors cutting turf on correct geometrical principles. Their clerks left them to become railway jobbers. Their domestic servants studied railway journals. They saw the whole world railway mad.' The period became known as the Mania, by which I refer to it throughout this book.

RAIL ROADS.

In November 1845, *The Times* calculated that parliament had that year projected 1,200 new railways in Britain, notionally requiring £500m in public subscription (or £50bn today). Some were for lines along parallel routes, some for trains running the length and breadth of the land. The freedom of the market place was given the job of regulating the industry, with no attempt to impose network coherence or national plan. Massive duplication occurred. When the Great Eastern company came to be formed in 1862, it needed the amalgamation of thirty-two approved railways in East Anglia alone.

Like all such bubbles, the Mania over-reached itself, bursting in 1847. The collective value of railway stock halved in a year. Companies collapsed and tens of thousands lost their savings. A contemporary cartoon

Railway mania: John Bull drunkenly accepts proposals for investing in railways, cartoon, 1836 had Queen Victoria pleading with her weeping husband, 'Tell me, oh tell me, dearest Albert, have YOU any railway shares?' Hudson was accused of fraud and fled the country. To Karl Marx in *Das Kapital*, the Mania was 'the first great railway swindle'.

The fire did not go out. As after 1836, enough capital had been committed to instigate a renewed round of construction, more vigorous than the first. Railways were voracious for money, materials and talent. Not since the rise of the British Empire in the 18th century had opportunity so beckoned to all classes. The nation hurled itself at the challenge of conquering distance. Victory needed iron, coal, timber, bricks, quarries, factories and forges. It needed cartographers, geologists, surveyors, engineers and men who could understand and handle money.

There were never enough of these. Many builders of the new railway came from the army, as military engineers, but most recruits were apprenticed on the job, few with any qualifications or regulation. Class and provenance were no issue. It was said that when George Stephenson, a Geordie, appeared before a Commons committee, MPs could not understand him. He recalled, 'Someone asked if I was a foreigner and another hinted that I was mad.'

Above all, the railway was built by hand. It needed muscle power, that of so-called navvies (after 'navigation' canals) to blast, dig, shovel, move and rebuild the earth. It needed horses to move everything. Construction of the railway was said to employ more horses than it supplanted on the highways. The railway might be new, but its facilitator was an archaic army of men and horses, traversing across open country at speeds that amazed contemporaries. It left in its wake a landscape scarred as never before, and all for two thin ribbons of steel.

Railways rendered obsolete a pattern of human movement that had been dictated by the speed of the horse since the dawn of history. A messenger or a coach could at best cover some eight miles an hour, although by the 1830s the famous *Tally Ho* was able to boast fourteen passengers carried 110 miles from London to Birmingham in eleven hours. Robert Stephenson's train could take 300 people in half that time, at a speed initially limited to 22 mph. Trains were soon running at 30 mph, while the Great Western and other lines rapidly reached 60 mph. The stage coach was dead.

Railways were noisy, dirty and, to many people, terrifying. There were frequent accidents. Thomas Carlyle described travelling from the Lake District to Euston as 'nine hours of tempestuous deafening and nightmare, like hours of Jonah in a whale's belly, flung out in Euston Square, stupefied for weeks to come'. Prince Albert travelled to Windsor to court Queen Victoria by a train in 1839, but she at first refused point blank to travel in one. In 1842, however, she took a train from Windsor to London and declared it 'free from dust and crowds and heat, and I am quite charmed with it'. But she forbade any train in which she was travelling from going faster than 40 mph.

Human experience was no longer circumscribed by physical distance. It had to obey not the sunrise but the national clock. Time had to be standardised as 'railway time', based on Greenwich. An early GWR timetable warned, 'London Time is kept at all Stations, which is 4 minutes earlier than Reading time, 7 minutes before Cirencester time, 11 minutes before Bath and Bristol time.' Universities and the Church generally opposed the coming of railways as immoral, so much so that Oxford's Christ Church cathedral to this day refuses to acknowledge railway time, still starting services five minutes 'late'.

The speed of transport fractured old patterns of trade. New markets opened to agriculture and industry alike. Track-side electric telegraphs were soon able to take the communication of information from the age of the horse to that of the internet. The new union of England, Scotland and Ireland was joined as never before, in bonds of steel. The centralisation of British government on the nation's capital received an almighty boost.

The railway tore open contemporary society. It redefined geographical identity and rewrote the conversation between London and the nation, town and country, rich and poor. It also introduced a new realm of classlessness. The Liverpool & Manchester's segregation of passengers in different buildings did not last. Two (initially three) classes of waiting-rooms and carriages survived, but the concourse, ticket office and platform became, like the church nave and the market place, a common space.

Travel beyond the bounds of one village or town had been confined to a few, mostly prosperous, people. Most humans lived, worked, played and died within single communities. Travel now became an obsession, abetted by Thomas Cook's innovation of rail excursions in the 1850s (see pp. 189–90). A train journey merged a private voyage with a public one, a coming together of people in the act of moving apart. Bradshaw's railway timetable, first published in 1839, was the Bible of the new mobility. It enjoyed pride of place on the family shelf, and was hallowed by Sherlock Holmes. Britain had acquired a new social congress, a national glue, under the aegis of the great god time.

In the fifteen years after 1832, an astonishing 4,000 miles of track were laid across Britain – without a bulldozer, a steam shovel or planning inspector in sight. A century later, it was to take teams of highly mechanised road-builders forty years to complete half that distance of motorway. And the job was done. By the 1850s, the skeleton of the national network recognisable today was complete.

The stations of the Mania

While the 1830s' boom produced mostly modest halts and wooden sheds, the 1840s' Mania saw more substantial stations being built. In bigger towns, structures were needed to cover trains and passengers together, as well as to display the ambitions of the new railway companies. The first requirement was a roof, quaintly called a 'shed', as are railway roofs to this day. With multiple tracks and platforms, these could be of unprecedented expanse. As the rail historian Christian Barman wrote, 'Not since the days of the great cathedrals had the constructors of buildings been faced with such a challenge.' Britain was suddenly to see structures on a scale not seen since the Middle Ages.

The early sheds were wonders of both engineering and materials science, notably at Newcastle, York and Paddington. They were being designed coincidentally with Joseph Paxton's 1851 Crystal Palace in Hyde Park. Brunel and Robert Stephenson both served on the Crystal Palace building committee, and Brunel sought to poach its engineers, among them the outstanding Charles Fox, for his Great Western company. Newcastle's John Dobson immersed himself in ironworks to invent malleable ribs for the world's first curved iron vault.

Elsewhere, new stations created enclaves, usually on the outskirts of towns, that developed a society of their own. They comprised ticket halls, waiting-rooms, staff housing, goods yards, warehouses and signalboxes, as well as stabling for engines, carriages and horses. Stations acquired some of the characteristics of a secular church, with its buildings, liturgies, priests and acolytes privy to the mysteries of an awesome technology. This demanded quasi-military discipline, without which the trains could not safely run. Uniforms were worn throughout. Hierarchy and obedience were absolute. Staff could not leave their posts until relieved. Signalmen were the most respected members of this clerisy.

Their life-and-death status was recognised with powers similar to those of police constables, and some were even known by the police nickname of 'bobbies' (after the founder of the police, Sir Robert Peel).

In smaller towns, the arrival of the railway was more of an event. The stationmaster was ranked below only the squire, the parson and the doctor, and his residence reflected this status. On the eccentric Ipswich to Bury line, stationmasters' houses even mimicked local manor houses (see p. 164). The smallest village and rural stations were the jewels of the railway. They remained true to the vernacular tradition of the earliest halts, often borrowing their character from their neighbourhoods. To Barman, 'No country in the world has a collection of minor stations that begins to compare.' None has a Stamford, a Boxhill or an Eggesford.

As for what should serve as the architectural style of the new railway, no one knew. During the first boom in the 1830s, station-builders took their cue from the prevailing Regency classicism. This was soberly late-Georgian at Manchester's Liverpool Road, grandly Doric at Euston, vaguely Italianate at Brighton. The last was so popular for early stations that Italianate was even dubbed 'railway style'. It seems to have conveyed reassurance to nervous early passengers.

At the time, however, Italianate was challenged by the Romantic taste for rusticity and the picturesque. John Nash and the Wyatt family were promoting decorative gothic, which became fashionable after the publication in 1833 of John Claudius Loudon's *Encyclopaedia of Cottage, Farm and Villa Architecture*. It popularised a stylistic pot-pourri of Tudor, gothic and Italianate, summed up in the concept of the *cottage orné*. Old-fashioned, familiar, even twee, Loudon's pattern-book designs were a god-send to frantic railway engineers, charged with getting their lines built and into service in a matter of months. It gave their stations a quaint, soft-edged personality. Euston's Grecian pomp gave way to Temple Meads quaint. It was as if Marie Antoinette had gate-crashed Brunel's drawing office.

In 1836, Augustus Welby Pugin published his architectural manifesto, *Contrasts*, calling for a full-blown revival of north European gothic. He dismissed the prevailing classicism as un-Christian, pagan. Although initially addressed to the Church, Pugin's message seeped into every branch of architecture and design. It swept over royal palaces, country houses and urban terraces. It obsessed the commissioners of the new parliament buildings at Westminster in 1836. The classicism of America's

Battle of styles: Greek Euston, *cottage orné* Caterham, French Slough

Capitol building, then being extended, was condemned as republican, if not French revolutionary.

Hence, at the very moment when the railway was seeking to find a new architectural language to express its confidence and dynamism, Victorian aesthetics offered no answer. The railway was enveloped by what came to be called the 'battle of the styles'. Mania entrepreneurs might regard this as a matter of scant importance. They did not need architects who hobnobbed with aristocratic or ecclesiastical patrons or perused sketches of the Grand Tour. The times required them to be practical men. But they still needed buildings, and where there was a building there had to be a style.

The *Builder* magazine, the journal of the trade, complained constantly about the lack of 'architects' on the railway, but it was a term of nuance rather than a classification. In the mid-19th century, architects, engineers and surveyors were not regulated professions. Railway companies certainly asked well-known names to design their hotels, such as Philip Hardwick at Paddington, Alfred Waterhouse at Liverpool and Sir George Gilbert Scott at St Pancras. Actual stations were mostly left to men who were first and foremost civil engineers, such as David Mocatta, Charles Driver, Francis Thompson, Thomas Penson and George Andrews. Most were employed by a single company but some, such as the elusive Thompson, worked for many. Only Sir William Tite and Scotland's remarkable James Miller were recognised architects with practices extending well beyond the railway.

As a result, the appearance of the British station, from the 1830s through to the 1880s, can only be called promiscuously eclectic. Brunel would sketch a design during a stopover at an inn, and hand it to his master mason to execute. His Bristol terminus was in neo-Tudor, his Bath station neo-Jacobean and his Paddington roof that of a gothic cathedral. In the south-east, David Mocatta was playfully Italianate. East Anglia's Sancton Wood showed a preference for Jacobean/Dutch renaissance. In the north, Hudson's architect, George Andrews, was elegantly classical. One of the few historians to study railway buildings, the American Carroll L. V. Meeks, even detected three stylistic periods, those of 'early, middle and late picturesque eclecticism'. He saw the fashions of the railway age as a ballet, 'in which sometimes one steps faster or leaps higher than the others, but all dance to the same music – the unfolding of a single tale'. It was as if station design were mimicking the undisciplined nature of the Mania itself.

The age of maturity

The railway historian Simon Bradley chose the 1860s as the time when revolution reached a sort of stability. Mergers and consolidations had turned the early companies into regional monopolies, or at least rival duopolies. New railway bills slowed to a trickle through parliament. The Great Western bestrode the west country, where it competed with the London & South Western. In the north, the London & North Western established its command over the so-called west-coast route to the Midlands and Manchester. The Lancashire & Yorkshire ruled the Pennines. The Great Northern sped over the flatlands of eastern England to Doncaster, at which point the North Eastern's territory began. Round them fussed smaller lines, some dynamic, some lethargic. The great pioneering days were over.

The station had become an established feature of the nation's life. For the railways, wrote historian Tony Judt, stations were 'their most visible incarnation, their greatest public monument . . . as organizers of space, as innovative means of accumulating and dispatching unprecedented numbers of people'. This centrality was captured in William Powell Frith's celebrated painting of Paddington in 1862. It portrayed chaos amid order, the railway as cauldron of society, young and old, rich and poor, working and leisured. Each of Frith's characters tells a story: a newly wedded couple leaving on honeymoon, a child going to school, a soldier saying farewell to his wife, a policeman arresting an escaping prisoner. Dickens in *Dombey and Son* depicted the mid-Victorian station in what could be Frith's painting: 'To and from the heart of this great change, all day and night, throbbing currents rushed and returned incessantly, like its life's blood. Crowds of people and mountains of goods, departing and arriving score upon scores of times in every four-and-twenty hours, produced a fermentation of the place that was always in action. The very houses seemed disposed to pack up and take trips.' The painting was hugely popular, touring the country and seen by 80,000 people at a shilling a view. Prints sold nationwide.

The confusion bequeathed by the Mania was now embedded in local geography. There could well be three, four or five stations even in modest towns such as Norwich, Chester or Carlisle. York and Bristol were rare in having just one. Most afflicted was London, where residential estate owners were strong enough to resist the railway's advance. The metropolis duly saw fifteen termini erected round its perimeter, a provision unique in the world. London south of the Thames remains to this day

Introduction

15

Chaos amid order: *The Railway Station*
by William Powell Frith, 1862

a crazy-paving of cross-cutting tracks, visible relics of the Mania. One advantage of this plethora was the opening in 1863 of the world's first underground railway, the Metropolitan, linking the northern and western termini to the City of London. It instantly led to a number of London companies staging a mini-Mania, with proposals before parliament for 174 miles of new track in the metropolitan area at a cost of £33m.

The rail historian John R. Kellett calculated that, if built, the 1863 proposals for London would have required 'four new bridges across the Thames and scheduled one quarter of all lands and buildings in the City of London for compulsory purchase and demolition'. Unlike in the 1840s, parliament would have none of it. It required the Metropolitan to link with the new District line to form a 'circle' line embracing almost all termini in a single circuit. Paris's Metro was not started until 1900 and New York's Subway in 1904. London was half a century in the lead.

The national network remained complex. Companies ran over each other's tracks and used each other's stations, sometimes happily, often not. A railway clearing-house had been established at Euston as early as 1842, where hundreds of clerks registered every journey over 'joint' workings and allotted revenue to companies appropriately. By the 1860s, the clearing-house was administering some 800 inter-company running agreements. Bradley notes: 'In their diversity of ownership, statutes, rights, duties, fees, privileges, exceptions, liveries, uniforms and general paraphernalia, Britain's railways at their zenith call to mind the unreformed societies of *ancien régime* France or the Holy Roman Empire.'

The contrast with the rest of Europe at the time was stark. Commercial duplication of lines and stations was chaotic, and while other countries struggled to match Britain's rampant entrepreneurialism, it at least meant that continental railways could be planned. Belgium's were nationalised from the start. Germany's had been taken over by the state by the time of Bismarck in the 1870s, when railway profits substituted for taxes to aid unification. Even in France, where government and professional conservatism stifled innovation, railways were able to benefit from centrally ordained coherence.

The same applied to stations. As Bill Fawcett conceded in his 2015 guide to railway architecture, 'In the 1880s world leadership in large station design passed to Germany, where state funding helped secure the building of central stations on a lavish scale.' While British towns and cities squabbled over building what were called 'joint' stations, most European cities were able to insist on just one 'union' station. Like opera houses, these became expressions of civic pride, displays of ever-increasing splendour. Europe saw majestic palaces of commerce rising not just in Paris, Berlin and Lisbon but in provincial cities such as Frankfurt, Antwerp, Toledo, Limoges or Leipzig. A common French joke about the British station was, '*C'est magnifique mais ce n'est pas la gare.*'

British railways may have stopped expanding, but pressure of business demanded their stations be constantly extended and rebuilt. Gordon Biddle estimates that by the 1880s some 9,000 stations and halts of various sizes had been constructed or reconstructed. Even as they grew in size, they remained similar in form. Passengers would arrive and leave under a porte cochère, full of shouting porters and stamping horses. They would pass into a ticket hall and, in the case of larger stations, on to a larger concourse.

Companies ran teashops and cafeterias, and these became notorious for their dire quality. Dickens wrote of their pies as 'bumps of delusive promise' and of 'scalding infusions satirically called tea'. Trollope excoriated 'that whited sepulchre . . . that real disgrace of England, the railway sandwich'. In 1848, William Henry Smith opened his first news-stand in Euston station. Realising that the railway could transport a commodity, news, that was as time-sensitive as passengers, he quickly secured a near-monopoly across the network. He later brought out cheap 'yellow books' designed to be read on trains. Only in 1905, when hit by the Great Western with steep rent increases, did Smith's decide to open shops on high streets. It was at Exeter station in 1935 that the young publisher Allen Lane hit on the idea of discarding cardboard in favour of paper-backing, further to lower book prices. After pondering dolphins and porpoises for the imprint, he decided on a penguin – and took the world by storm.

The largest city stations tended to be fronted by grand hotels, initially the biggest in the land, as at Liverpool, York, Glasgow and the London termini. These hotels dominated, and probably depressed, the hotel market throughout provincial Britain for over a century. Lesser stations also had to encompass company offices, giving some of them a presence they might otherwise have lacked. Examples survive at Bristol, Chester, Stoke and Perth. Smaller stations were usually composed of a single building, for passengers on one side and the stationmaster and his family on the other.

Beyond lay the business side of the station, the railway proper with its 'up' and 'down' platforms, to and from London. The origin of up and down allegedly lay in the old mine trackways, up to the pit and down to the harbour. Larger stations had vaulted sheds covering all platforms, rare versions of which remain at Beverley, Bournemouth and Carlisle. Most platforms were simply protected by glazed canopies, some with elaborate ironwork. The most extensive was at Tynemouth, the most richly decorative at Great Malvern. These canopies would usually be edged with ornamental wooden valances, reputedly a Brunel innovation, imitating a fabric pelmet. Such is their variety that their study has become a cult among enthusiasts.

As for architectural style, the mergers of the 1860s and 1870s seemed only to exaggerate the Mania's eclecticism. In the south, there was a shift from Italianate to French Renaissance, sometimes with both combined, as at Denmark Hill and Eastbourne. French influence was also strong at Slough, Norwich and Portsmouth. Italian was more secure in the north, as at Chester and Preston. Gothic at Middlesbrough, Carlisle and Perth contrasted with art nouveau at Darlington and Hull. Scottish stations varied from Flemish baronial to Swiss chalets.

A last gesture of Victorian entrepreneurialism took place on 15 March 1899, when the first train of Sir Edward Watkin's Great Central Railway steamed into London's newest, and most anti-climactic, terminus at Marylebone. A railwayman since the 1840s and a latter-day George Hudson, Watkin was on the boards of nine British railways. He built the Canadian Pacific and the Athens to Piraeus line. His final dream was to run expresses from the north of England to France through a channel tunnel. Watkin even began an Eiffel Tower at Wembley in celebration.

The Great Central was a commercial failure and Watkin's channel tunnelling foundered in the Folkestone mud. Marylebone became a national joke and narrowly avoided closure in the 1980s. Watkin died in 1901, the same year as Queen Victoria. His broken dreams marked the close of an era.

The twentieth century

The new century saw the evils of a fragmented, unregulated industry come to haunt it. A network still of some 120 separate companies was no longer fit for purpose. Trains faced growing competition from cars, lorries and motor coaches. Steel on steel was challenged by rubber on tarmac. In some places, the unthinkable began to happen. Passenger numbers started to fall.

Government inevitably began to flex its muscles. The immediate

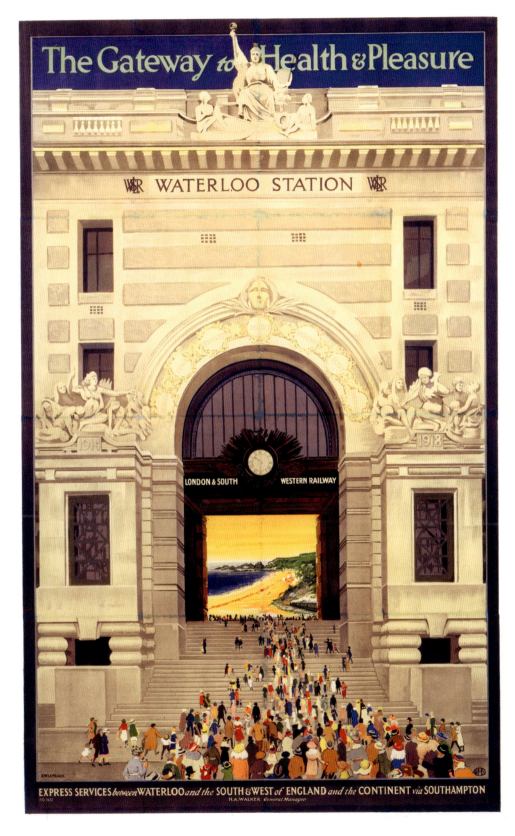

Waterloo: gateway to the post-war future

catalyst was the needs of the First World War. Troops and munitions had to be moved at speed. There was no scope for rivalry or argument. When the war was over, there was little opposition to the first systematic intervention in the industry, the 1921 Railways Act which led, two years later, to the formalising of the *de facto* regional monopolies into the so-called Grouping of four conglomerates: the London, Midland & Scottish (LMSR), the London & North Eastern (LNER), the Southern (SR) and the Great Western (GWR). Only the last was virtually unchanged, largely through its dominant presence in most of the south-west.

At the same time, stations atrophied, no longer with corporate rivalry as a spur to ostentation. Only in the south-east did the booming inter-war economy see continued expansion. Third-rail electrification of the network south of the Thames saw new stations built, while north of the Thames innovation was mostly on the suburban Underground. In the latter's case, the various companies were formally nationalised in 1933 under the London Passenger Transport Board.

For the few new stations a new aesthetic took hold. Some flirted with neo-Georgian. There were brief flourishes of art deco, as at Cardiff and Leamington Spa. But the advent of modernism saw a rejection of revivalism and of decoration in general. The boss of the new Underground, Frank Pick, recruited Charles Holden as his head of design, declaring in 1926 that London would be 'modern, not garbled classic or renaissance'. The two men visited Scandinavia in 1930 and saw its new architecture as a harbinger of a socialist society.

Holden called his stations 'brick boxes with concrete lids', as demonstrated at Southgate and Arnos Grove. Six years later, he travelled to Moscow to study Stalin's new Metro designs, but he had no truck with the dictator's bravura revivalism. The new Underground would be revolutionary and sweeping. It even embraced Edward Johnston's LT roundel and Harry Beck's 'electric circuit' Tube map, still London's most sacred design icons.

The Second World War completed what the Great War had begun. The new conglomerates were brought under state control for the duration, and nationalised in 1948. Shareholders were content to be compensated for near-worthless stock. The state acquired what was a mammoth transport corporation, embracing not just railways but docks, ferries, canals, road freight, property and the biggest hotel chain in the land. This proved so indigestible that, in 1962, the railway and its property assets were hived off into a new public corporation, British Railways. Its chairman was a former ICI executive, Dr Richard Beeching.

The early years of nationalisation have entered the country's industrial demonology. Passenger numbers continued to fall. Trains lost money. A steam-driven network fashioned in the chaos of the Mania could not compete with internal combustion and trunk roads. Steam engines were being supplanted by diesel and electricity, and were declared dead by a 1955 modernisation plan. Rural branch lines saw their market vanish to buses and motor coaches. Between 1945 and 1960, some 3,000 miles of under-used rail lines were closed, with little argument. The railway was becoming less a local service, more an inter-city and commuter one.

The railway that emerged bombed and battered from the Second World War was unlikely to spend money on stations. They were dark, dirty corners of the post-war economy, owned by 'everyone' and thus the responsibility of none. Where disused, they were demolished or left to rot. Stations lacked the untouchability of churches or the legal protection of historic buildings. In 1961, the railway's most historic building, the Doric arch at Euston, was destroyed on the decision of the prime minister, Harold Macmillan, eager to portray himself as a man of the future.

Where new buildings were needed, modernism ruled the day. The age was one of bleak economy. Gone was the day when the Southern's inter-war architect, J. R. Scott, might dabble in baroque at Waterloo, neo-Georgian at Ramsgate and art deco at Surbiton. The rebuilding of stations at Coventry, Birmingham and Euston adhered to the new party line. As railway historians Jeffrey Richards and John M. Mackenzie put it, 'The Victorians modelled their stations on cathedrals and palaces, Modern Man models his on shopping centres and office blocks.' Stylistic references to the great days of rail were anathema.

The Devastation

Hot from his demolition of the Euston arch, Macmillan took the view that a newly modernised railway should be 'made to pay'. It was a view he did not apply to the new motorway network. At British Railways, Beeching was duly instructed to this end. He produced a report in 1963 which proposed to close a further 5,000 of the 18,000 miles of Britain's rail network and 2,363 of its 7,000 remaining stations. He pointed out that some of these lines could muster barely a dozen passengers a day, and that he was merely accelerating a process already under way.

**Ice age on the branch line: passengers
made of snow,** *Punch*, 1953

The report led to an explosion of opposition and vilification – which, strictly speaking, should have been directed at Macmillan. On taking power in 1964, a new Labour government sacked Beeching, but significantly did not throw out his report. The proposals were largely implemented, including the closure of almost all the condemned lines and most of the stations. For all the abuse he received, Beeching's four years in charge of the railway were seismic. They saw the end of steam, the slimming of the regions and the creation of a new freight network. There was almost no labour unrest or service disruption and neither Beeching nor anyone else at the time could reasonably have foreseen that, a generation later, at least some of his closed lines might have a commercial future.

Public reaction to the closures crystallised nostalgia for a wider Britain that had departed with the Second World War. Beeching was the enemy of memory. As early as 1953, an Ealing comedy, *The Titfield Thunderbolt*, had depicted defiance to railway closures as a symbol of local identity and national pride. Church, squire and community were united against vulgar commercialism and a heartless state. The rebellious engine was driven by a vicar and fired by a bishop. (The film was stimulated by the rescue in 1951 of the narrow-gauge Talyllyn Railway in north Wales.) Trains and their stations had acquired the status of cottage hospitals and public libraries, woven into the blanket of the new welfare state.

Affection for railway lines rarely extended to their stations, of which 2,128 were eventually to close under Beeching. Secondary stations disappeared from cities such as Glasgow, Manchester and Nottingham. In Wales, twenty-seven stations in the Glamorgan valleys were destroyed and replaced by plastic platform shelters. Rarely was thought given to the architectural merit or possible reuse of railway buildings, almost all of which were neglected and decaying. Lucky ones survived to become offices or private homes, the best of which are listed below (see p. 45). Victorian architecture was unfashionable, especially where it fell into the category of industrial archaeology.

The 1960s and 1970s were to be dire for historic architecture generally, and there was little opposition to what became a systematic eradication of the railway's heritage. In 1977, a brave exhibition was held at London's Royal Institute of British Architects, entitled 'Off the Rails'. It called attention to the loss of historic stations by leaving them to decay and then classifying them as 'beyond reasonable repair'. It followed a similar exhibition on the loss of historic houses at the V&A Museum. The catalogue charted one tale of woe after another, including

most recently the sale for scrap of six beam pumping engines at the Severn Tunnel – 'there is no finer or more dramatic group of engines in the world' – rather than rescue and display them to the public. BR even turned down an offer of government money for repairing the roof of derelict St Pancras, lest it dilute the case for demolition.

In his 1979 study of station conservation, the founder of SAVE Britain's Heritage, Marcus Binney, described 'a downward spiral of dirt and dereliction which has dented the whole image of the railways . . . British Rail has acquired for itself an all too deserved reputation as the biggest corporate vandal and iconoclast Britain has seen since the Tudor dissolution of the monasteries.'

At the same time, little attention was given to the new buildings that replaced the old ones. Nationalisation appeared to have stripped the industry of pride. I can do no better than quote a 2015 'best station' blogger, who wondered if some heritage museum would ever see merit in commemorating the period by rescuing 'one of the old piss-stinking

Departed glory: Louth station

1970s bus-shelter-style platform buildings'. Was it conceivable, the blogger asked, that we would want to revive a restored Pacer unit on a scruffy litter-strewn platform, 'featuring Coke cans with old-school ring-pulls and polystyrene maxpax cups'. Throughout the entries in this book, I refer to the 1960s and 1970s as the Devastation.

Renaissance

This was the railway, rebranded as British Rail, that I joined as a non-executive board member in 1980. I served for ten years under three chairmen, Sir Peter Parker and his two successors, both confusingly called Sir Bob Reid. I admired the dedication of the surviving 'Beeching boys', front-line managers who regarded their former boss with awe. But, by the late-1970s, they were like generals in a defeated army, forced to plan a constant retreat in the face of the new mobility.

The prime minister of the day, Margaret Thatcher, disliked trains, having once been accosted on one, although she was sensitive to the public's affection for them. 'People love them too much,' she once told me while adamantly refusing to countenance privatisation. To politicians of her generation, roads and airports were the future and made first claim for infrastructure investment. Railways, blighted by militant unions, were yesterday. BR's culture was accordingly one of 'managing decline', and that was not good for morale.

Shortly after my arrival at BR, the demolition was announced of one of Francis Thompson's best stations, the Derby Tri-Junct, so named as the meeting of lines from Birmingham, Derby and the north Midlands. Its loss seemed an echo of the destruction of Euston twenty years before. I protested strongly to Parker, who said it was too late to halt the project. But he did appoint me to head the board's environment panel, with a brief to promote station conservation. The panel's secretary was the embattled but hardy St Pancras campaigner, Bernard Kaukas.

Railway conservation at the time was dismissed by most BR executives as the domain of steam engine necrophiliacs. Even the historic buildings movement was still wary of things Victorian. Listing stations for preservation was in its infancy. The environment panel plunged itself into visiting distressed railway heritage, if only to draw attention to its plight. I recall early trips to Glasgow, Gobowen, Bristol and the ever-worrying St Pancras. I take some pride in the fact that, to the best of my knowledge, no important station (other than Newmarket) was lost after 1980, though smaller ones continued to disappear. Life was a perpetual campaign to secure urgent listing.

Four years later, in 1984, BR won a prize for its renewed conservation work. When I presented it to the then chairman, the first Sir Bob Reid, he was baffled. His railway was receiving nothing but brickbats, and the welcome gesture brought him close to tears. I rashly asked for £1m a year for five years, to finance a new Railway Heritage Trust. It was to give small 'catalyst' grants to local managers in the hope of preventing some casual demolition or removal of a historic feature. Reid assented and I invited the enthusiast Bill McAlpine (later Sir William) to be RHT chairman.

McAlpine's estate outside Henley is a treasure trove of memorabilia. In among his meerkats, macaws and peacocks, he runs an authentic standard-gauge line, complete with tunnel and shunting yard. It is an array of engines and carriages, switchgear and signals, uniforms, head-gear, seats, cutlery and signage, all attended by a band of dedicated train addicts. Visitors to McAlpine's open days hear the clank of points and the wail of steam engines across the Chilterns. In a fold of the hills there even nestles a Victorian station.

The RHT's annual report became a catalogue of modest achievements, of ironwork restored, bridges repainted and valances replaced. The impact was huge, in my view a turning of the tide. Within a decade, Herculean efforts were going into saving and restoring stations across the network, from London's great termini to the smallest halts. Over the following thirty years, 350 stations received RHT grants. Rail enthusiasts who had ignored St Pancras or Derby in favour of rescuing a *Flying Scotsman* or a Gresley Pacific at last saw stations in the same heritage tradition. The restoration of Liverpool Street in 1991 was symbolic of a new dawn.

While Thatcher had refused rail privatisation, her successor, John Major, had no scruple. In April 1994, after half a century of corporate unification, Britain's nationalised railway was dismantled. Opposition from within the industry was ignored. The Treasury had an ideological conviction that the railway should be 'broken up', and privatisation became close to a parody of the 1840s Mania. Short-term targets drove out long-term coherence. For two years, passenger numbers, which had begun to rise, went into reverse.

This turbulent period is well described in Terry Gourvish's official history of the nationalised railway. At the time, BR managers argued strongly, and understandably, for management to remain as a single entity. Others, including myself, argued that if BR were to be dismantled, it should revert to the regional businesses of the Grouping era. This would institute 'competition by example' but retain the managerial hierarchy and responsibility for 'train and track', on which the railway had always depended for its efficiency and safety.

The Treasury would have none of this. Obsessed with 'horizontal segregation', it replaced the railway's quasi-military line of command with a chain of sub-contracts. Track, stations and other infrastructure were put into a single monopoly, Railtrack plc. This was to be sustained on rental revenues from train operating companies, chosen on government franchises. Public subsidy would go only to operators of loss-making services, none to Railtrack.

This Treasury hybrid was naïve, impractical and ultimately more costly to the taxpayer than BR. The managerial disciplines that had synchronised trains and track became a cobweb of legal contracts. I saw the manual for the management of Paddington station, which ran to hundreds of pages. Lawyers and accountants replaced middle-managers. Costs soared.

Within seven years, Railtrack was in administration and a year later the railway infrastructure was *de facto* re-nationalised as a public corporation, Network Rail. Public subsidy rose from £1.4 billion on privatisation to over £6 billion ten years later. The rail overheads soared. Whitehall's transport department had some forty officials overseeing the railway in the 1980s. By 2000, it and its agencies had expanded to some four hundred. Network Rail's subsidy dragged it under government control. For the first time in history, politicians really did run the railways, answering in the House of Commons for everything from rail strikes to investment decisions.

For all this tinkering with governance, privatisation could not be dismissed as a failure. Rail passenger traffic had been declining steadily since the war. Nearly 30 million passenger-miles in 1947 fell to about 17 million in 1982. These then stabilised, and when the initial post-privatisation slump passed, statistics began to rise strongly. By the end of the century, the number of railway journeys actually doubled. While BR would certainly have benefited from the boom in commuter travel, the new operating companies were undoubtedly faster on their feet. They introduced new ticketing and marketing. There were new liveries and improved on-board service. Privatisation also heralded a new attention to stations.

Historic buildings went from liability to marketing asset. The renovation of Paddington in 2000 was like that of a cathedral. It was followed in 2007 by the rebirth of St Pancras. Stations throughout the land emerged in a condition they had not seen since the 19th century. Although station design still seemed unable to free itself from what I call railway clutter – an obsession with unnecessary signage or ill-conceived advertisements – it was clear that the horrors of the Devastation were over and station architecture was treated with a new respect. The station moved at last into the canon of Victorian architecture, alongside the church and other civic buildings.

A remarkable feature of this renaissance was a surging interest in what are called, wrongly in my view, heritage railways. These are mostly leisure railways, but then so are many lines on the main network. The difference is that most employ volunteer rather than unionised staff. The number of such lines currently operational has grown to a phenomenal 150, not including museums and miniature railways. Owners are almost invariably charities, although operators are frequently commercial, with no support from government other than the Heritage Lottery Fund. There are more private railways in Britain today than in 1900.

Most have adopted traction by the once-despised steam, because passengers clamour for it and will pay for it. Many indeed charge a premium for services drawn by steam. Engines, carriages and stations must be the best maintained, cleaned and polished in the history of public transport. The largest enterprises, such as the North York Moors, the West Somerset, and the Ffestiniog & Welsh Highland lines, are as important to their local economies as when they were founded.

London Underground, which had seen little capacity added since the war, also began to spread its wings, despite a disastrous flirtation with privatisation in the late 1990s. Its manager and then chairman Denis Tunnicliffe engaged Roland Paoletti as design director, and the two men re-enacted the days of Pick and Holden. For the Jubilee Line Extension, opened in 2000, they commissioned the best British stations since the Second World War, with a railway 'cathedral' at Canary Wharf. Other signs of more expansionist times were dramatic new concourses constructed in a post-modern idiom at London's King's Cross, Birmingham New Street and Manchester Victoria.

By the dawn of the 21st century, what had been unimaginable in Beeching's day was reality. There was no more talk of managed decline. Passenger journeys passed their post-war peak and reached 64 million by 2015. A Channel Tunnel had been built and high-speed trains arrived in London on a new track from the Continent. A new underground railway, named the Elizabeth line, was built to link west and east London across the city centre. For the first time since Watkin's Great Central Railway, there was even talk of a new, albeit controversial, high-speed corridor to the north, from Euston to Manchester, Birmingham and Leeds. In March 2017 much excitement greeted the reopening of the Settle–Carlisle line, with a train drawn not by a diesel but by a steam engine. Trains were back in fashion. The railway station, an institution that had soared, stuttered and declined, again stood proud.

THE STATION
IN THE BRITISH IMAGINATION

The chief feature that today's visitor would notice on returning to John Schlesinger's 1960s Waterloo would be its colour. The station was black. It inhaled people and exhaled soot. Black were its engines, black its carriages, black its platforms and black the shirt collars and blouses of passengers at the end of every journey. This human conduit to and from the capital was funereal, as if carrying the souls of the nation to Valhalla. But in those days, all city buildings were black. Soot was the tribute paid by Britons to the great god, coal.

Even in those dark days, Britons enjoyed a love–hate relationship with their railways. For all the dirt and unreliability, branch lines were defended, engines romanticised, rail subsidies approved. Trains retained a curious public affection, far greater than other legacies of the industrial past. Canals, ships, mills and factories had their enthusiasts, but not on the scale of trains. As we saw above, it was this affection that saved BR from privatisation under Margaret Thatcher. Even though railways were cursed for their squalor and unpunctuality, there was something special about them.

In his book *The Fascination of Railways*, written in the early 1950s, the clergyman Roger Lloyd wrote that he had never met a rail lover 'who felt the slightest need to produce any moral justification for his pleasure'. While that might be said of most hobbies, Lloyd seemed to regard train-loving as the natural state of a true Englishman. In his case, this was partly the appeal of steam, which still lay 'at the heart' of his railway. He remarked that 'I should not bother to cross the road to look at an electric train.' It was hardly a real train.

I have put Lloyd's claim to the test. When George Stephenson was promoting his engine, *Rocket*, he invited the celebrated actress Fanny Kemble to ride on the footplate. She wrote afterwards of her exhilaration. The engine was an 'iron horse'. Its wheels were its feet, the piston rods its legs and the crankshaft its hips. Coal was its oats. Although not a steam fanatic, I did once drive, under supervision, a vintage engine on the Ffestiniog Railway in north Wales. Exhilaration was the word.

Steam power is not like internal combustion, its workings hidden behind screens, dashboards and buttons. Standing on the engine footplate, I could feel its potency, from the fire roaring at my feet, through the levers, dials and regulators to the hissing, bellowing pipes, chimneys and pistons. Like Kemble, I sensed the steam being a sort of blood supply, racing to fill each component with muscular energy. With the opening of the regulator, the creature surged forward like a thoroughbred, straining for speed, guided on its way by a thin metal line.

There is no doubting the role of these astonishing machines in the romance of rail, from its birth to the present day. But that romance survived the demise of steam. Long after its disappearance, I remember my puzzlement at noticing those dogged crowds of train-spotters still lingering at the ends of platforms. They were ritually noting down the movement of diesels and even electrics. Fascination went beyond Lloyd's love of steam, into a deeper truth about railways in general.

The Revolution

The railway is not just a train. It is an industry wedded to time. It requires the meticulous management of people and machines under the rule of that immutable icon, the clock. It demands of its acolytes powers of memory and skill, rather than art or imagination. It appeals to so-called nerds but in a manner that goes beyond crankshafts and timetables. The organisation of a railway is mesmeric, dedicated to certainty, reliability and predictability. Time is an absolute. Not for nothing did 'making the trains run on time' enter the psyche of 20th-century dictators. A late car journey is just one of those things. A late train journey is an offence against order. The railway stands proxy for all life's journeys, for our hopeful beginnings and our intended ends.

To the early-Victorian imagination, this proxy was widely seen as a monster. It was born of philistine capitalism, inducing in conservatives at every level of society a fear of change. The historian Eric Hobsbawn wrote that the word 'railway' foretold, for the Victorians, an unknown and probably dangerous future – much as in his post-war day did the word 'atomic' and perhaps today the word 'robotic'. The railway's energy seemed demonic, and the path down which it led frightening. Its promise of wealth drove men mad.

In describing the impact of railways on the Victorian imagination, the historian Michael Freeman pointed out that this impact was not just economic and social. It shattered the pre-Victorian sense of space, time and order. It distorted the perception of surroundings. Contours were wiped out. Distance became a straight line. The earth was torn open and its innards revealed. Steam engines arrived at the same time as Irish famine, Chartism and political revolution in Europe. 'The 1840s,' Freeman wrote, 'were a decade when there no longer appeared to be benevolence in either history or nature.'

With this alarm went a widespread dismay at the aesthetic of the new railway and its buildings. John Ruskin was fascinated by steam engines, marvelling at the 'Titan hammer-strokes beating out these glittering cylinders and timely-respondent valves . . . in noiseless gliding and omnipotence of grasp'. Yet when it came to stations, he was appalled. They displayed the worst manifestations of industrialisation. As he travelled the railway network, Ruskin saw his glorious landscapes ruined and images of his beloved Venice abused in station arches, columns and windows. He viewed ornamenting stations as pointless: 'Better bury gold in the embankments,' he wrote, 'than put it on ornaments on the stations . . . You would not put rings on the finger of a smith at his anvil.' Beauty in a building, he wrote, was 'what separates architecture from a wasp's nest, a rat hole and a railway station'.

It was Ruskin who loftily asked what sort of 'lucrative process of exchange' meant that 'every fool in Buxton can be at Bakewell in half an hour, and every fool in Bakewell at Buxton'. He was not alone. In protesting against the new Kendal to Windermere railway, Wordsworth turned to poetry: 'Plead for thy peace, thou beautiful romance/ Of nature; and, if human hearts be dead,/ Speak, passing winds; ye torrents, with your strong/ And constant voice, protest against the wrong.' To the young William Morris, 'Verily railways are abominations.'

Others greeted the railway more with awe than horror. Turner painted his *Rain, Steam and Speed*, one of the few early depictions of a train, at the height of the Mania in 1844. The engine mesmerised him, as it did the hare shown fleeing the engine down Brunel's line near Maidenhead. Two years later, Dickens used the pandemonium of railway construction as a metaphor for contemporary social disruption in his *Dombey and Son*. To Trollope, the railway was to be the epitome of greed and venality in *The Way We Live Now* (1875).

The Romance

Yet the impact of the train on public imagination changed over time. Familiarity alleviated fear, replacing it with an often exasperated affection. As we have seen, the ascendancy of the railway peaked at the end of the 19th century, and then began a long decline. It was no longer an agency of change, but a fixture of Britain's recent past, dusted not just with soot but with nostalgia. It became a symbol of communal collectivity, soon to be challenged by the introverted privacy of the motor car and by that offence against time and distance, the aeroplane. The railway might sometimes run late, but it was determinate. It ran on certain rails, not uncertain roads. This nostalgia was well captured by Tony Judt in a 2010 essay, 'The Glory of the Rails', in which he wailed that if we had lost our railways and their stations, 'We shall have acknowledged that we have forgotten how to live collectively . . . throwing away our memory of how to live the confident civic life.'

By the time of W. H. Auden's 1936 poem *The Night Mail*, which he wrote to accompany a documentary film for the GPO, the train had even become feminine: 'This is the Night Mail crossing the border,/ Bringing the cheque and the postal order . . . Pulling up Beattock, a steady climb:/ The gradient's against her but she's on time.' She was soon to be joined by T. S. Eliot's all-seeing railway cat, Skimbleshanks. For him, the Night Mail 'just can't go' until he 'gives one flash of his glass-green eyes/ And the signal goes "All Clear!"'

Railways found a new place in Britain's cultural narrative. Their ability to keep going through the turmoil of war was an emblem of British resilience. They began to feature in films, notably as the backdrop for the human turmoil of war in that most delicate of romances, David Lean's *Brief Encounter.* Filmed in 1945, mostly in wartime Carnforth, it told of love waxing and waning amid the banalities of tepid tea and biscuits, under the relentless station clock. As Judt later wrote, 'The scenes at Carnforth, juxtaposed with domestic life whose tranquillity they threaten, represent risk, opportunity, uncertainty, novelty and change: life itself.'

In 1946, children were likewise enthralled by the works of an English clergyman, the Reverend Wilbert Awdry. His sensitive, unconfident *Thomas the Tank Engine* cast, and still casts, a worldwide spell. Today, at the Thomas Land theme park in California, children who have never seen a train in their lives shriek with delight at Thomas and friends, as lovable as dinosaurs – and, to them, as extinct. A later film, *The Railway Children* (1970), depicted the railway as the link between a family's ostracism and the outside world, with its climax on a steam-enveloped platform as a train brings father home to a tear-jerking cry of 'Daddy, my Daddy.'

In all this, the star of the show was largely the train. The subject of this book, the station, was slower in coming on stage. Rail anthologies are rich in the anecdote and drama of engines, trains, lines, companies, but extraordinarily silent on stations. Steven Parissien, in his study of English stations, goes so far as to say their admirers were regarded 'as irritating anachronistic nuisances'. Bill McAlpine's railway library, without equal as a private archive, has hundreds of volumes on trains, but barely a shelf on station architecture. Nikolaus Pevsner, whose survey of England's buildings was meticulous, dismissed all but the grandest termini with little more than a passing line. He travelled everywhere by car. The volume on Glasgow runs to 700 pages, but gives just half a page to its majestic Central Station.

Yet the station was never wholly absent from the railway drama. It was not just the railway's public face but its portal, its point of arrival and departure. It embodied the transitional in life. I have always found it strangely moving that Tolstoy, who used the train as a tool of suicide in *Anna Karenina*, also fled the pressures of family life to die, as if symbolically, in a railway station. To me, these places convey civic pride,

Thomas's friends: the train
as fantasy and magic

commercial grandeur and human emotion, all in a single building. Zola was right to declare 'that our artists must find the poetry of stations as their fathers found that of forests and rivers'.

To many, the grand terminus was an imaginative successor to the medieval cathedral, if only because it was the first class of building to surpass the cathedral in size. G. K. Chesterton wrote of its 'vast arches, void spaces, coloured lights and, above all, its recurrence of ritual'. The French writer Théophile Gautier was even more dramatic. The station, he wrote, was 'the cathedral of humanity, the meeting place for nations . . . the centre of gigantic stars with steel rails stretching to the ends of the earth'.

Stations inspired much of John Betjeman's most affectionate writing, notably on London's Metroland (see pp. 88–9). His text to the black-and-white photographs by John Gay produced the finest of all station picture galleries. Philip Larkin, in *The Whitsun Weddings* (1964), watched scenes on passing platforms from his train to London, its lines now embedded in the concourse floor at Hull. It was the station as a stage-set for life's drama.

Most remarkable was the rise to 'most popular poem' status, long after it was published in 1917, of Edward Thomas's *Adlestrop*. It recalls a moment at a sleepy rural halt in the Cotswolds: 'one afternoon/ Of heat the express-train drew up there/ Unwontedly. It was late June./ The steam hissed. Someone cleared his throat./ No one left and no one came/ On the bare platform. What I saw/ Was Adlestrop – only the name/ And willows, willow-herb, and grass,/ And meadowsweet, and haycocks dry.' These lines became a requiem for the vanishing English station during the years of the Devastation.

A different sort of imagination was later captured by J. K. Rowling in her use of the station as gateway to a world of comradeship and magic in the Harry Potter series of books. Platform 9¾ at King's Cross was the point of departure for Harry and friends, as the busy crowd divided between the land of reality and that of make-believe. The 'platform' and the trolley embedded in its wall can still be visited by those who do not mind the queue. So can Hogwarts' station at Goathland.

The legacy

These artists were celebrating that central characteristic of almost all the stations in this book, Victorian architecture. They were aesthetic as well as commercial and social institutions. As such, they were vulnerable to the vagaries of contemporary taste. To understand their extraordinary appearance, we must try to think ourselves back into the imaginations of those who built and used them—and of those who initially distrusted them. For the strange feature of these stations, built in the heat of industrial revolution, was that they turned their back on the age in which they lived. They found inspiration not in the future but in the past.

The shed for Isambard Kingdom Brunel's Paddington might take its cue from the sensationally innovative Crystal Palace, as it had to be big and thus dependent on the new materials science, but when Brunel turned to lesser stations, he harked back to the Tudor and Jacobean eras. George Hudson, the 'Railway King', might have been a ruthless entrepreneur, but his architect, George Andrews, designed mostly in the classical revival. Charles Driver and F. Dale Banister sprinkled south-east England in medieval and renaissance cottages and villas.

Men whose practical imagination was necessarily radical sought to reassure their customers with the old and the familiar. To study Huddersfield's Palladianism, Battle's monasticism or Great Malvern's naturalism is to wonder at the variety of messages the new industry was seeking to convey. As we have seen, few designers of these stations were noted architects. They were engineers who had emerged from the chaos and opportunities of the early railway Mania. Their imagination was derivative and vernacular. We can almost imagine that, in matters of design, the rail industry, especially in its early years, felt constrained by some innate conservatism, by a desire to be thought not too radical, let alone dangerous. For commercial reasons explained earlier, British stations came nowhere near to the scale and grandiloquence of the great continental termini. But this appears almost deliberate, as if they were agreeing with Ruskin, and rebelling against the harsh aesthetic of iron and stone. The builders were playful, escapist, even mischievous, as they spread centuries of Europe's stylistic history across their façades.

Some saw the diversity and eclecticism of Victorian architecture as a political virtue. Writing in the 1860s, the president of the Royal Institute of British Architects, Alexander Beresford Hope, was overtly political. He championed eclecticism as emblematic of the British Empire. It would draw inspiration from 'Benares and Labrador, Newfoundland and Cathay . . . We must assimilate and fuse everything that we eclect [*sic*]' into what he called 'a progressive eclecticism'. After the early-Victorian battle of the styles, architecture should become a peace treaty, a resolution. The future, said Beresford Hope, would lie in the capacity of architects to sympathise with the legacy of their precursors and build a new style on that basis. Eclecticism was thus the cross-pollinator, the inspirer of a Victorian globalisation, drawing strength from diversity.

This was a sadly faint vision. By the third decade of the 20th century it had come to an end. The same architect who had designed the entrance to Waterloo in neo-baroque, J. R. Scott, was designing the modernist Surbiton. Just as the Victorians' picturesque eclecticism was a reaction against Georgian decorum, so the 20th century reacted totally against Victorianism. It rejected diversity and ornament in favour of minimalism. Renewal is a familiar feature in the history of style. But in the case of 20th-century modernism, it demanded obliteration, as if to put the past out of mind and temptation. Most of the stations listed in this book were vilified by inter-war and post-war modernists.

In the 1930s, the critic Roger Fry wrote contemptuously of 'a populace whose emotional life has been drugged by the sugared poison of pseudo-art'. He knew what people should be wanting, and he and his contemporaries would give it to them. He was not exceptional, even in his arrogance. A wider public sensed that the failings of the 19th century were embodied in a 'degenerate' architecture, and could somehow be atoned for by its destruction. Even a traditionalist such as P. G. Wodehouse had Bertie Wooster remark of the Victorians, 'It's pretty generally admitted that few of them were to be trusted within reach of a trowel and a pile of bricks.'

Leafing through the pages of John Minnis's epic tragedy, *Britain's Lost Railways*, it is hard to quarrel with his 'melancholy rule, that the finer our railway architecture, the more likely it was to be demolished in the name of progress'. It was tragic that the railway's commercial decline meant that the 1960s and 1970s condemned hundreds of stations to death at the very point when the reaction against modernism was beginning and a new awareness of the quality of Victorian design emerging. Every station-lover wishes that a particular favourite could have held on just one more decade in order to be saved. Had London's Broad Street not been destroyed when it was, it would today be 'listed' and probably encompass a thriving farmers' market.

I believe a chief reason for the neglect of British stations over the last half of the 20th century was that they were unknown. Enveloped in decades of dirt and soot, their architecture was invisible. The workmen who arrived in 1966 to reduce Adlestrop station to a pile of rubble would barely have noticed what they were destroying, any more than those who demolished London's Euston, Birmingham's New Street or Glasgow's St Enoch's. Yet these buildings were as much a celebration of the Victorian age as were treasured mansions of the Tudor, Stuart and Georgian periods.

In this book I want to present stations as among the most enjoyable buildings in the land, and the richest in stylistic references. From Robert

Stephenson and Brunel to the architects of the Edwardian era, they were created by free spirits who acknowledged no dictatorship of fashion. They delivered what may seem to some a film-set world of Georgian villas, gothic ticket offices, Tudor cottages, baronial waiting-rooms, Venetian palaces and Loire chateaux. A Victorian letter in *The Times* even suggested that the Midland Railway had become so obsessively historical that its guards should be 'costumed as beefeaters and its stationmasters as Garter Kings of Arms'. But we do not dismiss the revivalism of Inigo Jones, William Kent or Pugin as pastiche or, as modernists said, 'dishonest'. We welcome it as an exhilarating respect for the past, part of the great tableau of the historical imagination.

The Victorian railway was an enterprise so radical, so sensational, that it earned its champions the privilege of choice. As they could dictate distance, so they could dictate style. They could walk through a garden of paradise, and pick whatever fruit took their fancy. The only certainty is that these builders loathed boredom. They wanted to reassure and delight. They even wanted to tell stories. When Sir George Gilbert Scott reached the ticket hall at St Pancras station, it might be thought he could take a rest. Yet he adorned his column capitals with scenes from railway life as enjoyable as those in a medieval cathedral.

Today, we can at last respect Beresford Hope's plea to see beauty in our surroundings as a treaty, a marriage of old and new. We can see it in the architectural additions to King's Cross and Manchester Victoria. We see it in the new London Underground. We see it in station conservation generally. These may remain mostly Victorian constructions, but they can accommodate new spaces without insulting old ones. A capacity to stimulate the imagination by comparison is the legacy of a civilised environment.

E. M. Forster wrote that 'only a chill man' fails to endow his stations 'with some personality, and extend to them, however shyly, the emotions of fear and love'. Railway culture once treated stations as off-shore islands of its world. This is no longer the case. Other civic buildings, such as churches, town halls, institutes, libraries, even high street stores, are struggling to survive a technological revolution as great as that of the early railway, that of digitisation. Yet stations stand curiously firm and fit for purpose. They witness the timeless experiences of coming and going, meeting, greeting and parting. If we can look at them with a new eye, a new familiarity, my hope is that we will value and love them. Loving a place is the key to saving it.

THE HUNDRED BEST

The Five Star Stations

Bristol Temple Meads
Glasgow Central
Liverpool Lime Street
London King's Cross
London Liverpool Street

London Paddington
London St Pancras
Newcastle Central
Wemyss Bay
York

There are 2,560 stations on Britain's main rail network, with hundreds more on so-called heritage lines. I have tried to include all the more prominent ones that retain some architectural appeal, plus a selection of those smaller ones which aroused my enthusiasm. My criteria were entirely personal, qualities of architectural beauty, eccentricity or setting.

Limiting the choice to a hundred was painful. I restricted the list to stations still in use or within an operational enclave. A large number of former stations are now redundant, many of them inaccessible by train, and I list some of these below. I have omitted railway hotels, except those that are again part of the station enclave. Demolished stations, those tragic ghosts, can only be regretted and forgotten. I must also repeat, as I say in the Introduction, that this is a book about stations, not trains or railways.

A large number of my entries are inevitably in London. Its great termini were built as showpieces of the big railway companies, and as gateways to the principal lines of route. In addition, London's Underground stations were, and remain, among the earliest and finest in the world.

I have not included stations that have been neglected or defaced, no matter how historic. Saddest of these is Liverpool's Edge Hill, whose presentation – or lack of it—is a disgrace to the railway industry. Others have been disfigured by additions, ramps and unsightly additions, such as Brunel's once-charming Charlbury. I also decided that a single outstanding feature did not make a 'best station', such as Kettering's fine canopies, Scarborough's clock tower or Worcester Shrub Hill's tiled waiting-room.

This is not a list of the biggest or most picturesque stations. A different book could be written on the most isolated, which would embrace a dozen halts on the Cambrian coast and West Highland lines. Berney Arms in Norfolk is often proclaimed 'most isolated' station. Dixe Wills's delightful *Tiny Stations* is a reflection on the separate beauties of request stops, with a glorious chapter on my local halt of Penhelig in north Wales.

Two categories gave me difficulty. One was stations on routes where companies designed almost identical buildings. These included the Newcastle & Carlisle, the West Highland, and London Underground's Piccadilly Line. The other was the booming heritage railway. My admiration is boundless for those who devote time and love to these glories of Britain's industrial past. If their stations stray into twee-ness and fancy dress, that is the privilege of authenticity. In both categories, I could only choose what I regard as outstanding examples.

I have awarded stars, as is now the custom for public attractions. These do not reflect size or importance or general acclaim, merely *my* response to a particular place. This complicated the constant question, 'What is your favourite?' As with my previous books on churches and houses, I find it hopeless to protest that all are favourites in their own way. I cannot avoid the generalisation that Britain's finest stations remain the great London termini. All were lucky to survive the Devastation – some by the skin of their teeth—and my choice of 'best' is between St Pancras and Paddington. Of these St Pancras gives me the greatest thrill.

Finally, I am acutely aware of the often fierce partisanship of rail enthusiasts. I can only apologize to those whose favourites I have overlooked. I am also aware that, in describing stations and their builders, I have ventured into what remains under-researched territory. For the avoidance of doubt, where sources conflict, for instance on dates and named architects, I have relied on Gordon Biddle's various works. I welcome corrections, additions and subtractions, sent to my publisher. There is always room for another hundred best.

STATIONS NO MORE

A list of beautiful stations demolished in the 20th century would be long and painful, and is included in the appendix to Gordon Biddle's *Britain's Historic Railway Buildings* and John Minnis's heartbreaking *Britain's Lost Railways*. Stations still standing but no longer operational (often inaccessible) can still be worth seeing, if only from outside. I list below and opposite some that caught my eye. I am sure readers could add many more.

Alton Towers	Maldon East
Ashby-de-la-Zouch	Manchester Central
Bath Green Park	Melrose
Bexhill West	Monkwearmouth
Elgin	Nottingham London Road
Fenny Stratford	Petworth
Glasgow Kelvinside	Sandon
Glendon	Southampton Terminus
Gosport	Stamford East
Halifax	Thurston
Llanidloes	Welshpool
Louth	Wingfield
Lytham	Wolverhampton Low Level

opposite: Stations reborn: Bath Green Park (*above*), Gosport

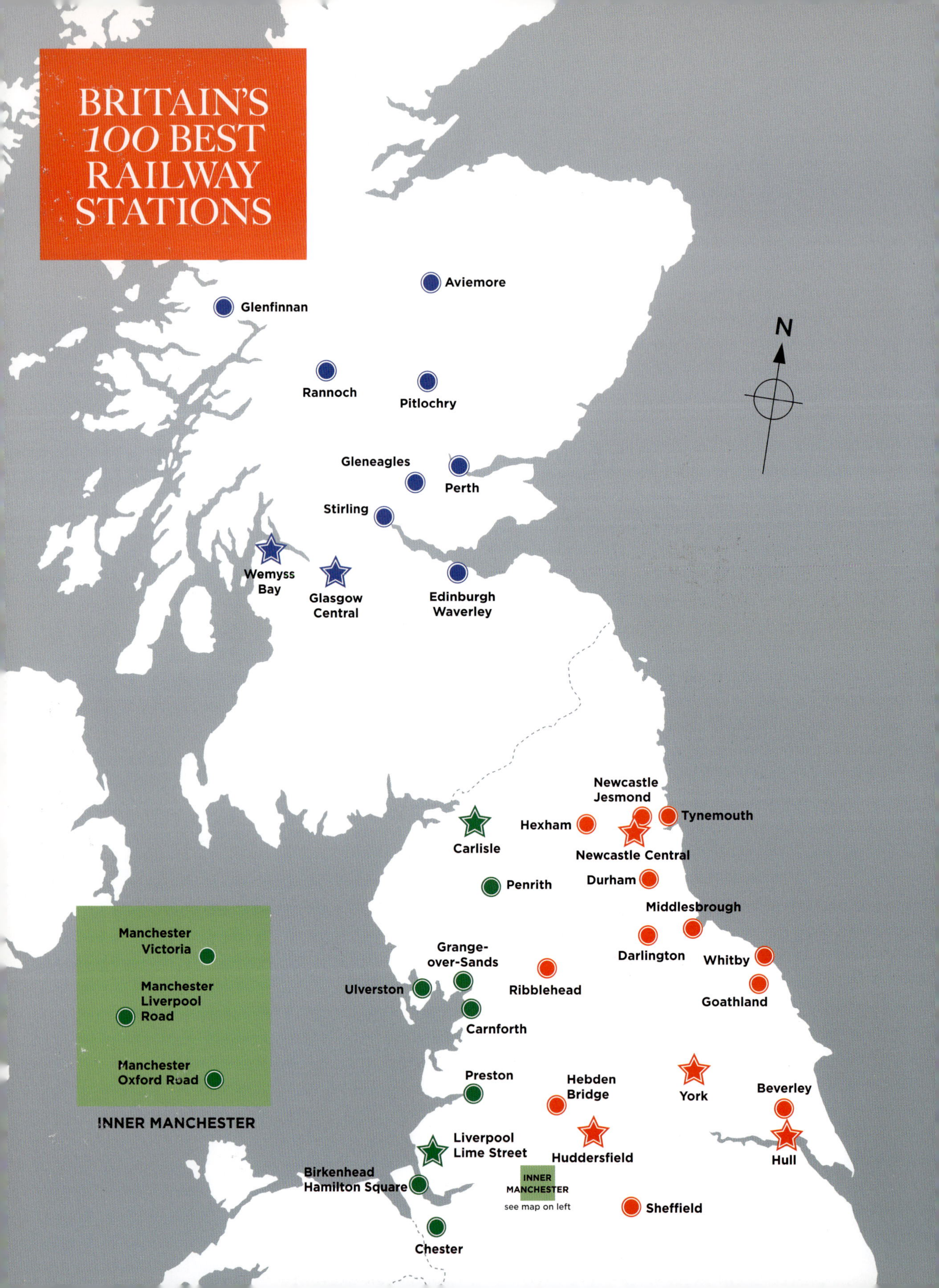

BRITAIN'S *100* BEST RAILWAY STATIONS

N

Aviemore

Glenfinnan

Rannoch

Pitlochry

Gleneagles

Perth

Stirling

Wemyss Bay

Glasgow Central

Edinburgh Waverley

Newcastle Jesmond

Hexham

Tynemouth

Carlisle

Newcastle Central

Penrith

Durham

Middlesbrough

Manchester Victoria

Manchester Liverpool Road

Manchester Oxford Road

INNER MANCHESTER

Grange-over-Sands

Ulverston

Ribblehead

Darlington

Whitby

Goathland

Carnforth

Preston

Hebden Bridge

York

Beverley

Liverpool Lime Street

Huddersfield

Hull

Birkenhead Hamilton Square

INNER MANCHESTER
see map on left

Sheffield

Chester

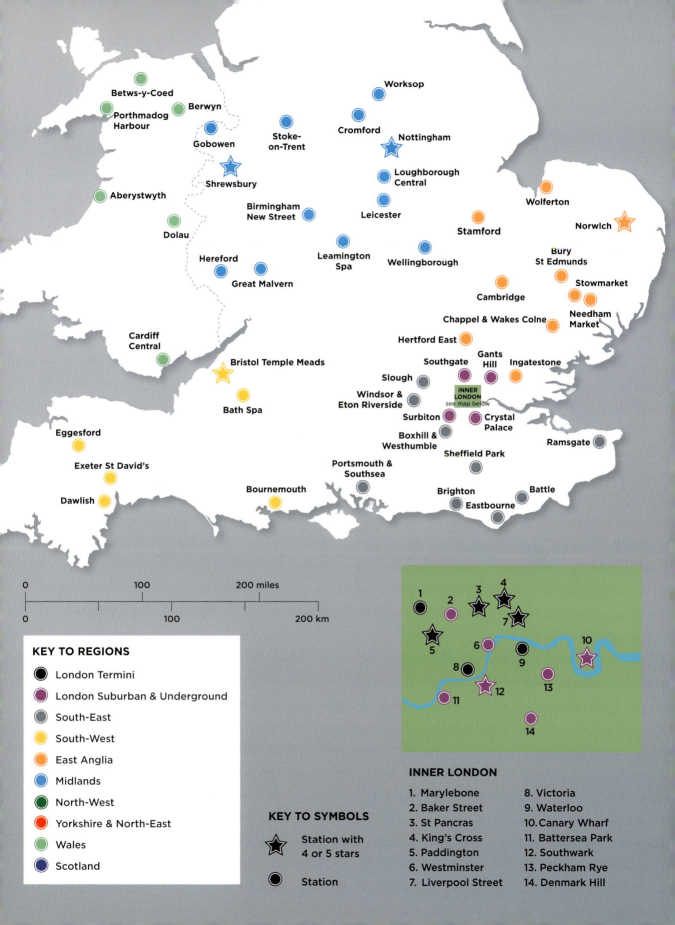

Worksop

Betws-y-Coed

Porthmadog
Harbour

Berwyn

Gobowen

Stoke-
on-Trent

Cromford

Nottingham

Shrewsbury

Aberystwyth

Dolau

Birmingham
New Street

Loughborough
Central

Leicester

Wolferton

Norwich

Hereford

Great Malvern

Leamington
Spa

Wellingborough

Stamford

Bury
St Edmunds

Stowmarket

Cardiff
Central

Bristol Temple Meads

Cambridge

Chappel & Wakes Colne

Needham
Market

Hertford East

Bath Spa

Eggesford

Exeter St David's

Dawlish

Slough

Windsor &
Eton Riverside

Southgate

Surbiton

Gants
Hill

INNER
LONDON
see map below

Crystal
Palace

Ingatestone

Boxhill &
Westhumble

Sheffield Park

Ramsgate

Portsmouth &
Southsea

Bournemouth

Brighton

Eastbourne

Battle

KEY TO REGIONS

- ● London Termini
- ● London Suburban & Underground
- ● South-East
- ● South-West
- ● East Anglia
- ● Midlands
- ● North-West
- ● Yorkshire & North-East
- ● Wales
- ● Scotland

0   100   200 miles

0   100   200 km

KEY TO SYMBOLS

★ Station with
4 or 5 stars

● Station

INNER LONDON

1. Marylebone
2. Baker Street
3. St Pancras
4. King's Cross
5. Paddington
6. Westminster
7. Liverpool Street

8. Victoria
9. Waterloo
10. Canary Wharf
11. Battersea Park
12. Southwark
13. Peckham Rye
14. Denmark Hill

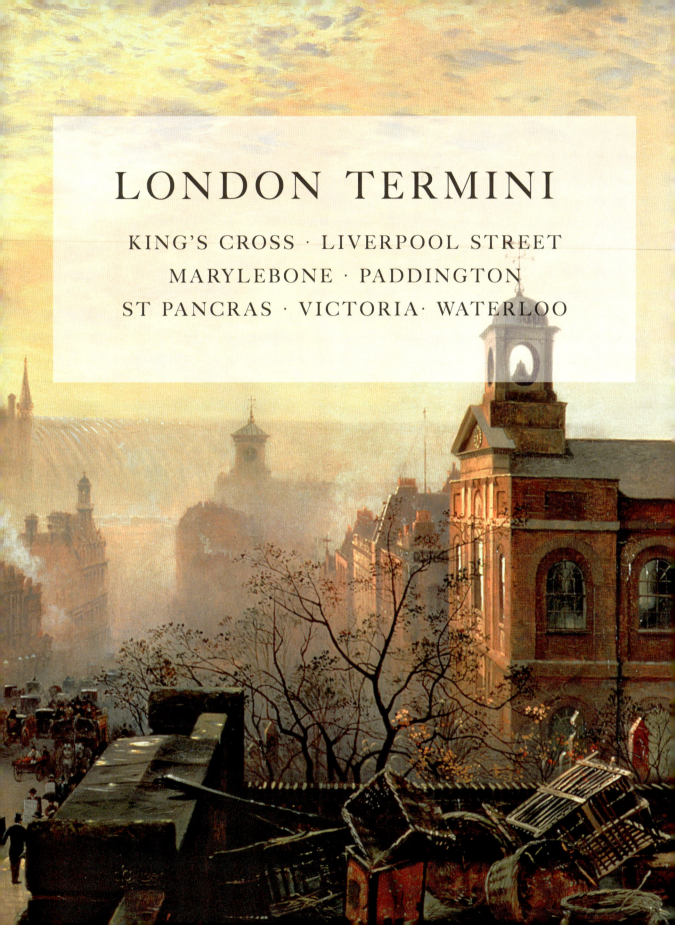

LONDON TERMINI

KING'S CROSS · LIVERPOOL STREET
MARYLEBONE · PADDINGTON
ST PANCRAS · VICTORIA · WATERLOO

LONDON: THE TERMINI

Central London was a repelling magnet to the railway. Neither government nor the rail lobby could overcome the hostility of the city's landed estates to tracks and termini jeopardising their rental values. As a result, the London termini were not the majestic hubs built in Paris, Berlin or Milan. Trains came to a halt in what were initially suburbs. The first versions of Paddington, Victoria, Waterloo and Liverpool Street were hundreds of yards short of their present locations. Only the railway companies crossing poorer land to the south and east were able to penetrate the City of London. Even then, none of the southern routes, with the exception of Holborn, could get beyond the north bank of the river. The result was that London had an astonishing fifteen termini.

The surface railway map of London is thus curiously lopsided. Termini from the north and west are ranged along the line of the Marylebone and Euston Roads. Termini from the south are along the line of the Thames, but the southern access lines are a cobweb of cross-cutting tracks, displaying how the early companies struggled to get as close as they could to their new markets. The result was a chaos of junctions, as at Borough Market and Clapham Junction. Trains to the south-east go from Victoria in the west, crossed by trains to the south-west from the more easterly Waterloo.

For the companies, the London termini were their showcases, although only Euston, Paddington and St Pancras were architecturally impressive. The Devastation (see p. 24) put most if not all the London termini under varying degrees of threat, although only Broad Street completely vanished. Saddest was Prime Minister Macmillan's approved destruction of the original Euston, its replacement so miserable that it is now planned for demolition and rebuilding. But the recent revival has delivered gains, including the magnificent restoration of King's Cross, Liverpool Street and, most spectacularly, St Pancras. I have omitted lesser London termini as insufficiently outstanding.

KING'S CROSS

★ ★ ★ ★ ★

At the height of the competitive frenzy that consumed London's railways in the 1860s, King's Cross was plain Jane, the poor kid on the block. Built in 1852, it was overshadowed by neighbouring St Pancras, muscling on to its patch fifteen years later, the epitome of style and glamour. But that was the 19th century. Come the 20th, King's Cross was suddenly the beautiful Cinderella and St Pancras the ugly sister. To have its roof expressed in the arches of its façade was 'honest'. St Pancras was now a monstrosity, a ragbag of pseudo-historical references. When stations were lined up for execution at the time of the Devastation in the 1960s (see p. 24), it was St Pancras that was condemned. King's Cross, seen as a precursor of modernist virtue, was to be saved.

Every Victorian terminus reflected the ambition of its owners. The Great Northern Railway (GNR) had, throughout the 1850s, forced its bitter rival, the Midland, to pay to use its tracks into King's Cross. Parliament felt the Midland had grown too big for its boots, so the GNR regularly ensured that its trains into King's Cross would be held up and passengers even forced to disembark short of the platforms. When, in 1865, parliament finally conceded the Midland its own terminus, its promiscuous architecture took revenge. The Midland was always extravagant, but never more so than at St Pancras (see p. 71).

King's Cross had opened in 1852 for trains running up the east side of England to York and Edinburgh. It was a route of long, flat stretches of track and high-speed timetables. The company became home to great steam engines, to its engineer Nigel Gresley's Atlantics and Pacifics and the *Flying Scotsman*. To the GNR, trains ran on rails and when they reached a

Cubitt's engineering as architecture

destination, they stopped. It was an engineer's railway. All its stations needed was a roof to keep off the rain, with bricks to support it.

The company's construction at the time was in the hands of that most productive clan, the Cubitt family, celebrated somewhat apologetically in a new square behind today's station. Sir William Cubitt built the line, and his son – Joseph – was company engineer. His nephew – Lewis – was given King's Cross to build. Cubitt's design could hardly have been simpler. It was of two adjacent roof spans, for arrivals and departures, each with a single platform plus sidings. The side walls were of yellow London bricks and the roofs, made of laminated wood rather than iron, terminated in two glazed arches. Economy was all.

The station was completed two years before Paddington and fifteen after Euston. It was an instant success, especially for daily commuter passengers with the new 'season tickets'. But space was limited and when new platforms were needed, they had to be outside the west wall. The front of the station acquired a scruffy settlement of sheds, stalls and, later, Underground entrances, nicknamed the 'native village'. In 1854, Cubitt supplied the obligatory hotel, the Great Northern, but it was anything but grand, on a curved site detached from the façade. The curve was dictated by a former road, which in turn followed a bend in the Fleet River, which still runs underground. The building looked, and still looks, like a terrace that has wandered north from Pimlico, much of it built by Cubitt's brother, Thomas.

King's Cross station is everything that St Pancras is not. As early as the 1860s, the *Quarterly Review* hailed it as 'simple, characteristic and true: no one would mistake its nature and use'. The twin arches look Georgian in their simplicity. They are slightly chamfered, their semi-circular windows filled with a grid of glass panels in white frames. These are crowned by a modest Italianate clock tower, as on a provincial town hall. The tower was later criticised by purists as twee, and should be accepted as Cubitt's concession

pages 54-5: The concourse:
modernism disciplined by history
opposite: Contrast in style: King's
Cross from St Pancras

to architecture. The clock was said never to show the same time as that at St Pancras.

The main station interior is dominated by Cubitt's two shed roofs, each 100 feet wide, divided by brick arches stretching into the distance. Simple iron ribs on bare brick walls are adorned with circles in their brackets. It has the architectural grace of great engineering. G. K. Chesterton wrote of 'cloudlands of great smoke, that range o'er range/ Far floating, hide its iron heavens o'verhead.../ What poet-race shot such cyclopean arches at the stars?'

The modern concourse to the west of Cubitt's shed, added in 2009, could hardly be more contrasting, a textbook exercise in brazen modernism tempered by historical context. It was the outcome of a heated running battle between the architect, John McAslan, and officials from English Heritage. McAslan had to find space for a new ticket office and range of shops to the west of and parallel to Cubitt's building. He duly constructed a new roof across what had been open space between the station and the Great Northern Hotel.

This roof is exhilarating. It is composed of a semi-circular fan vault of white tubes, emerging from the old station wall like a giant palm tree run riot. The fronds soar and then fall, answering the curved façade of the hotel. They might be considered thick and overpowering, but succeed because, thanks to English Heritage, the old station was never allowed to disappear. The brick wall is dominant. Scroll brackets are retained inside the ticket office. The hotel has a new Italianate façade, while in front a retail mezzanine performs an elegant sweep, echoing the curve of the vault.

The 'native village' in the forecourt survived into the 1960s, when British Rail decided to further abuse Cubitt's façade by building a new travel centre straight across it. This was removed in the 2009 reordering when an open piazza was reinstated, finely displaying the original façade. With the side of St Pancras rising to the west, this has become the focus of the new King's Cross/St Pancras district, one of London's more successful urban rehabilitations. It has none of the pomposity of the great continental set pieces.

Fragments of Victorian buildings survive among the modern blocks, humanising a new cultural and

university quarter. Diverging styles in casual harmony compose a charming, typically London, cityscape.

Attached to the west side of King's Cross, the original parcels building has been retained as The Parcel Yard pub. Its warren of upstairs rooms is now a concoction of bars and restaurants. Corridors lead to private corners, with sofas, newspapers, books, sawdust and seclusion. Nowhere on the railway would I rather bury myself away for peace and quiet. I could spend days here and no one would notice.

LIVERPOOL STREET
★ ★ ★ ★ ★

The Great Eastern Railway (GER) at Liverpool Street was long regarded as hell on earth. From the turn of the 20th century to the Second World War, it was the world's busiest commuter terminus. Under its noble shed, exhausted engines and battered carriages charged hither and thither in a frenzy of soot and steam. Passengers likened themselves to cattle, if not sardines. Between the wars, turn-round times were reduced to ten minutes by uncoupling incoming engines and coupling a new one to the rear. Doors were painted with coloured stripes according to class, giving the suburban lines the epithet of 'Jazz' trains. One wit suggested that criminals be condemned to travel all day between Liverpool Street and Romford in preference to execution. Even for Betjeman, who adored Liverpool Street, it was 'a great dragon belching out thousands of people at breakfast time', and then 'drawing them in again, with their white exhausted faces, after tea'.

The GER was formed to co-ordinate the East Anglian companies in 1862. The company was eager to bring its passengers closer in to the City than its old terminus in Shoreditch. The GER duly acquired the site of the old Bethlem hospital at Liverpool Street, next to the North London Railway's Broad Street station, and evicted 3,000 people from their homes. The new station opened in 1874 but it was not to serve some genteel Metroland; indeed, the GER was allowed to expand fifteen years later only on

condition of providing twopenny tickets for a day return. Thousands of City workers (many of them evicted by the railway) duly migrated into the poorer suburbs of Hertfordshire and Essex. The GER became known as 'the poor man's line'.

The builder of Liverpool Street was a Scotsman, Edward Wilson, who worked on various railways before becoming the GER's in-house chief engineer. He had, within a cramped site, to supply separate platforms for main-line passengers and commuting hordes. He also had to dig down deep to enable GER trains to run on to the subterranean Metropolitan line (see p. 88). There were also to be company offices and a hotel. It must have been the toughest architectural commission in London.

Further platforms were built to the east in the 1890s, with access from Bishopsgate. These were by Wilson's nephew, John, and the architect William Ashbee. The Great Eastern Hotel, built in 1884, was extended down the Bishopsgate frontage. The resulting jumble of platforms, bridges and exits was bewildering and unpopular. It was recorded that 27,000 unclaimed items accumulated in its lost luggage office in 1897 alone.

That Liverpool Street has all but gone. In 1974, British Rail decided to demolish both Liverpool Street and adjacent Broad Street and replace them, as it hoped at King's Cross, with a single terminus. Broad Street was no contest. Once the third busiest station in London, its ramble round north-west London from Richmond had lost out to the expanding Underground (part of its route has become the new London Overground). At the time, I walked its semi-derelict platforms with Betjeman and saw collapsing canopies, disused tracks and trees growing from splitting platforms, with the pulsating towers of the new City rising round about. It seemed the last cry of a dying mode of travel.

Liverpool Street did not capitulate so easily. With the blood of Euston still on the British Rail carpet, the opposition was this time better able to marshal its

opposite: Liverpool Street's
ecclesiastical wonder

forces. With Betjeman, Spike Milligan and others to the fore, a public inquiry was achieved, leading to one of the great conservation triumphs of the 1980s. It was commensurate with the saving of Covent Garden and Piccadilly Circus.

Victory led to the rebuilding of most of the site, albeit much of it in reproduction, an example of architecture for once honouring history. Liverpool Street was adapted rather than demolished, its restoration financed by air rights over part of its tracks. There followed an internal battle within BR to save Wilson's office range at 50 Liverpool Street, a saving that was critical to the Victorian character of the site. The outcome required the office range to be completely rebuilt in 1985–91. A final skirmish saved the two-storey arcade of shops across the road. Liverpool Street is a reminder that urban renewal is about choices, not inevitability.

Today's station offers variations on a Victorian theme. The separate entrance gateways to Liverpool Street and Bishopsgate are new, marked by two towers with lantern tops. They carry GER cartouches. New also is the internal concourse, the shopping arcades and, most extraordinary, the entire eastern shed. BR's in-house architects, Nick Derbyshire and Alastair Lansley, were meticulous in retaining or replicating Wilson's proportions, details and fittings. As for Wilson's rebuilt 50 Liverpool Street, it now looks across a small piazza at the bland flank of the Broadgate Centre next door. Only a rather tacky canopy and new lamp standards strike a jarring note. In the centre of the square is a statue of Jewish refugee children, the *Kindertransport* from Nazi Germany, who arrived at the station from the Harwich ferry in the 1930s. We can only imagine their terror at the pandemonium of Liverpool Street at the time.

The station interior is Derbyshire's masterly completion of what we assume would have been Wilson's original conception had he had the space to achieve it. The entire space is on two levels and its success depends on the tension between them. A sweeping upper-level mezzanine curves over the lower concourse, linking the two entrances along the rear walls of Wilson's office building and the Great Eastern Hotel next door. On one of these walls is a magnificent Renaissance memorial to GER staff who died in the Great War. Wide stairs and escalators lead

above: Great War memorial on concourse
opposite: The new entrance: twentieth-century harmony

down from both entrances. Here is a ghost of the drama of old Euston's great hall.

Looking east from the upper level, we should get a sweeping view of the roof and walls of Wilson's original shed and its modern replica to the east, like the view down the nave of a great cathedral. This view is marred by the most serious shortcoming of the Derbyshire scheme, the continuation of the retail gallery over an impenetrable wall of platform barriers. This is the same visual blight that afflicts Waterloo, but in the 1990s was removed from Paddington.

To appreciate the glory of the shed roof other than in glimpses, we must go behind the barrier and down the eastern extension of the gallery. The roof is on a par with Brunel's Paddington, and it is hard to believe Wilson did not have this parallel in mind. He even created two transepts, Paddington-style. The central two bays are divided by a row of doubled columns the length of the central platforms. These columns are like trees rising to a cluster of struts, with intricate pierced spandrels to the brackets. In the rebuilt portions, even the original acanthus capitals have been reproduced. They form a magical forest, now brilliantly repainted. On every side are lancet windows, paired, tripled and quintupled. As Betjeman wrote, 'Let gothic lancets spring and soar and iron ribs disclose the sky.'

The Great Eastern Hotel next door has also been saved, at least in part. Its redbrick façade in a vaguely renaissance style – Pevsner calls it 'neo-Chambord' — is by Charles Barry's son, also Charles, and contrasts pleasantly with the yellow brick of Wilson's gothic next door. It turns the corner well into Bishopsgate, where it meets the later range by the flamboyant Colonel Sir Robert Edis (see p. 64). This offers a variegated façade, in a darker red brick, linking to the Bishopsgate entrance. The Great Eastern Hotel has been redesigned with complete disregard for its former self, rather in the style of a corporate headquarters. Some reception rooms have been retained, including a former masonic temple and a '1901 Restaurant', both in lush Maples decor.

The lack of a good interior view of Liverpool Street is partly redeemed by the modern piazza to the north of the station in Exchange Square. Here we can take a cup of coffee in the shadow of Wilson's semi-circular end screen. Especially at dusk, it offers the best

spectacle in London of these great works of engineering. But why should it have taken so many battles?

MARYLEBONE
★ ★ ★

'A branch public library in a Manchester suburb,' suggested Betjeman. 'Council offices for a minor provincial town,' retorted Alan Jackson. Marylebone is as unobtrusive as the neighbourhood from which it takes its name. Its traditional image was that of tweedy Home Counties characters, up in town to see their solicitor before dropping in to watch some cricket at Lord's. A. G. Macdonell in *England, Their England* had its porters 'going on tiptoe', with barrows with rubber wheels, and trains giving 'only the faintest of toots upon their whistles so as not to disturb the signalmen'. It was, he wrote, the terminus of 'a dreamer among railways, a poet, kindly, absurd and lovely'. A crueller story is of a Roman Catholic complaining to his confessor, 'There's nowhere in London I can meditate in quiet and in peace.' 'But have you tried Marylebone Station, my son?' replied the priest.

Marylebone was London's last new terminus, the final throw of expansionist ambition before the 1923 Grouping and eventual nationalisation. It opened in 1899 as an ambitious attempt by Sir Edward Watkin, chairman of the Manchester, Sheffield & Lincolnshire Railway (MSLR) to reach London and merge with the Metropolitan, of which he also happened to be chairman. Watkin was dubbed 'the second Railway King', in memory of George Hudson. His plan was to complete the MSLR's entry into the capital on Metropolitan tracks. One day he hoped the route would continue south to a channel tunnel (see p. 88).

As the 1880s became the 1890s, Watkin's

opposite: **Marylebone: renaissance in suburban scarlet**

ambition met serious opposition from the artists of St John's Wood, while the cricketers of Lord's were equally ferocious. The former protested that the trains would convey 'not only passengers but coal, manure, fish and other abominations'. The latter complained at the digging up of the sacred turf of Lord's. The result was costly tunnels and cuttings. By the time the MSLR reached Marylebone Road, Watkin had given it a grander name, the Great Central Railway, but it was haemorrhaging money. Some 4,500 'persons of the labouring class' had to be evicted, but by now the companies were ordered to re-house them. The MSLR had been nicknamed 'The Money Sunk and Lost Railway', but was now the GCR, the 'Gone Completely' one.

That did not stop Watkin boasting the most luxurious rolling stock anywhere. He invented the on-train buffet car, with mezzotints of exotic destinations adorning its ceilings. First-class seats were in teak and plush velvet. Commuters were treated as club members. But there were never enough of them. In the early days, passengers were numbered in dozens. Things improved under a dynamic manager, Samuel Fay, after the Great War, but departure boards that once boasted Sheffield and Manchester soon boasted Great Missenden and Monks Risborough. After Beeching's cuts, Marylebone's surviving passengers were exclusively from the north-western Home Counties.

There had been no money for a grand terminus. The company engineer, H. W. Braddock, was told to build one with a few 'architectural details'. His exterior was in a plain Queen Anne style. Smartness was confined to the ticket hall, its walls and windows lined with terracotta, as was the main entrance arch. This was a place into which Sherlock Holmes might slink from his house in neighbouring Baker Street without attracting attention – although, oddly, Marylebone was the only London terminus not named in frequent references to Bradshaw in the Holmes novels.

In the 1960s, Marylebone was expected to go the way of Broad Street. Writing in 1969, Jackson concluded, 'Marylebone seems unlikely to last much longer . . . the killing could be done without too much pain.' But the station was still open in 1984 when there was a proposal to turn its line of route into a concrete road for coaches. When this idea died the death, closure notices appeared. Given the failure of Watkin's vision, it was ironic that the station was saved by privatisation. Marylebone's Great Central Railway was revitalised as Chiltern Railways in 1996, and runs as far as Oxford and Birmingham.

Today, the station still has a sleepy, suburban air to it. The old ticket hall is a branch of M&S. The interior concourse has a white terrazzo floor with red stanchions, bright and pleasant but utilitarian. Classical façades survive for the small shops. Instead of the intended sixteen platforms there are now just six, from which birds can be heard singing from adjacent gardens. The only note of swagger is the GCR logos that festoon every wall and railing. Marylebone's discretion meant that it was much used for filming. In the Beatles' *A Hard Day's Night* (1964), it stood in for Liverpool Lime Street. In *Khartoum* (1966), troops left to relieve General Gordon on a train bound for Denham.

Odder was the hotel built to accompany Watkin's modest terminus. The company could not afford one at all and turned to the furnishing magnate Sir Blundell Maple as promoter. His architect was the larger-than-life Colonel Sir Robert Edis, also busy at the Great Eastern (see p. 62). Edis was a colourful member of the aesthetic movement, designing mostly London houses in the spirit of arts and crafts. He also rose to become the commanding officer of the Artists Rifles and a member of the first London County Council. He was cartooned by Spy as 'Architecture Militant'.

Edis ensured that the hotel, named The Great Central, opened in time for the first train in 1899. His building completely obscured the station from Marylebone Road, as if it were an embarrassing relative up from the provinces. No expense was spared. The style is full-blown neo-Jacobean renaissance. The exterior was coated in then fashionable terracotta, with a bold tower overlooking the main road. It had no fewer than 700 rooms, and even a fitness cycle track on the roof. But, like the station, it lacked customers. It never prospered and in 1945 became an office block, the headquarters of British Rail as humble '222 Marylebone Road'. It was here in a gloomy office in 1980 that I was inducted on to the BR board by Sir Peter Parker. I left the meeting

Marylebone's terracotta welcome

wondering what grim future I, and the then demoral-
ised railway, had in store.

By the end of the 20th century, the building had at
last realised its original ambition, as the Landmark
Hotel. The rear porte cochère was restored as a
covered link to the station. Edis's interiors were
reordered round a winter garden atrium. Columns,
palms and Italianate façades soared eight storeys to
the roof. Everywhere was reinstated in Maples
marble, unlike Edis's poor Great Eastern. It is one of
the most stylish hotel revivals in London.

PADDINGTON

★ ★ ★ ★ ★

There is magic in the air at Paddington. The departures board tells of rolling Wiltshire downs and Devon moors, of Welsh hills and Cornish ozone. The great shed is a cathedral of iron. This is one man's domain. A statue of Isambard Kingdom Brunel broods over the bustling platforms as if his giant ego refuses ever to depart the place. The Great Western Railway (GWR) was his canvas and Paddington its centrepiece (see p. 144).

The line from Bristol to London began construction in 1835. Three years later, the first service at the London end ran from Maidenhead to a station just north of Paddington at Bishop's Bridge Road. This was pending an abortive proposal to continue east and share Euston with the London & Birmingham Railway. The service to Bristol commenced in 1841. Plymouth followed in 1849 and Swansea in 1852. But it was not until 1854 that Brunel was allowed to penetrate the Bishop of London's Bayswater estate and build a proper terminus at Praed Street in Paddington.

Here Brunel brought his trains into a shallow cutting. Inclined ramps on the west and east sides separated departing and arriving passengers, while the south end was enclosed by what, in the 1850s, was the grandest hotel of its day, the Great Western. This was designed by Philip Hardwick, builder of Euston. His twin corner towers in a French Italianate style (since removed) loomed over the Bishop of London's estate. Scruffier hostelries soon emerged in the adjacent streets, embarrassing successive bishops by their numerous brothels.

Paddington quickly usurped Euston as the aristocrat among termini. It was here in 1860 that William Powell Frith set his painting *The Railway Station*, depicting a disparate group of passengers preparing to board a GWR express, described in the Introduction

(see p. 15). The GWR alone held aloof from the 1923 Grouping, retaining its traditions and its personality. As Betjeman recalled, it kept fast to its 'green livery for engines, brown and cream for carriages and stations, its own radishes and watercress in the dining cars, and its own most excellent brand of whisky'. The poet recalled that it took boys to Eton, undergraduates to Oxford, huntsmen to Badminton, sailors to Plymouth and coal owners to Cardiff. It even hired announcers with 'refeened' accents.

P. G. Wodehouse wrote of 'that air of well-bred reserve which is characteristic of Paddington trains . . . for only the best people, cultured men accustomed to mingling with basset hounds, and women in tailored suits who look like horses'. According to Alan Jackson, the phrase 'rush hour' was not to be uttered as being beneath Paddington's dignity. To the satirist Paul Jennings, the very initials GWR suggested 'the sort of noise made by a large, round-eyed but essentially domesticated dog, worrying playfully through Mendip tunnels'. It was at Paddington that Michael Bond found and named his celebrated bear.

This distinctive ethos survived even 1948 nationalisation. Staff on what became the Western Region of British Railways continued to hold themselves as a tribe apart. I can recall even in the 1980s the region's civil engineers refusing to let Brunel's personally drawn surveys go to the National Railway Museum archive at York, as 'we still use them'. Reproduction was out of the question. As the sacred sheets were rolled and unrolled in the civil engineer's private coach I was appalled, but the sense of a railway as a timeless continuum was glorious.

As a station, Paddington was and still is all but invisible from outside. Brunel described it as 'in a cutting, and admitting of no exterior, all interior and all roofed in'. The concourse was developed on the site of what was briefly the hotel garden, an area

opposite: **Paddington's 'letter from home'**
pages 68-9: **Brunel's great waves of iron**

known to this day as the Lawn. The ramp down from Praed Street remained little more than a tradesman's entrance. The western arrivals side was more dignified, but in the discreet style of a Bayswater terrace. Its wall remains as part of the Crossrail interchange.

Otherwise, the station was to make its impact, as it still does, inside. The building was planned during the construction of the Great Exhibition of 1851, on whose committee Brunel served. He poached all he could from Sir Joseph Paxton's Crystal Palace, including his civil engineer, Charles Fox. For architectural detail, he hired the young Matthew Digby Wyatt, of the Wyatt architectural dynasty. For artistic ornament, Wyatt in turn hired Owen Jones, again from the Crystal Palace. Brunel's provincial stations tended to be satirised as 'Brunel's barns', but here they were on metropolitan show. It was engineering as architecture, architecture as engineering.

To gaze up at the station roof on a bright afternoon, with the sun glancing off the girders and ribs, is to sense what earlier ages must have experienced in a medieval cathedral. There can be little doubt that Brunel had such structures in mind. The roof has three spans, a central nave of 102 feet and two aisles of 70 feet each. Their longitudinal vaults were interrupted by two crossings. These were initially thought to be for lifting wagons from one track to another – there are similar ones at Liverpool Street—but no devices for this were ever installed and the purpose is now questioned. It is more likely that they were taking a cue from Salisbury cathedral.

The roof is ridge-and-furrow, with rainwater channelled into downpipes inside the structure's cast-iron columns. Wyatt's most distinctive signature is on the curving girders that sweep down to the piers. These carry arabesque reliefs, whose colouring by Owen Jones has been restored. At the northern and southern end of each vault are semi-circular glass screens or lunettes. These were decorated by Wyatt with swirling curlicues, fore-tastes of art nouveau. They rank among London's most elaborate works of decorative art.

Wyatt is also credited with the principal – and extraordinary – feature of the interior, the internal façades to platform 1. The wall is divided by the two transepts, each with complex Venetian window bays. These have Moorish openings and reliefs. Details are picked out in Jones's olive-grey colours. One of the bays, for the old GWR boardroom, has exotic domed windows and balconies and could be a stage set for *Romeo and Juliet*. Beneath the window is a Charles Jagger war memorial (1922) showing a soldier standing solidly, almost defiantly, not with a gun but reading a letter from home. It is a most moving effigy.

Paddington has been well treated by history. In 1916, pressure of numbers required a fourth span to be added to the west side of the station. In a stroke of respect for the past, the GWR's in-house engineer, W. Armstrong, made a facsimile of Brunel's adjacent roofs, complete with Wyatt curlicues in its end screen. Then, in the 1930s, the GWR's prolific architect, Percy Culverhouse, brought his emphatic thirties style to the side office building behind the hotel, with giant GWR lettering. Culverhouse showed Hardwick's hotel no mercy. What had been London's first grand hotel was gutted.

In the 1990s, the Lawn was encased in a glass screen, with Wyatt's curlicues re-created in the great lunette. An attempt in 2000 by Network Rail and the architect Nicholas Grimshaw to demolish the Edwardian fourth span was defeated after a single-handed battle with the conservation group, SAVE Britain's Heritage. The rebuilt northern access from the new Metropolitan Line station offers a delicious glimpse of the shed roof from outside. Arriving passengers can step straight from the escalator on to the canal quayside, as if on to a Venetian gondola for their onward journey. Brunel would have approved.

opposite: Great Western
boardroom in Moorish mode

ST PANCRAS
★ ★ ★ ★ ★

It was the evening of 6 November 2007. The vast shed was packed. All was darkness. Suddenly giant spotlights of mauve, purple and blue spun across the roof parabola and the Royal Philharmonic exploded with a William Walton march as billowing clouds of dry ice drifted in from the night outside. We expected to see a mighty steam engine thundering into view. Instead, there slid three gleaming snakes of steel. Eurostar had arrived. The actor Timothy West boomed out Tennyson: 'Let the great world spin for ever / Down the ringing grooves of change.' For many of those present, it was the moment, after thirty years of battle, that St Pancras was saved.

I have a print on my wall of John O'Connor's 1884 painting of St Pancras from Pentonville Road (see pp. 48–9). It shows the terminus at sunset, its towers and turrets glowing over the roofs of London. Another print shows the interior of William Barlow's shed in 1869, the vault towering over the diminutive trains herded like cattle beneath. The two pictures encapsulate the Victorian marriage of architecture and engineering, of art and materials. The ideal of a railway terminus as a civic signifier, initiated at Euston in 1837, was brought to a climax at St Pancras.

In the 1840s, George Hudson's Midland Railway was boisterous and belligerent, eager to break out of the boundaries implied by its title. Its trains reached north to Carlisle and south to Bournemouth, but its rivals lobbied parliament to prevent it having a London terminus. To get there, its trains had to rent tracks and platforms from the Great Northern at King's Cross. In 1865, with Hudson long gone, parliament relented and the company acquired land from Lord Somers' estate, demolishing seven streets and evicting 10,000 of his tenants. Railway companies were to a large extent

responsible for the early suburbanisation of working-class London.

The company asked its engineer, William Barlow, to hasten forward with a design for something dramatic. To reach it, trains had to bridge the Regent's Canal, unlike King's Cross next door which tunnelled beneath it. This meant an elevated causeway to an elevated station. A side track to join the Metropolitan Railway, to get northern coal to south London, was driven through old St Pancras churchyard to the west, to widespread horror at the disturbance of graves. The cost was enormous. Barlow's original estimate of £1.7m ended up costing nearer £4m.

Barlow's achievement was to span five tracks in one great leap. Earlier London roofs, at Paddington and Liverpool Street, had needed aisles and subordinate arches, with a maze of tie bars to stabilise the walls. Barlow's roof was a single arc, with its cross ties buried under its floor in the form of horizontal girders. Until Jersey City Station in 1888, this 243-ft span was the largest in the world.

The company now ordained another grand gesture, commissioning the most celebrated architect of the day, Sir George Gilbert Scott, to design a hotel. It would be the most luxurious, not just in London but in the world. It would also cost fourteen times as much as the Great Northern's hotel next door. Scott's building, however, had to conform to Barlow's existing entrance ramps to his shed, hence the distinctive plan of an entrance wing on to Euston Road with a curved quadrant forecourt to reach the station.

By 1865, Scott was the nation's most prolific architect, and a workaholic. At the time, he was completing his grandest commission, the Foreign Office in Whitehall, where he had lost a two-year battle with Palmerston to build in the gothic style. Palmerston demanded Italianate, and Scott had to do as his client required. At St Pancras, however, he was able to have his way – although not, as is often rumoured, by using an aborted design for the Foreign Office. He was a follower of Pugin, but his was an eclectic gothic, adapted to new engineering and new materials.

For what he would regard as his masterpiece, Scott sought inspiration from across Europe. The historian J. Mordaunt Crook detects the Cloth Hall at Ypres in the hotel tower, and the town hall at Oudenarde in the gabled entrance front. The station's biographer,

above: Gothic shadows on railway faience
pages 72–3: Barlow's St Pancras: the great shed

Simon Bradley, sees echoes of 'Bruges, Salisbury, Caernarvon, Amiens, Verona'. Scott himself saw the work as 'on so vast a scale as to rule its neighbourhood, instead of being governed by it' — the cry of the starchitect down the ages. His self-esteem was unbridled, declaring not just that St Pancras was the finest building in London, but 'my own belief is that it is possibly too good for its purpose'.

The hotel attracted instant celebrity, not least for its innovation of a ladies' smoking-room and bedside telephones. The latter could connect visitors to live West End shows, I think a courtesy never repeated since. But it had just one bathroom per floor and business was never good. It closed in 1935 and was used as an overnight hostel for train crews and offices for British Rail catering. Nor were there as many passengers as to Euston and King's Cross.

As for St Pancras's appearance, just as it had been the child of fashion, so it fell victim to fashion. As the 20th century progressed, Victorian architecture lost is élan and St Pancras came to embody all that was worst in stylistic eclecticism. The historian John Summerson derided St Pancras for its 'disintegration of architecture and engineering'. The *Times*'s architecture critic, James Richards, joined a growing chorus by comparing it unfavourably with King's Cross, which he dubbed 'the sane architecture of the 19th century'. St Pancras's fate symbolised the 20th century's approach to the buildings of its predecessor. My parents regarded my enthusiasm for the place as inexplicable.

Bowing to this fashion and for a heart-stopping period in the 1960s, BR tried to clear the entire site for redevelopment and concentrate rail services at King's Cross. Yet another battle was joined, with the new Victorian Society in the lead. In 1967, the government was prevailed on to list St Pancras 'grade one' for preservation, but this did not stop its dereliction. In the early 1980s, I explored the entire building from the catering stores in the basement to the pigeon-infested attics in the roof. It was like Hadrian's villa in Rome. To call attention to the building's plight, we in 1982 staged a party on the hotel's dirt-encrusted grand staircase, with trumpeters blasting from the gallery overhead. A sympathetic developer, Trevor Osborne, held an annual St Pancras Day dinner in a gloomy, dust-sheeted dining-room. Throughout those desperate years, the splendour of Scott's creation never dimmed.

Restoration still seemed doomed until, with the turn of the century, the spell was at last broken. A developer, Manhattan Lofts, and a hotel chain, Marriotts, joined forces and, with the switch of Eurostar's terminal to St Pancras from Waterloo in 2007, the dream was realised The hotel was a triumph, with its staircase of exposed iron beams and medieval murals, its morning-room, ladies' smoking-room, bars, corridors and grand entrances all back in place. Nothing so defines the rebirth of the British station at the end of the 20th century as the new St Pancras and the opening of its rightly called Renaissance Hotel.

There were a few wrong turnings. A team led by the former BR architect, Alastair Lansley, magnificently restored Barlow's shed, but Foster & Partners were used as consultant on the new domestic extension at the north end of the station. It is a plain, unimaginative roof with a characterless side entrance facing King's Cross, a masterpiece reduced to banality. Better by far is the hotel extension in a Gilbert Scott style by Richard Griffiths on the west side of the site.

Nothing can detract from Barlow's vast interior. The best view is from the statue of John Betjeman gazing upwards from the south-west corner (see p. x). From here, the curving roof can be seen launching from the redbrick walls and soaring upwards on wings of iron, painted pale blue to imitate sky. The northern glazed arch, just slightly pointed, is marred by the Foster roof, but is still spectacular, as if liberating space into the light of day. Openings on the west side of the station give on to refreshment rooms and the old booking hall, now converted into a bar. The corbelled capitals in its rafters depict engine drivers, guards and signalmen. They remind me of the medieval capitals in Wells cathedral.

The station platforms rest on 800 cast-iron columns. This undercroft was used to store one of the Midland's principal imports to the capital, barrels of beer from Burton-on-Trent. Today, it lends an added dimension to the modern terminus by having some of its roof removed and made open to the upper concourse. By retaining Barlow's iron columns and brickwork, the lower concourse reflects the architecture of the station, while forming an avenue of cafés, boutiques and bistros. The grandest of stations is reduced to the cosiest of high streets. St Pancras is truly a station apart.

VICTORIA
★ ★ ★

Poor, unloved Victoria. Today, it is London's second-busiest terminus after Waterloo with, most of the time, the atmosphere of a football crowd leaving a stadium. Yet if we lift our eyes from the turmoil, we can still glimpse a building both eccentric and enjoyable. Until the Grouping of 1923, Victoria was two stations, adjacent but not connected, the result of four companies in the 1850s fighting to penetrate the Duke of Westminster's Grosvenor estate and get close to the West End. The estate refused to allow a viaduct from the Thames as being too intrusive, so trains had to descend a steep incline from Grosvenor Bridge into a semi-cutting through Pimlico. The track into the station was even laid on rubberized sleepers to minimize vibration, and a glass roof was required to avoid soot falling on the Grosvenor estate washing-lines.

Collaboration between the companies did not last. In 1862, the London, Chatham & Dover Railway (LCDR) decided to build a terminus of its own to the east, abutting Wilton Road. Mostly serving Kent and dubbed 'the Chatham side', it survives as a rare example of the first generation of London termini. Its quiet Italianate side wall appears to have been designed to melt into the background of neighbouring Pimlico. Inside is its original train shed, designed by the engineer, Sir John Fowler, builder of the Metropolitan Railway. It has a charming two spans, with crescent struts above slender columns, forming Victoria's one corner of relative tranquillity.

The LCDR and the London, Brighton & South Coast Railway (LBSCR) now entered a long-running feud. The former, serving Dover, adopted the slogan

of 'Gateway to the Continent', giving it the edge in exotic romance. It ran Pullman trains to Dover and, from 1924, the famous Golden Arrow train to the Dover Ferry, and on to Calais and the Flèche d'Or to Paris. It became synonymous with the romance and opportunity of Europe. I remember that just to step on to the platform was to have one foot in the Boulevard St-Michel. This made Victoria's Chatham side the point of entry into London for dignitaries arriving from Europe. In the case of royalty, a red carpet and guard of honour would be supplied in Hudson's Place with horses and carriages drawn up for the short ride to Buckingham Palace.

Yet the LCDR could never quite shake off the down-market character of its south-east London and Kent catchment area. The *Railway Magazine* in 1918 remarked that its 'locomotives were excellent but the carriages were always poverty-stricken rabbit hutches'. The LBSCR fought back at every turn. Although its old station was devoid of distinction, it defiantly ran a rival boat-train to Newhaven, and a luxurious *Southern Belle* to Brighton (later the *Brighton Belle*, see p. 117). To Alan Jackson, the Brighton side was 'redolent of soft, leisured southern counties, with its theatre and racing type, its ageing nouveau riche, its adulterous couples and its Brighton belles'.

This class distinction was most celebrated in Oscar Wilde's *The Importance of Being Earnest* when Jack Worthing appalled Lady Bracknell by disclosing that his origins lay in a capacious handbag residing in the Victoria left-luggage office. His protest that at least 'it

Southern baroque: Chatham side (*opposite*) and Brighton side (*above*)

GOLDEN ARROW
PULLMAN DAY SERVICE TO PARIS

EVERY DAY OF THE YEAR
FROM LONDON (VICTORIA)

SOUTHERN
BRITISH RAILWAYS

the Grosvenor Hotel to the north. This opened in 1906. Its style is Edwardian neo-baroque, with scrolls, pediments and female figures. A large porte cochère faced on to the forecourt.

The LCDR immediately retaliated with a new frontage on to the same forecourt, completed two years later in 1908. Designed by Alfred Blomfield, it deliberately juts out further than the LBSCR's canopy, but as it had to turn the corner into Wilton Street, it upset its own symmetry. The arch is more triumphal, the females more voluptuous, the walls more laden with devices. It might be termed competitive baroque.

All this became pointless with the 1923 Grouping. The following year, the new Southern Railway ended the nonsense and broke through the dividing wall between the two concourses. Little else changed. There were constant proposals for rebuilding and expansion, including a 1970 plan for a 'sleeper service to Moscow'. What happened instead was that both concourses became more like an airport, a shopping mall masquerading as a transport facility. Even the Gatwick Express was sent round to the tradesmen's entrance.

At least Tess Jaray's abstract design for the concourse floor on the Chatham side, commissioned by British Rail's environment panel in the 1980s, is still in place. In place, too, is a relic of the first Victoria, the Grosvenor Hotel on Buckingham Palace Road. It was designed in 1860 by J. T. Knowles in an effusive French Renaissance style. The façade drips with friezes, fronds and relief busts in carved roundels, whose identity I have yet to crack (Pevsner cannot get beyond Victoria, Albert and Palmerston). The cornice suffers from sculptural indigestion. The interior, an elegant confection of plasterwork and faience, has been admirably restored.

LONDON TERMINI

was the Brighton line' met the famous rejoinder, 'The line is immaterial.' This was funny only because the audience knew it was indeed material.

Throughout the 19th century, the street frontages of Victoria were a shambles of mean façades and sheds. That this should be the face of the railway just hundreds of yards from Westminster Abbey and Buckingham Palace was considered a national disgrace – while at the same time Paris was building the Gare du Nord. The LBSCR was the first to act. It replaced its roof and expanded its tracks to parallel Buckingham Palace Road, while it built itself the present range of offices and hotel rooms adjacent to

Victoria romantic: Gateway to the Continent

WATERLOO
★ ★ ★

Waterloo is Britain's biggest and busiest station. It hosts 94 million journeys a year. Seen from the air, it is like the Nile delta, disbursing its torrent of humanity into the sea of inner London. I once sat in its control room and watched electronic trains slither like eels in and out of platforms in constant syncopation, marvelling that it worked at all. Even today, the personality of Waterloo is well captured in John Schlesinger's 1961 documentary, *Terminus* (see p.1).

Few of Waterloo's passengers have time or the inclination for its looks. Whether they are emerging from the Tube or climbing the steps of the north portal, they move like robots along their pre-ordained routes. If they have eyes at all, it is for the information gantry over the platforms. Waterloo is a conveyer belt.

In the 1840s, the London & South Western Railway (LSWR) pushed east from the old London & Southampton's 1831 terminus at Nine Elms, demolishing 700 terrace houses but swerving to avoid the Archbishop of Canterbury's palace at Lambeth. The station was completed in 1848 and became notorious for confusion, an apparent chaos of tracks, diversions, bridges, alleys, offices and booths. Office workers jostled with soldiers making for Aldershot, sailors for Portsmouth, race-goers for Epsom and travellers to board ship at Southampton. Platform numbers did not follow sequentially; indeed, they had no rhyme or reason.

Triumphant peace over Waterloo

The chaos was ridiculed in *Three Men in a Boat*, where the heroes wander around Waterloo desperately searching for a train. They are hilariously misdirected by one official after another. Eventually they tip an engine driver half a crown to take them to where they want to go, accidentally depriving an express of its engine. Another story has a Devon farmer and his wife, totally lost, concluding, 'It was no wonder the French got licked here.'

In 1900, the LSWR board began a complete rebuilding, a task not completed until 1922. The design was by the LSWR's in-house architect, J. R Scott, a man of diverse talents (see p. 106). His layout was in the form of a fan of twenty-one platforms, terminating in a spacious crescent-shaped concourse. This was 260 yards long, backed not by the customary hotel, but by a curving wall of offices adorned, as at Victoria, with baroque details inside and outside.

Scott's boldest gesture was his entrance arch, facing north across the Thames towards the City. It is a work of elephantine Edwardian baroque, adapted and dedicated after the Great War as a memorial. Above the arch are medallions centred on a starburst with a clock. On either side are elaborate sculptural groups by Charles Whiffen, one allotted to 1914 and depicting war, the other to 1918, depicting peace. Overhead is a statue of Britannia triumphant. Inside the arch are the names of the LSWR war dead.

The most evident problem was that such an imposing gesture needed a grand forecourt to make its point. In the event, all it had was the obstruction of the Hungerford Bridge viaduct, bang in front. Scott hoped this might one day be removed, but it was not. Recent restoration has gone some way to respecting Scott's work, but the south end of Waterloo Bridge remains a miserable failure of London planning. We can only groan at what Paris would have made of such an opportunity.

Waterloo was extended in 1994 as the London terminal of the first Eurostar service to the Channel Tunnel. This saw the addition of Nicholas Grimshaw's train shed, curved both laterally and longitudinally like a glass banana. In 2007, it fell foul of yet more poor planning, as Eurostar's trains were diverted north to St Pancras. The shed now extrava-

gantly houses five platforms for commuters from suburban Windsor.

Restoration of Scott's interior at last forms a coherent architectural whole. The curved office façade has been given a rather plodding mezzanine, with overhead shops and cafés. It displays three neo-baroque memorials, honouring the two world wars and the original Battle of Waterloo. From its terrace, there should be a view of Waterloo's train shed, twenty acres of ridge-and-furrow glass and hero of Schlesinger's documentary. This may lack the panache of a Paddington or Liverpool Street, but it remains Britain's largest expanse of glass roof. Sadly, it cannot be appreciated because of a floor-to-ceiling barrier laden with train information and advertisements. Waterloo is polluted by commerce. If posh Paddington can be cleared of gantries, why not Waterloo?

LONDON TERMINI

opposite: Climax of Edwardian baroque
pages 80–81: The 20-acre roof with the Eurostar shed on the right

LONDON SUBURBAN & UNDERGROUND

BAKER STREET · BATTERSEA PARK
CANARY WHARF · CRYSTAL PALACE
DENMARK HILL · GANTS HILL
PECKHAM RYE · SOUTHGATE
SOUTHWARK · SURBITON
WESTMINSTER

LONDON: SUBURBAN & UNDERGROUND

The multiplicity of termini round the outskirts of Victorian London did have one significant benefit. It spread the commuter footprint extensively out to the Home Counties and relieved what would have been intolerable overcrowding at fewer central stations. It was also a catalyst in the building of the world's first underground railway, the Metropolitan, to link the northern and western termini with the City of London. This developed into what remains the world's finest urban rail network, overground and underground.

Few suburban stations north of the river were outstanding, since the big companies were more concerned with their long-distance business. At Liverpool Street, crowded suburban platforms were emphatically segregated from more elegant 'express' ones. To the south, however, the (mostly up-market) commuter enjoyed priority. Here the London, Brighton & South Coast's Charles Driver was the star architect, pioneering an eclectic mix of Italian and French Renaissance. His only equal was the London & South Western's J. R. Scott, who brought a brief flourish of 'moderne' to stations such as Surbiton.

The Underground offered more limited scope for architecture, but inter-war nationalisation gave free rein to London Transport's Charles Holden, notably on the Piccadilly line. The use of different architects in the 1990s by the Jubilee Line Extension team continued in the Holden tradition, delivering some of the most exciting new stations in the land.

BAKER STREET

★ ★ ★

Gaily into Ruislip Gardens
Runs the red electric train,
With a thousand Ta's and Pardon's
Daintily alights Elaine;
Hurries down the concrete station
With a frown of concentration,
Out into the outskirt's edges
Where a few surviving hedges
Keep alive our lost Elysium – rural Middlesex again.

Baker Street was and remains the fountainhead of middlebrow suburbia. The Metropolitan Railway company's colonisation of north-west London had its laureate in John Betjeman, whose poem on the demise of rural Middlesex gently mocked its faux gentility. He was fascinated by the area, incanting its destinations like a litany: Harrow, Wembley, Wealdstone, Kenton, Perivale, Pinner. But his was a sceptical romance, conscious that those predominantly youthful commuters were being sold a pup. They were destroyers of the rural bliss they craved. They would settle into suburban torpor, while 'Of their loves and hopes on hurrying feet/ Thou art the worn memorial, Baker Street.'

The Metropolitan was the brainchild of Charles Pearson, surveyor to the Victorian City Corporation. Since the 1830s, a tangle of railway lines from the north and west had laid siege to London. There they ran up against landowners who feared what these dirty and noisy incursions might do to their rents. No railway penetrated south of what are now the Marylebone and Euston Roads. In the 1850s, Pearson sought a railway that could gather up longer-distance passengers from Paddington, Euston and King's Cross and bring them into the City at Farringdon.

Pearson's associate was one of those towering Victorian engineers, a Yorkshireman, Sir John Fowler, who devised 'cut-and-cover' construction directly under main roads to avoid the need to buy and demolish houses. It was soon dubbed 'trains in drains'. A new Metropolitan board secured legislation to dig a large ditch down the middle of the Marylebone and Euston Roads. Two tracks were laid in it and the road replaced overhead, the task taking ten years and causing a decade of traffic chaos. The entire length of these roads lies on top of Fowler's railway.

The first trains ran at the start of 1863, with Gladstone and other dignitaries in the front carriage. Despite ventilation shafts in the pavements above to let out the smoke, and tales of toxic air and 'a descent into Hades', the railway was an instant success. Thirty thousand people a day immediately used the trains to get to the City, despite arriving covered in soot. The company declared a first-year dividend of 6.5 per cent. Five years later, a second line was opened from Baker Street north to St John's Wood and beyond.

By the 1870s, under the chairmanship of Sir Edward Watkin, the Metropolitan's ambitions grew to become a national network. Watkin wanted to link it with his Manchester, Sheffield & Lincolnshire Railway, which he also chaired, and with the South Eastern Railway (on whose board he served) through Kent to the coast. He dreamed of taking trains from Baker Street under the Channel to France. He even began to build an abortive 'Eiffel Tower' at Wembley to attract business to his line.

An easier ambition awaited in rural Middlesex. Most railways headed for population. The Metropolitan headed for open space and created its own population. Against its steam-rolling, Middlesex had no defence. By 1915, the company was responsible for developing fourteen suburbs from Neasden to Amersham, containing around 4,600 houses. Dubbed 'Metroland' by the company's salesmen, the name stuck.

opposite: Gateway to Metroland

Meanwhile Baker Street station went from strength to strength. The Metropolitan company rebuilt its headquarters there in 1911, with Chiltern Court as a block of luxury flats over its entire site. The block was instantly fashionable. Its blue plaques recall Arnold Bennett and H. G. Wells as early residents, and Conan Doyle obligingly located Sherlock Holmes nearby. There was even talk of opening a branch of Harrods on the ground floor. The present Metropolitan Bar is an echo of those days, festooned with ornate shields and coats of arms of putative Metroland grandees.

Travellers alighting today at Baker Street station get a surprise. Rather than the familiar circular 'tube' or grubby 'sub-surface' platform coated in advertisements, they enter a museum. Following restoration in 1983, Baker Street has been returned to its original appearance. The twin platforms are concave, wide-arched and in brick, flanked by recessed bays with sixteen ceiling vents. These were once open to the sky to let out the smoke. The vents are now lit artificially but the illusion of daylight is effective.

The platform alcoves contain their original wooden seats, with signs in Victorian script. Metropolitan roundels carry the date of the line's opening, 1863. The lamps are original and there is an air of remarkable dignity to the place. Modern trains seem an intrusion.

At the foot of the steps dividing the original western platforms from the later St John's Wood branch is an iron arch with an adjacent war memorial. The lion on top is magnificent and prominent. The footbridge over the track displays photographs, admirably captioned, of Baker Street's past, although it is hard to read them without being knocked off one's feet by passing commuters. The modern Bakerloo and Jubilee lines are buried far beneath.

The ascent from this Victoriana to the street above is an enjoyable contrast of styles. Above, all is Edwardian, a series of passages and concourses in clinical white tiling, overcrowded with travel clutter. Elements of the arts and crafts design of the day can still be detected in the occasional ironwork, light fixture or war memorial.

In January 2013, Transport for London celebrated Baker Street's 150th anniversary by running a restored steam train, drawn by the 1892 Locomotive No. 1. It ran from Paddington through Baker Street to Moorgate, pulling a reconstruction of an original first-class carriage, restored at the Ffestiniog works in north Wales. It ran at midnight to allow the air to clear before the Tube resumed, something a rail manager can only do if he really is boss of the railway. Tickets costing £150 instantly sold out. Someone pointed out that TfL's finances would return to profit if they ran it every night.

BATTERSEA PARK
★

As we sat on a train passing Clapham Junction, my father announced it was 'the world's busiest railway station'. A man sitting opposite said quietly from behind his newspaper, 'Chicago Central, I think,' and continued reading. My father knew Chicago well and was mortified. Today, Chicago Central is no more and Clapham ranks only fourteenth in Britain, but from the north end of platform 6 is a view of trains swerving this way and that towards Victoria and Waterloo that matches any railway vista I know. In the distance, a line veers to the north and disappears towards the lonely oasis of Battersea Park station.

There is not much left of old Battersea. It has been rebuilt more drastically than if flattened by an earthquake, but a fragment of the old community clings on to life beneath a tangle of railway bridges on Battersea Park Road. Here lurk a pub, a tenement, a church hall, a school and, overshadowed by bridges, an extraordinary pocket palazzo. It might have been dropped from a railway wagon on its way to Venice.

The station is a relic of the race in the 1850s to cross the Thames into Westminster. The London, Brighton and South Coast (LBSCR) had run to London Bridge since 1842, but the move in 1854 of the Crystal Palace from Hyde Park to Sydenham Hill, and the opening of Battersea Park, brought traffic

opposite: **'As if I were running a theatre'**

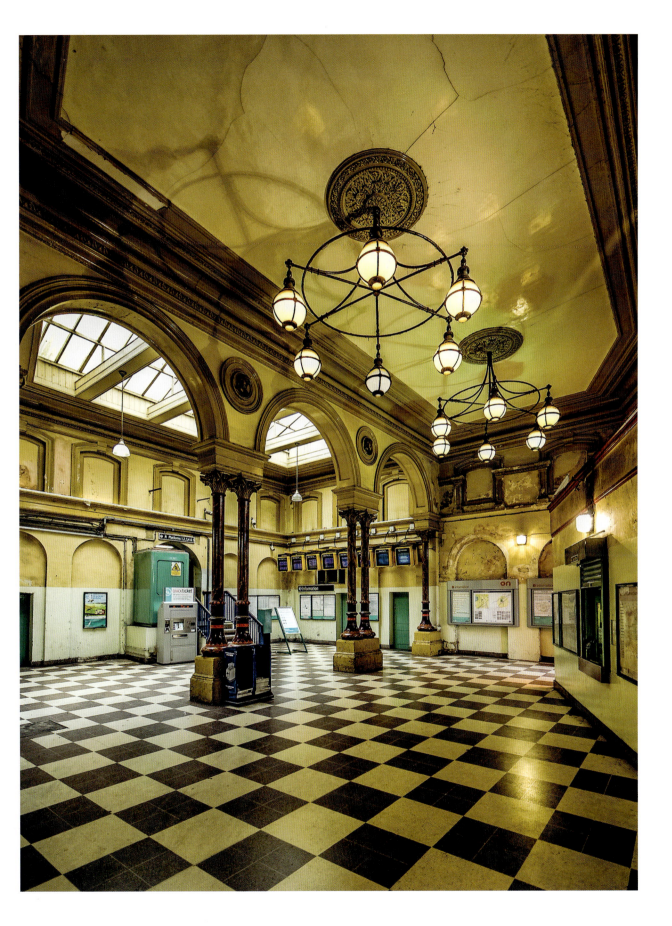

from west London. To all this, the Duke of Westminster's Grosvenor estate in Pimlico turned a deaf ear. Trains could reach Battersea Wharf on the Thames South Bank in 1858, where a station was hopefully named Pimlico, but passengers going north had to pay a toll to walk across the new Chelsea Bridge.

In 1867, a second station south of the wharf was built to serve Battersea Park. This survives, squeezed bizarrely between two bridges, one leading east to Waterloo, the other south to Clapham. The station is invisible from along the road in either direction. The building is almost certainly the work of the LBSCR's versatile architect, Charles Driver. He worked with Joseph Paxton on Crystal Palace and with Joseph Bazalgette on the Thames Embankment and on the Abbey Mills and Crossness pumping stations. He built stations, seaside piers, landing stages and, grandest of all, the Station of Light in São Paolo in Brazil. He left £1 million on his death in 1900. Even among Victorian builders he was a giant.

Battersea Park station has three storeys, with arched windows and incised keystones, flanked by floriated capitals, the bricks in red and yellow. The roof has a heavy, prominent cornice with a touch of French Renaissance to it. This eclecticism continues within. The ticket hall is in the form of a theatre atrium, divided by pairs of slender columns supporting wide arches. The spandrels facing the staircase carry cameos of young women in dramatic guises. The columns are of extraordinary refinement, with elaborate ringed bases and voluptuous capitals. These were restored in the 1980s in imitation scagliola, making the entire hall look, as the station manager suggested, 'As if I were running a theatre.' When the station was again restored in 2013, the scagliola was sadly overpainted a dull cream.

The ticket hall serves as foyer for the drama beyond. A wooden staircase and other passages ascend to overhead platforms. These have a breezy, seaside feel. The columns on platform 1 are like those below, again with rings. The canopies have ornamental valances. The view from here is tremendous, to the south over the rooftops of Wandsworth and to the north into the vastness of the Battersea Power Station development. This is the joy of south London railways, superior to north London's subterranean caverns.

above: Battersea voluptuous
pages 94-5: Escalators to the light of capitalist day

CANARY WHARF

★ ★ ★ ★

London's Jubilee Line Extension (JLE), which opened in 1999, was as fraught as any project in the capital's railway history. Begun in 1990, it was hit successively by the 1992 bankruptcy of Canary Wharf, the failure of the 2000 privatisation of the Tube and an ongoing feud between the Treasury and the then London mayor, Ken Livingstone.

Yet the project ploughed on. London Underground's director, Denis Tunnicliffe, and his design chief, Roland Paoletti, fought for the quality of their stations at all costs, comparing themselves with their pre-war forebears, Frank Pick and Charles Holden (see p. 98). The JLE duly ran 70 per cent over budget and was two years late, but it was built. Its eleven stations offer an architecture no other city can match – although the Tyne and Wear Metro does at least mount a challenge.

Paoletti chose star architects for his stations. North Greenwich went to Will Alsop, Westminster to Sir Michael Hopkins, Southwark to Sir Richard MacCormac and the JLE's centrepiece, Canary Wharf, to Lord Foster. All were told to design for future traffic growth, and to admit natural light wherever possible. Paoletti wanted to avoid 'the labyrinthine tunnels and formless *ad hoc* spaces' of existing Tube stations. His ambition, he said, was to 'allow heavy engineering, which is so often static and inhuman, to become instead resourceful and brilliant and active'. Almost all the stations conform to the 'un-decorated' neo-brutalism of the 1990s, with occasional homage to Charles Holden.

At Canary Wharf, which opened in 1999, Foster honoured Paoletti's grandiloquence. Within a decade, 40 million passengers a year had made it the busiest non-junction station on the network. The interior is vast, scooped out of an old dock basin with entrances at either end of the 300-yard Jubilee Park. The two main entrances are each 'semi-conoid arches' laid on their sides, one wide and sprawling, the other more upright. Each is a carapace, an oval glasshouse by day, and at night the inside of a turtle shell.

The cones offer no hint of what lies below. Banks of escalators lead down to a vorticist vision of vanishing perspectives and inclined planes. Seen from below, these entrances are thrilling, appearing to suck Canary Wharf's workers up from the dungeons of public transport into the light of capitalist day.

When the station opened, the *Observer* described the subterranean concourse as 'a cross between Canterbury cathedral and the set of *Aliens*'. At least in daylight, its concrete greyness deprives it of the visual delight of the great Victorian sheds, and if any cathedral is recalled, it is austere Durham. The JLE's biographer, David Bennett, finds 'purity of form' in the central space, where uncluttered panels, tiles and aluminium surfaces 'beat out a vertical rhythm along its curvature'. The artificial skylighting 'floods the roof as silvery as the sheen across a field of barley under a full moon'.

There is no denying the grandeur. A line of concrete piers strides down the centre of the space, their outline softened by being elliptical in plan. The roof above is divided into two barrel vaults, articulated by concrete ribs fanning out to the walls, a clearly ecclesiastical form. The concourse is flanked by an ocean of the retail outlets on which Canary Wharf floats. Here the station degenerates into a conventional shopping mall, with none of the character of, for instance, the new St Pancras.

In the centre of the concourse are tunnels down to the platforms, giving the lower floors a massiveness similar to the station at Westminster. Here is a canyon of concrete piers, steel rails and laminated glass walkways, intersected by swooping escalators. The platforms have little personality.

Canary Wharf is like much of Foster's brutalist work, impressive in scale but cold and hard. What is masterly is the manipulation of space, and as such is in the great railway tradition. Canary Wharf is an antidote to the claustrophobia of stations on the earlier Victoria line and the northern section of the Jubilee line. Already by 2013, Canary Wharf had won the accolade of being cited as London's favourite Underground station, a prize appropriately shared between the newest and the oldest, Baker Street.

CRYSTAL PALACE

★ ★

What is going on, a visitor might ask. The station's booking hall is, like Denmark Hill's, that of a prosperous suburb served by the London, Brighton and South Coast Railway (LBSCR). Penetrate beyond the booking hall, however, and we emerge on to a balcony over an atrium that falls away at our feet to the platforms below. Its walls are stripped bare to their brickwork. It might be the staircase of a derelict Russian palace, abandoned on this south London hill by some proletarian revolution.

The station was built for visitors to the Crystal Palace, which was moved to Sydenham Hill in 1854. The move greatly excited the LBSCR, then eagerly promoting suburban south London, and it duly built a terminus for its line from London Bridge. The palace was a success, notably for its massed-choir concerts. At one in 1859, 2,700 singers performed Handel to an audience of 81,000. This needed a station that could move passengers at the rate of 12,000 an hour.

The company's rival, the London, Chatham & Dover Railway (LCDR), followed ten years later with a station higher uphill immediately beneath Crystal Palace Parade. It boasted a pedestrian tunnel direct into the palace forecourt. The two stations were known respectively as the Low Level and the High Level.

These survived in use until the Crystal Palace went up in flames in 1936. Tragically it was never rebuilt; the surrounding park is a ghost of its former glory. The High Level station was demolished in 1961, although its tunnel survives and was being restored at the time of writing. To Gordon Biddle, it resembles 'a Byzantine crypt . . . built by cathedral craftsmen from Italy'. The Low Level station on Anerley Road remains in good condition. First built in 1854, it was rebuilt by the LBSCR's F. Dale

Banister in 1875. It comprises two pavilions flanking a ticket hall. The company's fondness for Italianate walls and French roofs is evident. The building displays arched windows, prolific vegetation on the capitals and much blind arcading.

The ticket hall's roof is medieval, open to the rafters and supported on crescent-shaped ribs pierced with foliage patterns. The dark green paint goes well with yellow stock bricks. Doors lead through to the atrium balcony. The station was required to handle thousands of people at a time and, being on a steep hillside, meant a series of decks, parapets and flights of steps. The dramatic effect is today marred only by the insertion of steel and glass lifts, completely out of keeping. Can no one design these things in context?

The platform area was once covered by a large shed, supported by arcaded retaining walls. The shed has gone, replaced by insipid plastic shelters. But out along the platforms we can wander in the open air, with trees waving overhead, a place of departed glory with an aura of crowds vanished into thin air.

DENMARK HILL

★ ★

Denmark Hill station was built in 1865 – 6 for the fast-expanding suburb of 'South London's Hampstead' and was clearly intended to impress its new and wealthy clientele. Today, this mildly bohemian corner of 'medical' south London embraces both King's College Hospital and the Salvation Army's William Booth College. The latter towers over the station and is by Giles Gilbert Scott, in his full Bankside Power Station mode.

The station, like many in hilly south London, perches over the tracks where they enter a tunnel. The old ticket hall is by the London, Brighton & South Coast company's (LBSCR) Charles Driver, in his signature of Italianate walls, but the roof in the French style. A spreading central hall is flanked by single-storey pavilions. Yellow brick and red dressings are fashioned into arched windows beneath a strong cornice, precursors of Driver's Battersea Park and Peckham Rye. The pavilions are semi-domed. The hall is fronted by a generous canopy with ornate brackets.

When the ticket hall was gutted by fire in 1980, a group of spirited locals put forward a proposal to turn it into a real ale pub, appropriately named the Phoenix and Firkin (now just the Phoenix). Initially, beer was to be brewed in-house, with the commendable complicity of British Rail at the time.

The pub has restored the proportions and atmosphere of the old hall. The roof is open to the rafters, from which hangs a magnificent railway clock. A large mural of a phoenix adorns an end wall. At first the pub shared space with the ticket office, but that has since been relocated next door. Tickets should surely be sold over the pub bar. On Devon's Tarka Line, the Rail Ale Trail offers discounted beer on possession of a rail ticket (see p. 148).

The platforms below have been restored, although with a clashing modern footbridge that partly blocks the view of the track. Beyond, trains disappear beneath graceful road arches and thick greenery. It is a mirage of countryside towards what is really deepest Peckham.

above: South London's phoenix on a hill
opposite: Relic of a ghostly palace

GANTS HILL
★ ★

Gants Hill is outwardly the most unprepossessing station in this book. Whatever personality London's interwar suburbs once possessed – neo-Tudor, neo-Georgian, whatever – seeps away in this characterless part of Ilford, once Essex now Redbridge. At its heart is a roundabout junction of six roads. Circling it are unobtrusive steps let into the pavements. We descend them, and wow.

London's Underground network expanded rapidly between the wars, first under the Underground Electric Railways Company of London and then under the nationalised London Transport in 1933. Both were led by the inspirational Frank Pick and the stations were mostly the work of his chief architect, Charles Holden. The latter's designs were strongly influenced by a visit paid by him and Pick to Scandinavia in 1930, where they were much moved by Gunnar Asplund's central library in Stockholm. The two men bequeathed London a railway legacy, in a style that might be termed proto-modernist, that remains largely intact.

Holden's stations are so specifically his that I find it hard to choose between them. Sudbury Hill, Arnos Grove, Southgate and Piccadilly Circus all make strong claims, although their appeal is largely in the design of their ticket offices. Gants Hill is more impressive, and something of a mystery. Holden visited Moscow in 1936 and studied its emergent Metro system, although whether to advise or to learn is obscure. In reality, London and Moscow stations have little in common. Stalin's Moscow was an exercise in grand Russian nostalgia, harking back to the palaces of the 19th century. Holden's stations are small, ascetic and emphatically forward-looking.

Gants Hill was planned in the late 1930s but not opened until 1947, after seeing war service as a munitions factory. The ticket hall is a simple chamber lit by art deco lamps. From here, a staircase and two escalators lead down to a subterranean concourse. The escalators are lined with metallic panels and Holden's signature uplighters on bronze pillars, the wall advertisements are decorously framed, like paintings. It feels as if we are descending to some grand dance hall.

Below is a different world, indeed an echo of Moscow's platform-level concourses. Thickly squared piers divide a central nave from the side aisles containing the platforms. The ceiling is a single barrel vault running its entire length. The walls below are tiled and the floor is white terrazzo. In the centre are circular wooden seats surrounding yet more uplighters. We await the arrival not of a train but of a jazz band.

above: **Underground time, LT-style**
opposite: **Gants Hill awaits its jazz band**

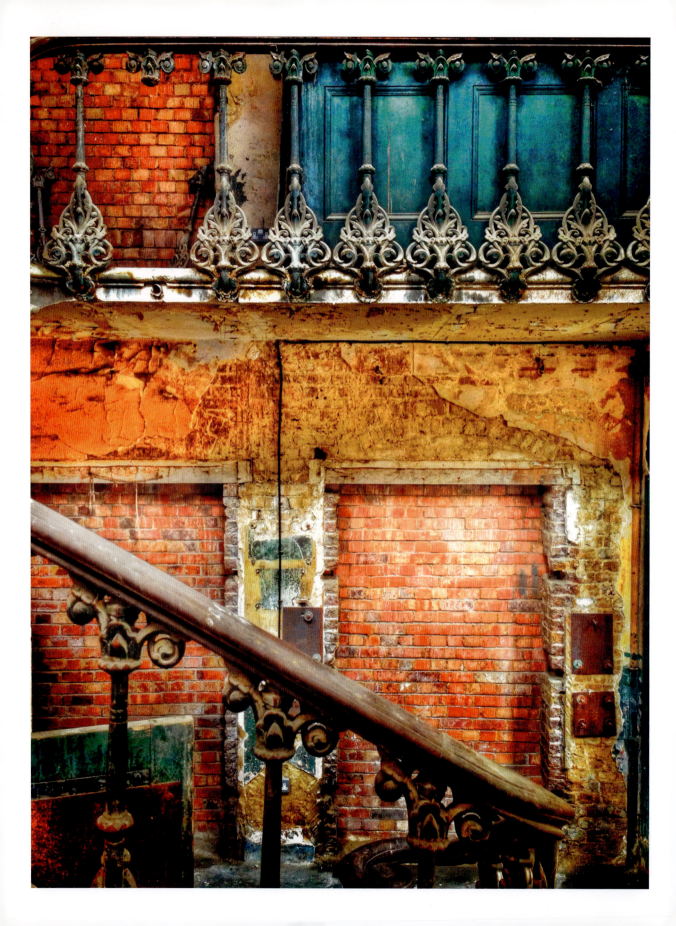

PECKHAM RYE

★

At the time of writing, Peckham Rye station is a phoenix still hiding in its ashes. It lurks behind a near-derelict 1930s shopping arcade, where Peckham Rye remains un-gentrified and exotic. The local council has long been intending to restore the area in front of the building, but has yet to do so. When it does, the old façade should emerge in all its Victorian glory.

The station was built in 1866 at the junction of those old rivals, the London, Brighton & South Coast Railway (LBSCR) and the London, Chatham & Dover (LCDR). The LBSCR was hoping passengers would change here for the new Crystal Palace Low Level station. The building is by Charles Driver, with much of his favoured ornamental ironwork. He set his building back from Peckham Rye, squeezed into the angle between the two companies' tracks. The platforms, like the tracks themselves, were on viaducts – to the dismay of the local washing.

Driver's station is a classic of his French Renaissance style (see p. 97), the rage of the 1860s. It is three storeys, with pink and yellow alternating brickwork. The windows are round-arched, linked by a foliate frieze and with a heavy cornice on top. The roof is convex, with fish-scale tiles. Driver's iron cresting has gone but is in store and should be reinstalled.

Most of the interior was rebuilt in the 1930s. Lavatories of the period survive (the Gents still with stern warnings against venereal disease). Upstairs is Driver's original waiting-room, a grand saloon extending the width of the building and capable of holding hundreds of people. It has no fewer than four open fireplaces. It was used as a billiards room until the 1960s and has been derelict ever since. Balconies, stairs, railings and roof ornament are littered with Driver's proto-art nouveau designs.

The station, like its forecourt, is awaiting restoration. The intention is to turn the grand waiting-room into a dining area, whether fashionably semi-derelict as now, or fully refurbished. It should then honour the local motto of 'Proudly Peckham'. I hope open fires can one day blaze in the fireplaces behind Driver's ironwork, and orchestras can serenade commuters on their way home.

SOUTHGATE

★

Southgate is the most distinctive of Charles Holden's stations for Frank Pick's Piccadilly line (see p. 87). Built in 1933 on the borders of Barnet and Enfield, it is on a circular island site, flanked by a quadrant of single-storey shops. Although the station was restored in 2007, it badly needs another make-over.

The building departs from Holden's spare neo-Georgian seen at Sudbury and Arnos Grove and is closer to what is termed the 'streamline moderne' of the early London cinemas. The form of the building is a wide, single-storey concrete drum, with another shallow drum of clerestory windows above it. This is crowned by a feature in the form of a Tesla coil with a ball on top. It is like the lid of a pressure cooker or a child's spinning top. Holden's sense of proportion is masterful.

The circumference of the building's exterior is composed of shop fronts above a dado of jazzy tiling. In the forecourt stands a Holdenesque obelisk with octagonal seating round it, crowned by an umbrella canopy below a giant London Transport roundel. When

opposite: Art nouveau Peckham-fashion
pages 102–3: Southgate's 'suburban moderne'

lit at night, the composition is a stunning affirmation of modernism in a London suburb. Southgate makes Holden's other stations seem plodding.

The interior maintains the excitement. The ticket hall is lit by uplighters round a central pillar and desk, its symmetry spoiled only by the closure of the side entrance and by clunking ticket barriers. One day, we hope technology will render these obsolete.

Beyond is Southgate's glory, a softly chamfered arch announcing London's finest Tube entrance. A central staircase, generously wide, is flanked by two long escalators. The descent is between bronze panels attended by a parade of stately uplighters. They are like footmen carrying torches. The colours are all mellow creams and browns, a taste of caramel.

The concourse below may lack the dance-hall effect of Gants Hill but it is well proportioned. The arched openings to the platforms on either side are picked out in coloured beading.

SOUTHWARK
★ ★ ★ ★

The location of Southwark Underground station is pointless, just a hundred yards from Waterloo East. Apparently it was built at the insistence of the local Southwark council since Waterloo was in Lambeth. A little nearer Tate Modern would have made more sense. The main entrance on to Blackfriars Road is single-storey, built in 1999 before the rest of the site was developed. It is shaped as a quadrant.

Within lies the jewel of the Jubilee Line Extension (JLE) stations. In contrast to the line's prevailing brutalism, we have the work of Sir Richard MacCormac, idiosyncratic and hard to place in the modernist spectrum. MacCormac said his design, neither harsh nor cold, was influenced by the 19th-century German classicist Karl Friedrich Schinkel. I find Holden more in evidence.

Southwark is better approached by train than from the road. The platforms are sophisticated, lined in unpolished steel and almost devoid of advertisements. Arches give on to a lower, two-level concourse, reminiscent of Holden's Gants Hill. Hidden

strip-lighting converts the steel-lined chamber in to a 'tunnel of light'. There are elegant portals on to the platforms and equally elegant railings. Stairs to the escalators are divided by what MacCormac called 'two heroic curved pylons rather like streamlined funnels'. The effect is theatrical.

Escalators to the upper concourse rise through steel tubes lit by portholes, as if in the belly of a submarine. Riding up from below, we see the opening at the top first as a distant ball of light, growing and then bursting at the top into an expanse of blueness. Here we reach an intermediate concourse. It has the form of a semi-circular atrium, one side of which is a curved wall covered in over 600 triangular blue tiles. This rises 130 feet and was designed by the Russian artist Alexander Beleschenko. The panels are deep blue at the base and grow lighter as they rise to the apex. The opposite wall has the openings for the escalators.

Overhead daylight is filtered by stark concrete struts, like the beams of a veranda jutting out into the sky. The concourse is open and, like the platforms, un-defaced by notices or advertisements, only some unfortunate potted palms. If greenery is needed, it should be a spreading vine. Better by far would be to call on the Tate Modern down the road to lend some of its more discreet paintings to adorn the walls, as does the Louvre to its eponymous station in Paris.

Two exits leave from either end of the atrium. One is to Waterloo East, signalled by an acute triangular opening, like the prow of a ship. It leads past steel-panelled walls, with advertisements hung only on one side so as not to spoil the purity of line. The Waterloo East entrance is an impressive curved chamber, making good use of the iron and brickwork of the old overhead line.

The other exit is to the Blackfriars Road ticket office. This is MacCormac's homage, to Schinkel or Holden according to taste. It is a single sweeping circular hall, with an opaque glass kiosk in the centre. A pillar rises to a circular lantern. The character of the station seen from outside changes at night, when the inside shines like a beacon into the street.

opposite: **Submarine-blue at Southwark**

SURBITON

★ ★ ★

At a loose end, I once found myself reading a novel called *The Smiths of Surbiton*. It was a bestseller in the early 1900s, and described the daily round of a young Edwardian couple in that particular suburb. Like critics at the time, I found it tedious, the reason for its bestseller status being that thousands of suburban Smiths identified with it.

Surbiton was south London's Metroland (see p. 88). At some point in the 1930s, the new regional monopoly, the Southern Railway, decided its forward-looking identity required it to 'go modern'. The company's chief architect, J. R. Scott, had designed the baroque entrance to Waterloo and turned his hand to clean neo-Georgian at Margate, Ramsgate and Hastings stations. By the late 1920s, the Southern was rebranding itself the 'Southern Electric', and Scott responded by adopting a novel design seen largely in factories and cinemas. He was an architect both eclectic and talented.

Richmond and Surbiton are two survivors of Scott's later work, Richmond being threatened with demolition at the time of writing. Surbiton was originally in open country outside Kingston-on-Thames, and was known as 'Kingston-on-Railway'. Opened in 1938, it was, said Pevsner, 'one of the first stations in England to acknowledge the existence of a modern style', although this is less than kind to Charles Holden. It is one of London's most polished works of interwar modernism. The style was variously nicknamed 'moderne', 'super-cinemary' and even 'Odeon'. Its cleanness of line is humanised by the faint echo of art deco classicism. As Steven Parissien says, it brings 'a touch of international glamour to this architecturally commonplace corner of Greater London'.

Southern Odeon at Surbiton

From the terrace of The Surbiton Flyer pub across the forecourt – recalling a steam engine of that name – the station might be from outer space (or perhaps Los Angeles). The entrance block rises some three storeys in creamy-white concrete, faced with a large rectangular panel of four glazed windows. Each window is vertically slatted. This entrance block is offset to the left by a linking range of shop fronts with, behind it, an elegant, faintly Italianate tower adjoining the station footbridge. Its windows are horizontally slatted, with a clock set into the wall.

At ground-floor level an awning snakes Bauhaus-style round the entire frontage. All the fascias, doors and windows have been preserved and modern signage does not intrude on the original façade, not even a BR logo. Above the main window, Surbiton Station is written in a bold sanserif typeface. A diminutive version of this frontage is replicated with a smaller entrance on the far side of the track, with three rather than four windows.

The building's overall sense of dignity is continued inside, in the spacious ticket halls, stairs, bridge and platforms. The halls have black and ochre door surrounds and concealed lights. The original wooden doors and seats have been retained and restored. Seen from the platforms, the tower and footbridge resemble the bridge of an ocean liner.

Surbiton station is marred only by a six-storey office block towering over it at close quarters. Who allowed this?

WESTMINSTER
★ ★ ★

Parliament's Portcullis House is as large below ground as it is above. Above, we see façades of vertical pilasters and stove-pipe chimneys with which the architect, Sir Michael Hopkins, sought to complement the late-Victorian Norman Shaw building next door. It is a rare modern London building that respects an earlier neighbour.

That said, the trees that fill the atrium of Portcullis House offer little hint of the mighty forces straining below. Escalators to one side give access to the Underground station concourse and ticket hall. Here

all is different, for below the existing District and Circle lines had to be inserted a station for the new Jubilee Line Extension (JLE).

Rather than just dig a seven-storey basement, the presiding architect, John Pringle, formerly of Hopkins Partners, left the completed Portcullis House floating on a raft above a crater, in effect a giant escalator hall. Into this crater he inserted a box made of a grid of Herculean concrete struts. The need for this was that the site was already criss-crossed by the ducts carrying the District and Circle lines. If the JLE's brutalism (see p. 93) is anywhere vindicated, it is here. Westminster is a Piranesian catacomb, although Pringle preferred to cite the dug-out churches of Petra and Cappadocia as inspiration.

The sub-street level concourse leads directly into a tangle of escalators, lifts and tubes giving access first to the District line ducts and then, far below, to those of the Jubilee line, situated vertically one above the other at the foot of the crater. Instead of the usual Underground labyrinth of tunnels, there is a series of flying bridges. Nor is there room for posters or other clutter. This is a hymn to the gods of concrete.

Riding the escalators, we see how 'the box' sits inside its space. The girders holding the walls apart are like arms straining every muscle to do so. All fastenings, nuts, bolts and nail-heads are left exposed. The side walls are raw slabs of concrete, as if hacked from rock. Pringle's intention was that the 'grillage of beams and columns against the walls should cast dark and light shadows that accentuate the drama'. The space, he says, 'has the feeling of a huge engine room'.

The walls are supposed to have 'a cliff-like appearance . . . revealing the bones of the station without covering it up by false linings or finishes – to show it warts and all'. In some places, the concrete was bush-hammered and sand-blasted to give varieties of surface. This soon gave way to dirt and discoloration, which it seems impossible to clean. It is the architecture of the noble savage.

In comparison, the station platforms are suffused with a blue-grey light, soothing rather than exciting. This is perhaps intended to calm visitors before the political histrionics above, or to calm them afterwards.

pages 108-9: **Piranesi comes to Westminster**

catta, Architect.

Published by W.H. Mason, at his Repository of

SOUTH-EAST

BATTLE · BOXHILL & WESTHUMBLE
BRIGHTON · EASTBOURNE
PORTSMOUTH & SOUTHSEA
RAMSGATE · SHEFFIELD PARK
SLOUGH · WINDSOR & ETON RIVERSIDE

G. Earp, junʳ delᵗ

, 81 King's Road, Brighton, June 14ᵗʰ 1841.

SOUTH-EAST

Railways in the south-east catered for three markets: commuters, seaside holiday-makers and traffic to the ports of Dover and Southampton. The London, Brighton & South Coast (LBSCR) established an early and commanding presence in Surrey and Sussex. Two companies, the London, Chatham & Dover and the South Eastern, fought over Kent. Hampshire and points west were largely the domain of the London & South Western into Waterloo.

The earliest stations were typically Italianate. It was even known for a time as 'railway style', notably those by the LBSCR's David Mocatta, whose Brighton station was later much altered and given a splendid train shed. By the 1850s, the South-East region had become the showcase of railway eclecticism. Architects such as Sir William Tite, Charles Driver and F. Dale Banister seemed able to turn their hand to gothic, Tudor, classical and even French Renaissance. We find manorial Tudor at Windsor, monastic at Battle and cottagey at Boxhill. France was in evidence at Slough, Portsmouth and Eastbourne.

Twentieth-century electrification saw the rebuilding of a number of new stations in an uncertain style, notably J. R. Scott's neo-Georgian at Ramsgate. The south-east is also home to one of the earliest and most celebrated heritage railways, the Bluebell line.

BATTLE

★ ★ ★

'Alight for 1066', says a sign at the station. Were the Conqueror to arrive at Battle today, he would find a warmer welcome than before. Proximity to the Channel Tunnel means that even directions to the town centre are in French.

Battle is railway gothic in its purest form. The South Eastern's normal stock-in-trade was Italianate, so its architect, William Tress, was here demonstrating the railway's search for a local language. Built in 1852, Battle was influenced, says Gordon Biddle, 'by the proximity of the Benedictine abbey and its massive gatehouse at the head of the High Street'. The station is tucked into a cosy cutting some way from the town, with the quiet dignity of a monastic retreat.

The building is in the form of a two unmatched and steeply gabled wings, linked by a small waiting-room. One is a house of two storeys, the other a ticket hall. The hall is lit by traceried gothic windows. The linking room has a large dormer window with bargeboards. The two-storey wing, once the stationmaster's house, has lancet windows with lozenge glazing bars. Multi-coloured tiles cover the steep roofs. It is most picturesque.

We enter the ticket hall as if into a small chapel. The roof is open, with red-painted rafters and a hooded baronial fireplace. The mildly ecclesiastical waiting-room also has a fireplace, although its bookshelf is sadly lacking in theological works.

The station's most distinctive feature is a two-bay loggia between the ticket hall and the platform, composed of two gothic arches. It might almost be a fragment of a cloister. Here we can sit and gaze up at the dense canopy of woodland opposite. As for an approaching train, might that just be the rumble of Norman hooves?

Ecclesiastical gothic on the South Eastern

BOXHILL &
WESTHUMBLE

★ ★ ★

Were I to tire of travel, I should apply, Betjeman-like, for the post of stationmaster at Boxhill & Westhumble. My visit was on a warm summer's day, with the soft outline of Box Hill on the North Downs in the distance, like a Tolkien landscape. Passing trains were mere irritants. The manor in which Fanny Burney lived, a pub and a scatter of cottages were hardly visible. This is as perfect a rural halt as I know.

It was not until the 1860s that the London, Brighton & South Coast Railway (LBSCR) built a line from Leatherhead to Horsham. The stations were assigned to the company's architect, Charles Driver, a master at adapting any and every style to a building's setting. At Boxhill, the LBSCR had to negotiate steep contours

and the even steeper requirements of the local landowner, Thomas Grissell of adjacent Norbury Park. Grissell was a builder (of Nelson's Column and the Houses of Parliament), and knew all about dealing with contractors. As a result, the new track can be seen from the platform to snake back and forth, rendered invisible from Grissell's house and from the local school. The station was required to be 'of an ornamental character'.

Driver did as required. His station is a marriage of his favourite styles, French chateau with elements of Venetian gothic and Swiss chalet. To outward appearance, there is more roof than wall, the building being composed of sweeping gables covered in layered patterns of slate. The façade to the platform is of two steeply gabled wings, separated by a large off-centre bay with ornamental tower. At one end is an elaborate porch resting on extravagantly floral

Venetian columns. The windows are paired Roman-esque openings. The only concession to the railway is two platform canopies, comparatively simple and, on my visit, in need of renovation.

The station sits in a dell, so thickly treed that to wander to the end of the platform is to feel lost in the woods. We are not alone in appreciating this. The platform sign carries lines from the local Victorian author, George Meredith, declaring that 'Nowhere in England is there a richer foliage, or wilder downs and fresher woodlands.' The former ticket hall, with roof rafters as in a medieval hall-house, is occupied by a friendly coffee bar cum bicycle shop called Pilgrim Cycles. The Pilgrims Way runs nearby.

BRIGHTON
★ ★ ★

In 1841, at the peak of the Mania (see p. 7), Brighton was maturing as England's most fashionable seaside resort. It needed a station to match. The London Brighton & South Coast company had the good fortune to have as its architect David Mocatta, master of so-called 'railway Italianate'. He was a pupil of Sir John Soane and scion of a wealthy Jewish family. Within a decade, he inherited a family fortune and retired, England's railway heritage being the loser. By then he had graced the Brighton line with a series of elegant stations, as well as the Balcombe viaduct and Clayton tunnel entrance. Almost all are altered or vanished.

For Brighton, Mocatta designed a terminus and company headquarters in the form of a Regency villa (see pp. 110-11), with a train shed tucked behind. The steepness of the contours meant that it was posi-tioned on a hill, almost a mile from the beach, although at least arriving visitors would have had a fine view down Queen's Road to the sea. The villa had nine arches beneath pedimented windows, and was coated in creamy stucco.

In the 1880s, the building and its setting were transformed and the shed was rebuilt. Drastic changes were made to Mocatta's façade, with a wide canopy over the forecourt. A new road was also cut directly across the station frontage to give access to the valley below.

The forecourt canopy at least is a fine one, with rococo ironwork to complement Brighton's promen-ades and piers, but the effect is to strangle Mocatta's work. Only by walking up the adjacent Guildford Road can we look down and see his original building, waving amid the surrounding roofs like a drowning Regency buck. His roof balustrade and prominent clock are just recognisable.

Brighton's pride and joy is unquestionably its shed. Built in 1883 by the company's engineer, H. E. Wallis, it is of two spans curving northwards round the side of the hill, where they end in semi-circular lunettes. The rhythm of the columns and trusses is a miniature of the great shed at York, and forms one of the handsomest smaller roofs in Britain.

The line's celebrated glory, the *Brighton Belle* Pullman from Victoria, survived until 1972. The seats were moveable armchairs, set amid luxurious walnut panels, red velvet and tassels. I joined it on what must have been one of its last after-theatre runs, for a supper of scrambled eggs with smoked salmon. The only other passenger was the actor, Laurence Olivier, returning to his Brighton home. He had fought a long and successful battle to retain kippers on the *Belle*'s menu. He saved the kipper but could not save the train. Since nothing is beyond salvage to a railway enthusiast, volunteers are reassembling the *Belle*'s surviving coaches, determined to bring it back to service. I look forward to the first serving of 'Kippers Olivier'.

opposite: Boxhill's sylvan bliss
pages 118-19: Seaside elegance: Brighton's miniature York

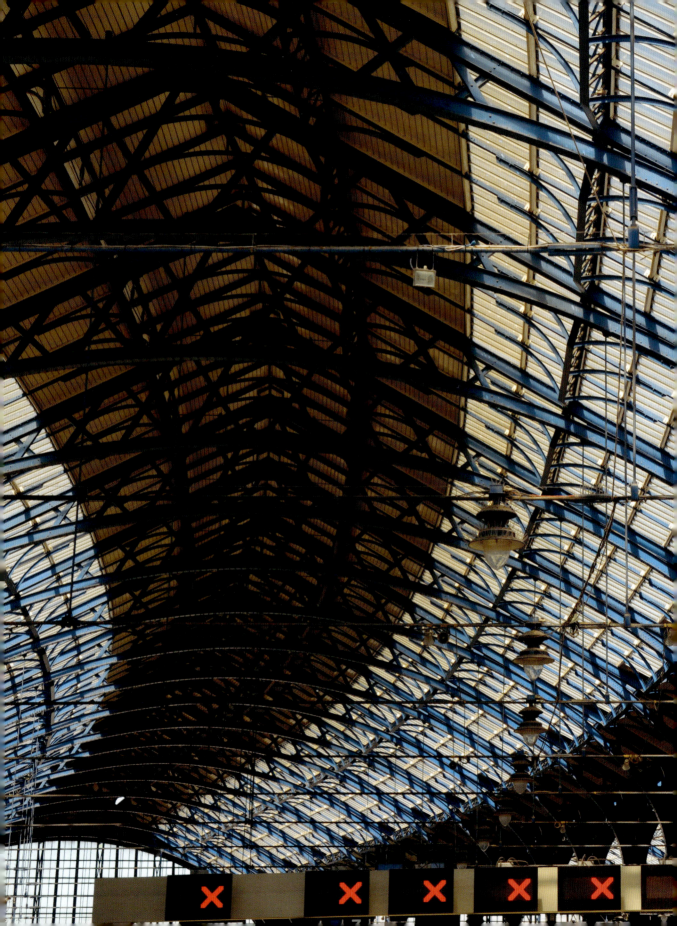

EASTBOURNE
★ ★

This jolly place seems a far cry from the genteel
resort that was planned as a rival to Brighton by the
local landowner, the Duke of Devonshire. An original
station to serve the embryo resort was built in 1849.
The present re-sited replacement came in 1886. It is
a curved structure following a bend in the road, its
eccentric roofscape beaming out over the centre of
Eastbourne in a confident smile.

The station was designed under the architect to
the London, Brighton & South Coast Railway,
F. Dale Banister, in the 1880s. It was in the then
fashionable French Renaissance style, adapted with
extraordinary versatility. The roof comprises three
elements, a domed quadrilateral covered in fish-scale
tiles at one end, followed by a big-boned clock tower
with heavy cornices and coat of arms, and completed
by a pagoda-like pavilion with a lantern attic. Ian
Nairn (in Pevsner) called it 'an exorable multitude of
funny motifs'.

The building material is a light-hearted yellow
brick with redbrick dressings, the exterior with a
welcoming canopy and white valances. The walls
beneath give the station that sense of careless
messiness you get on an Indian railway. Indeed,
I would not be surprised to find Eastbourne
station in Calcutta. It just needs a few more hawkers
and loiterers.

The interior concourse is bright and sunny. A glass
ridge-and-furrow roof is supported on colourful iron
columns, greeting arriving holidaymakers with a
sense of seaside. The walls echo the exterior, again in
yellow brick with red dressings. Some of the doorways have ornate floral capitals and carved
headstones, as if the craftsmen had been told to rifle
through their pattern books and reproduce anything
that took their fancy.

A touch of Calcutta on the south coast

PORTSMOUTH & SOUTHSEA

★ ★

Central Portsmouth is a monument to the unknown town planner, a city of inexplicable decisions. The more merciful is the survival of its Guildhall and its station. The latter is a classic of the Francophile chic of the London, Brighton & South Coast (LBSCR) in the 1860s, looking out over its bleak surroundings like a great-aunt fallen on hard times.

Trains from London to Sir William Tite's extant but disused Southampton terminus arrived in 1840–1. Of the same date is the colonnaded terminus at Gosport, built to serve Portsmouth, when the navy refused 'on security grounds' to allow railways into the port area. Gosport was later used by Queen Victoria to take ship to Osborne on the Isle of Wight. Both stations were firmly Italianate and Gosport survives as a tragic ruin. By 1848, the navy had relented and allowed a railway to penetrate the old town. Its terminus was rebuilt in its present form in 1866. This was shared by the LBSCR and the London & South Western, but to an LBSCR design. A later, high-level extension to reach the Docks had the effect of elbowing the station sideways.

The station was presumably designed by F. Dale Banister, LBSCR's chief engineer at the time and also responsible for Eastbourne. It is in the company's emergent French chateau style, and could be a *hôtel de ville* on the Loire. In red brick with stone dressings, it has a central pavilion with steep roof, decorated upper storey and five bays of windows.

opposite: Portsmouth-sur-Loire

Wings on either side culminate in miniature versions of the central pavilion. A pretty canopy over the porte cochère is unobtrusive and has fine ironwork. All this is bruised by the aggressive line to the Docks abutting its eastern wall.

Inside is a tall, robust ticket hall, its blind arcading filled with unimpressive works of modern art. The old terminus survives behind in the ground-level platforms, their original ridge-and-furrow glass roof forming a sunny canopy over the concourse. The ironwork has been carefully repainted in the company colours of white and blue.

To the right, stairs rise to the platforms at first-floor level for the Docks extension. These platforms offer a good view of the station façade below. A surprise treat is a stroll south towards the trees, from where can be seen the square in front of the city's fine Guildhall. In the distance is Portsmouth's spiky millennium monument. Some judicious tree-cutting would reveal an even better view, of Portsmouth harbour.

RAMSGATE

★

At the end of the Great War, the towns of the Kent coast struggled between remaining holiday resorts or turning their attention to London commuters. By the mid-1920s, the electrified and newly grouped Southern Railway decided on the latter. Its architect, J. R. Scott, was on a personal voyage from his neo-baroque entrance at Waterloo to the 'moderne' of Surbiton. At Ramsgate, Margate and Hastings, he and his team designed clean-limbed neo-Georgian buildings, fit for the discriminating traveller who wanted to be modern, but not too modern. They are similar to the electricity sub-stations built at the same time.

Of the three, Hastings has been replaced and Ramsgate is the more impressive of the remaining two. Completed in 1926, it sits overlooking an expansive forecourt, a mile from the sea. The station is essentially a bold rectangle, fronted by three giant windows with chamfered stone arches and scroll keystones. This façade is flanked by low wings

forming an arc, as though welcoming travellers into its arms. The windows almost exactly copy the three end windows of New York's Grand Central station, built ten years earlier and influential among station-builders in Europe and America. The canopy over the entrance is suspended from four large stays running up the façade and fixed with ornamental shields.

The interior of the hall is light and sophisticated. As in New York, the windows flood the booking hall with shafts of light. The decoration might be that of a Wren church. Brick walls give way to a plaster ceiling of low elliptical arches. An end wall is composed of a square arch, as of a church sanctuary. The company's coat of arms sits in the centre in place of a cross. Today, the arch encloses nothing more significant than a retail outlet. Handsome art deco chandeliers hang from the ceiling. The building appears ready for something more important than selling tickets.

above: 'Modern but not too modern'
opposite: Dignity of age on the Bluebell line

SHEFFIELD PARK
★ ★

The contrast between the commercial and 'heritage' sectors of the railway is less glaring today than it was under British Rail. But it remains in evidence, and nowhere more so than on the Bluebell line. This was the first of the standard-gauge railways to be allowed to operate after nationalisation, opening in 1960 just two years after its closure by BR and its rescue by local enthusiasts. It thus predates the Beeching closures.

The rescue echoed *The Titfield Thunderbolt*, an Ealing comedy based on a similar campaign to save the narrow-gauge Talyllyn line in north Wales. There was initially fierce opposition to such rescues from the rail unions, who did not want non-BR staff anywhere near the main network. The reason was clear when I asked the manager of another heritage line how much he paid his engine drivers. He replied, 'We charge them £50 a trip, and there is a long waiting list.' And they had to be experienced train drivers.

The Bluebell Railway originated with the London, Brighton & South Coast Railway (LBSCR) in 1882. The name then was the Lewes & East Grinstead Railway but was changed to something more picturesque. Today, it runs for eleven miles from Sheffield Park north to East Grinstead, and is a museum on wheels. The rolling stock includes a restored *Golden Arrow* Pullman and the Wealden Rambler restaurant cars. In 2013, a Herculean effort reconnected the Bluebell to the national network at East Grinstead.

Sheffield Park station, which competes with Kingscote and Horsted Keynes as best on the line, is a classic of the LBSCR's 'Queen Anne' rustic revival of the 1880s. It is built of red Sussex bricks with a tile-hung first floor, deep gables and bargeboards. The

eaves are adorned with arts and crafts willow patterns. Woodwork is in the company's maroon and cream. The canopies are deep, with decorative valances.

The station is immaculate. The columns have splayed capitals and gas lamps. The fireplaces and ticket grilles, the signalling equipment and tokens can never have looked so smart. Every bit of metal is polished and ship-shape. Flowers appear to have been planted yesterday.

The place is perpetually crowded with enthusiasts, while the uniformed staff are all volunteers. It boasts two cafés, a museum, two bookshops, two signal-boxes, waiting-room and ticket hall. Platforms are crowded with that heritage signature, old luggage. Fences are blazoned with advertisements for Weet-abix, Ovaltine, Woodbines and Virol – 'growing boys need it' – which seem less offensive for being antique.

Only when we reach the engine shed and the magnificent Bulldogs and Bulleid Pacifics is a grain of dirt to be spotted. The shed is filled with surplus steam engines – the line has some thirty in stock – in various states of dilapidation. Fathers and sons wander among them in rapt adoration.

If this all seems a little unreal, it is not. Sheffield Park is a Victorian building on a tourist line, and as such is no different from dozens of small stations on the main network. For its management to respect its Victorian appearance is no more trouble than to respect a Victorian pub or church. Ingrained in Britain's railway culture is still the idea that such stations are for 'leisure', and somehow not of today. If Sheffield Park can be presented as immaculate as well as historic, so can any station in the land.

SLOUGH

★ ★ ★

Slough is nowhere as slough-like as round its station, a jewel cast by planners among architectural swine. Given the town's reputation for drabness, we might think it would care for the setting of its rail gateway, but no. The station at least is listed for preservation, and is a true Victorian eccentric. It looks like a French chateau sailed by the Great Western Railway (GWR) down the Loire and deposited by the Thames to glare across the meadows towards Eton.

It was from here that Prince Albert boldly boarded one of Brunel's trains back to London in November 1839, after his first courting of the young Victoria at Windsor. The following year, the GWR, with an eye to a main chance, built the young couple a special carriage in Louis Quatorze style. It was not until June 1842 that Victoria could be induced to use it. She wrote that she reached Buckingham Palace in just half an hour from Slough, in a train 'free of dust and crowd and heat, and I am quite charmed by it'. In 1849, a branch line was built to Windsor for the growing royal needs (see p. 130). Victoria became a frequent but always nervous rail traveller, commanding that her train go no faster than 40 mph when she was aboard.

Slough station soon proved inadequate, but it was not until 1887 that a new station was built, with almost identical buildings on the up and down platforms. The style was emphatically that of the moment, French Renaissance, executed with great panache by the GWR's chief architect, J. E. Banks.

Each frontage is composed of a central projecting block with two wings, culminating in corner pavilions. Gordon Biddle describes the contrast between the roofs and the brick walls as 'icing all on top, with plain cake underneath'. The three pavilion roofs have bulbous concave domes with fish-scale tiles, pierced by bull's-eye windows and crowned by spindly ornamental ironwork. The central pavilion has a gable with an impressive clock. The only blemish is that the forecourt canopy rather cuts the main windows on the façade in half. The interior platform buildings are red brick and equally elegant.

The down-side building is so close a replica of the up side that it takes time to work out which side you are on, but it is slightly smaller. Across the forecourt glowers Slough's aggressively modern bus station, with the appearance of a basking shark. All we can say is, how fashion changes.

At the end of the 19th century, Slough's most celebrated staff member was a dog, Station Jim. He padded the platforms, collecting money for rail charities in a box strapped to his back. His custom of barking his thanks as a coin clinked was much loved by children. On his death in 1896, Jim was stuffed and displayed in a case on platform 5. The inscription reads: 'He would sit up and beg, or lie down and "die"; he could make a bow when asked, or stand up on his hind legs . . . If anyone threw a lighted match or a piece of lighted paper on the ground he would extinguish it with a growl. If a ladder was placed against the wall he would climb it. He would play leap frog with the boys; he would escort them off the station if told to do so, but would never bite them.'

above: **Station Jim**
pages 128–9: **Fish-scales and bull's eyes at Slough**

WINDSOR & ETON RIVERSIDE
★ ★ ★

Nowhere was Mania rivalry (see p. 7) more absurd than round the slopes of Windsor Castle. Two companies were eager for royal patronage, the Great Western (GWR) on its branch from Slough (see p. 127) and the London & South Western (LSWR) from Waterloo through Datchet. Both spent ten years fighting Eton College to cross its land. The college, like Cambridge University and cathedrals such as Durham, held that proximity to a railway induced immorality in the young. After much wrangling, both companies eventually reached Windsor the same year, 1849, with termini just two hundred yards apart. There were even two

sets of royal waiting-rooms. Queen Victoria showed diplomacy by using both. Her preference was reputedly for the LSWR as she could alight at Nine Elms, a shorter ride to Buckingham Palace.

Since the GWR's conversion of its Windsor Central terminus to a shopping mall – with a side platform carrying the bulk of tourist traffic – the more charming station is the LSWR's Windsor & Eton Riverside. To travel to it over the water meadows from Staines is a rare experience of semi-rurality in suburban London. The line curves gently to a halt amid sleepy platforms under the castle cliff. It is how one should arrive at a castle.

The building was designed in 1851 in a neo-Tudor style by Sir William Tite, architect of the Royal Exchange in the City, an MP and president of the early Royal Institute of British Architects. Stations for which he was responsible stretched from

Eggesford, through Carlisle to Perth. Given that he described much of his work as neo-gothic, it was odd that he was among those who lobbied against Sir George Gilbert Scott's gothic design for the Foreign Office.

At Windsor, Tite clearly felt Tudor to be the style for the young queen. His station is like a modest Elizabethan country house, with buttresses, gables and mullioned windows. A large bay window lights a booking office as if it were a medieval hall. One might expect a wimpled lady to peer from the ticket window. The station concourse is quietly manorial, more appropriate to horses and carriages. Were a

above: **The cavalry gate**
opposite: **Tite's deferential medieval at Windsor**

train to intrude on its peace, it should surely be drawn by a steam engine.

The royal platform is flanked by an exceptionally long brick wall of twelve bays. This is punctuated with bright blue doors, intended for the 'entrainment' of cavalry attending the monarch, a railway version of a mews. The road side of the wall is decorated with black bricks depicting monograms of the royal couple, V R and P A, alongside those of the L S W R and its chairman, W C, for William Chaplin. Such was the presumption of a Victorian railway tycoon.

The wall terminates at the east end of the platform in a lodge for the royal party, firmly at a distance from the station concourse. Above it is a small tower, supposedly so staff could be warned of the royal party's imminent arrival. The lodge, now offices, contained waiting-rooms, although why the Queen should need to wait for a train is not clear.

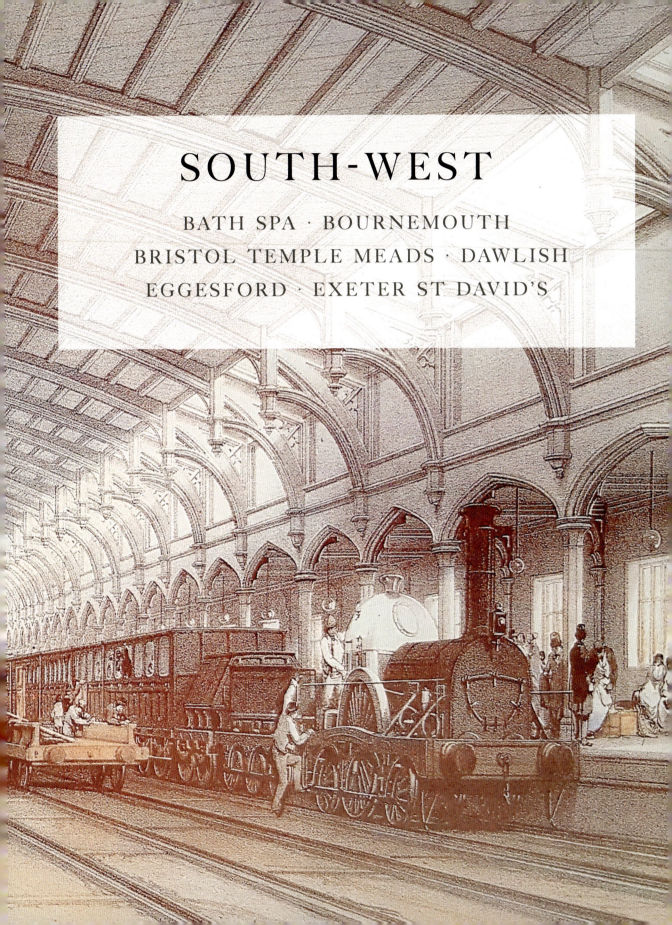

SOUTH-WEST

BATH SPA · BOURNEMOUTH
BRISTOL TEMPLE MEADS · DAWLISH
EGGESFORD · EXETER ST DAVID'S

SOUTH-WEST

The railway in the south-west is still stalked by the ghost of its prime creator, Isambard Kingdom Brunel (see pp. 140–44). His Great Western Railway (GWR) and its affiliates dominated the region to an extent unknown elsewhere. He was challenged only on the fringes, to the north by the Midland Railway and the west by the ambitious London & South Western (LSWR), which thrust south through Devon and Cornwall. Brunel's twin termini at Paddington and Bristol still stand, but his local stations tended to be more modest affairs, mainly wooden sheds with offices inside. They were nicknamed Brunel's barns. Most have gone or been much altered.

A feature of many Brunel stations is evident in the extra space between the tracks, due to the reduction in their width in the 1880s from broad to standard gauge, most noticeably at Bath. Brunel is also sometimes credited with the platform veranda or glazed canopy with fretwork valance, which became the signature of Britain's early railways.

By the 1850s, the LSWR was spreading west from Southampton and Portsmouth, offering a rival, and shorter, route to Devon and Cornwall. It derided the GWR as the 'great way round' of reaching Exeter. It was also running on standard-gauge track, giving it greater flexibility towards London. The LSWR built fine stations at Bournemouth and Exeter, where competition with the GWR produced chaotic duplication of both lines and stations.

BATH SPA

★ ★

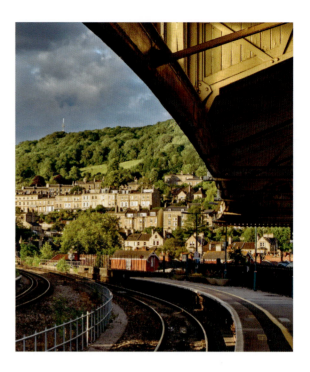

By the summer of 1840, Isambard Kingdom Brunel's navvies had battled their way up the Avon valley as far as Bath. Here they encountered his hated contours, needing cuttings, bridges, tunnels and embankments, all involving delay and expense. By the time the line had reached the site of the new station, it had crossed the river twice, linked by a twenty-arched viaduct. Brunel at least honoured the town by lining the cuttings with dressed stone and building bridges to allow sightseers to view the trains passing below. Only David Mocatta on the Brighton line built arches as handsome as these.

To get close to the centre of the town, the station required the co-operation of the owner of the riverside land, Earl Manvers. He demanded a symmetrical building that would sit well at the end of Manvers Street, but this did not correspond with the track alignment. The result meant a skew building behind a curving quadrant façade. The platforms were on an embankment behind, requiring the platforms to be elevated on the first floor.

Brunel's station, opened in 1841, was of local stone, but curiously owed nothing to Bath's prevailing Georgian style. He had used Tudor at Bristol's Temple Meads, but here brought his stylistic vocabulary forward to Jacobean. To this day, it looks out of place. Over the entrance is a projecting bay window beneath three simple Dutch gables. It could be a requisitioned 17th-century manor, although the ground floor nods at Georgian with round-headed windows and decorative fanlights.

The ticket hall leads up to the platform level, where Brunel's original shed, similar to that at Bristol, was dismantled in the 1890s. The climb from the hubbub below is a pleasant one. Rosebay willowherb sprouts in the middle of the track. To the south rise Bath's encircling hills. Church steeples tower over stone terraces against a wooded backdrop. On a quiet day, one can sit here and enjoy wafts of lilac and jasmine.

Mention must be made of Bath's 'other' station, the disused Green Park, formerly Queen Square. Built by the ever-competitive Midland Railway in 1868–9, it was closed in 1966. The Midland was clearly eager to outdo Brunel. Green Park is a miniature palace, with a five-bay *piano nobile* with Ionic columns. This is flanked by end bays with pilasters, topped by a parapet balustrade. The old station building is now a brasserie and its iron train shed a car park. We must admit that this, rather than Bath Spa, was the station fit for Beau Brummel.

above: Sylvan vista: view from platform
opposite: Bath Spa's Jacobean intrusion

SOUTH-WEST

Renaissance reborn at Bournemouth

BOURNEMOUTH

★ ★ ★

The London & South Western Railway (LSWR)
station at Bournemouth is an oddity. Built in 1885
initially as a terminus, it was clearly intended to
impress the clientele of the booming resort of the
1880s. Indeed, the town rejected an earlier design as
looking too much like a station. The company also
had to move it to the town's outskirts, where the
chief engineer, William Jacomb, made it look more
like a conservatory. The result is essentially a
brick-walled train shed.

The face the station gives to the world is puzzling.
The two-storey entrance façade runs for twenty-two
bays, the station offices being little more than
ingredients of the wall. There is no central feature to
indicate the main door. But the Victorians were good
at walls and this is a fine one. It is of red brick, each
bay with a trio of slender windows. Each is framed by
a prominent scrolled buttress, a pilaster and a
triangular finial. The only variation is that the
fourteen left-hand buttresses have bigger scrolls. The
scrolls have tiny pediments.

The cramped ticket hall and other station offices
are tucked into the ground floor of this façade, while
the grander upper storey is merely the thickness
of the wall. It is a paltry antechamber to what is
revealed inside.

Bournemouth has one of the most dramatic shed
roofs of any station, with the atmosphere of a great
Victorian exhibition hall. The space is awesome. It is
a longitudinal ridge-and-furrow canopy supported on
a mass of latticed girders. These rest on ornamental
brackets springing from the external walls. At each
end is a giant arched glass screen. The interior walls
are of red brick with stone dressings, smartened with
white door and window surrounds, and bold white
cornices. The roof members are painted dark blue,

with the swirling ironwork of the brackets picked out in light blue. On a sunny day, the scene is exhilarating.

For many years, to arrive at Bournemouth was to enter a sort of Hades, a black canyon of sooty emptiness. Inevitably, demolition threatened and battle ensued, with victory won only in 2000. The renaissance of Bournemouth was the true turning of the tide in English station rescue.

BRISTOL TEMPLE MEADS
★ ★ ★ ★ ★

Temple Meads stands with York and Newcastle in the trinity of great English provincial stations. It was to the Bristol suburb of Clifton in 1828 that the 21-year-old Isambard Kingdom Brunel came to recuperate from serious injuries sustained during the building of his father's Thames Tunnel. Five years later, during which time he won the competition to design the new Clifton suspension bridge, Brunel secured the post of engineer to the new Great Western Railway (GWR), becoming chief engineer on its incorporation in 1835. He was just twenty-seven.

Brunel proceeded to build a railway stretching from Bristol to London inside six years. It was one of the great feats of engineering history. He surveyed, planned and supervised every mile of track, every

bridge, cutting, station and shed. He dreamed that the GWR's customers would join his steamships in New York, reach his docks in Bristol and ride on his trains to London, without leaving company property. A titan in an age of titans, the man was self-confident to the point of arrogance, a ruthless taskmaster, micro-manager and poor delegator.

Brunel walked his own lines. He designed, drew and recorded everything. He marshalled his navvies like Napoleonic armies, their work rate as prodigious as their death rate. Brunel was popular but only because he paid well. By 1845, the *Railway Times* was already lauding him as 'neither a rogue nor a fool, but an enthusiast blinded by the light of his own genius . . . never so happy as when engaged, regardless of cost, in conquering some, to ordinary mortals, impossibility'. He burned out and died in 1859, at the age of fifty-three.

Brunel's most celebrated error was to choose, and refuse to compromise on, the 7-ft gauge track (later plus ¼ inch). All other companies had opted for the Stephensons' standard gauge of 4ft 8½ inches. Brunel proved to an 1845 royal commission that his gauge was steadier and more able to carry heavy loads, but the majority was against him. An 1846 act ordained standard gauge for all new railways and the GWR was left fighting a losing battle. It first introduced third rails on shared lines, mostly in the Midlands, but gradually it switched to standard, and at

opposite: Bournemouth: Italian elegance
above: 'Brunel's parish church': the Temple Meads shed
pages 142–3: Medieval homage: Wyatt's castle on a hill

crippling expense. One line after another was converted over the 1880s, with the final stretch from Exeter to Truro completed in May 1892.

When it came to stations, Brunel was an engineer's engineer, concerned more for the simplicity and efficiency of his line than for the convenience of passengers or the beauty of buildings. In Bristol, he avoided troublesome land acquisition by placing his terminus on a location some distance from the city centre – inconvenient to this day. It is a complex site, the product of serving three competing companies, lucky only in choosing the same location for all of them in a city that had little flat ground for railways.

Brunel's original terminus is not easy to discern. It fronts on to the main road with, behind it, a long wall up an incline to the present station's entrance. The first station was an office block with a train shed tacked on to its rear.

At the time, Brunel's rival (and later friend) Robert Stephenson was dignifying his London to Birmingham line with an austere classicism, notably at Doric Euston. Brunel occasionally employed Italianate, but he seems to have regarded gothic as the language of the future. It was the victor in the style wars that had engrossed the commissioners of the Palace of Westminster in 1836. The new station opened in 1840.

The surviving offices are a simple rectangular building of four storeys with Tudor windows and a crenellated roofline. Brunel had wanted romantic towers on each side but this was vetoed on grounds of cost. The façade was originally flanked by two gateways, for arriving and departing carriages. Only one survives. The building is undeniably modest and was dismissed by Pugin, as 'mere caricature . . . full of pretension', although he was kinder about Brunel's 'medieval' shed behind.

Here, arriving trains had to cross Bristol's Floating Harbour and enter the station on a viaduct. Brunel saved the need for a concourse by gathering his passengers on the ground floor below the tracks, with steps up to the platforms. Meanwhile the company offices occupied a mezzanine over the buffers. This economised on space but fumigated the clerks working at their desks above.

Brunel's original shed survives, one of England's great railway relics. As we have noted so often

elsewhere – as at Paddington – the design was essentially that of a church nave. Trains entered and left as might a processing choir, while the side platforms served as aisles beneath decorative hammer-beams. If Paddington was to be Brunel's cathedral, Temple Meads was his parish church. The original shed later became a much-abused space. It was lengthened in the 1870s, lingering on as a terminus for the Midland Railway's trains from the north. It was briefly a goods area in the 20th century, but this closed in 1965. British Rail then barred its future use as a station by building a signalling centre across its entrance.

The old shed was used variously for storage, as an exhibition hall, an 'interactive science centre' and even an abortive museum of the British Empire. Its inconvenient location told against it. The building is now a venue for weddings, exhibitions and conferences, but there are plans to bring it back into some form of railway use, involving the welcome removal of the signalling centre.

No sooner had Brunel's work been completed than a different company, the Bristol and Exeter Railway (B&ER), arrived from the south-west with a terminus at right angles to Brunel's shed. An extra curving platform was then required to enable GWR trains to run through on the new track to Exeter. A headquarters for the B&ER was designed by a local architect, Samuel Fripp, and still stands on the right of the station approach. Its twin turrets and bold gables evoke the residence of a Jacobean grandee – the 17th-century facing Brunel's 16th.

As business expanded, the two companies merged and a new station was needed. In 1878, with Brunel long dead, Matthew Digby Wyatt, who had worked with Brunel at Paddington, supplied the company with a new entrance on the cusp of the curve linking the GWR and the B&ER tracks. As at York, this graceful curve was the shed's dominant feature. It was designed by Francis Fox, son of Paddington's Charles Fox and consultant on the Simplon Tunnel, in its day the longest in the world. The roof now sweeps past the entrance to the old terminus, as if paying Bristol the briefest of respects before dashing on to the south-west.

The present Temple Meads is, in essence, Wyatt's creation, although Wyatt deferred to his former master's medievalism in adopting that style for his façades and platforms. His entrance sits at the head of a long rising approach, like a castle on a hill. Crenellated walls and turrets rise above canopies which spread like skirts down both sides of the forecourt. The building has lost its decorative features and French turret, bombed in the war, but it still holds centre stage.

The interior might be a church narthex, a lofty gothic passage containing the ticket office and waiting-rooms. It was altered in the 1930s by the GWR's Percy Culverhouse in a sub-art deco style with much ceramic tiling. More recently, Network Rail has defaced the walls with notices and advertisements, but the nobility of Wyatt's design survives.

Fox's shed is splendid. Its walls are of brick with sandstone dressings, the roof a web of spars and struts, curving into the open air at each end. It was doubled in size by Culverhouse in 1935, and forms an exhilarating portal to the west country. No less so is Bonapartes Café Bar, like a baronial great hall. To me, Temple Meads is a fine station, if somewhat lacking in heart. However, great things are promised of it in coming years, as the centre of a high-tech 'hub' for Bristol. It should prove the inspiration for a hundred future Brunels.

DAWLISH
★

The star on this stage is the sea, sometimes angry, mostly at peace. The down platform is virtually on the beach. On a fine day, we can enjoy a vista from Exmouth and the Dorset coast round to the red sandstone cliffs of Devon. Inland, the Haldon Hills rise steeply over the pretty resort.

The South Devon Railway was scene in 1846 of Brunel's most swiftly abortive experiment, an atmospheric railway. This involved a piston descend-ing beneath the locomotive into an iron tube in the bed of the track, with a leather flange along the top, along which it was sucked by compressed air. The leather leaked, the grease froze or was eaten by rats.

Points and crossings failed and trains could not reverse. After under a year of chaotic service, even Brunel had to admit defeat.

Brunel's sea-wall railway survived, along the south bank of the River Exe and round into Newton Abbot. At Dawlish, it runs above the beach, cutting the town off from the sea. On rough days, the waves beat against the station wall and drench the rails. In February 2014, a storm famously removed more than 100 feet of track. There has been talk of driving a new line inland, or even twenty-five yards out to sea, as yet to no avail.

Brunel's station was wooden and burned down in 1873. The present one dates from 1875. It is hand-somely Italianate, like a row of seaside townhouses, composed of projecting bays, heavily rusticated and stuccoed. The ticket hall rises to a fine ceiling.

The down platform on the sea side is in grey stone with bricked-up round-headed windows, defying the waves to do their worst. Viaduct arches and an ironwork colonnade carry the track along the beach, such that bathers could almost swim into the carriages at high tide. The station is best seen from the breakwater below, with a surreal view of express trains snaking past as if over the sand.

Dawlish station was given a handsome new footbridge in 2012, made of glass-reinforced plastic to defy the sea air. It was a faint hope. The station platforms are like the bridge of a battered trawler, their white paint perpetually stained with rust. Waiting passengers can at least taste the salt on their lips.

pages 146–7: Dawlish: the tang of salt on the lips

EGGESFORD

★

The line from Exeter to Barnstaple is a journey through paradise. It follows the path of the River Taw past rolling fields and bulging hedgerows, dotted with cattle and sheep and heavy with hawthorn blossom in spring. The line was the creation in 1854 of the North Devon Railway, but was taken over by the London & South Western Railway (LSWR), eager to steal territory from its rival, the Bristol & Exeter (affiliated to the Great Western).

The stations are built in local stone and are simple halts. All show a zest for gardening. The railway is today marketed as the Tarka Line, after the otter, or as a 'Rail Ale Trail' of Devonian pubs, some offering discounted beer on production of a train ticket.

The station was built on land belonging to the Earl of Portsmouth, who required that all trains stop there for his convenience. They still do, as the station is the token exchange point for the surviving block signalling on the line – ensuring that two drivers cannot enter the same length of track.

Approaching Eggesford, the Exeter train clatters along a single track beside a stream. There is no other sign of life. The picturesque station comprises what looks like a row of village cottages, more medieval than Victorian. The government's historic buildings list attributes it to Sir William Tite, no less, architect to the LSWR and responsible for the equally quaint Windsor & Eton Riverside as well as Perth and Carlisle. The design must have been an afternoon doodle for the busy man.

The platform's single- and double-storey cottages have steep roofs and asymmetrical gables, made of a stone known as mudstone rubble. The only indicator that this is a coherent work of architecture is that the roof gables all have the same coping steps, or kneelers. Two bay windows project on to the

Eggesford: mudstone picturesque

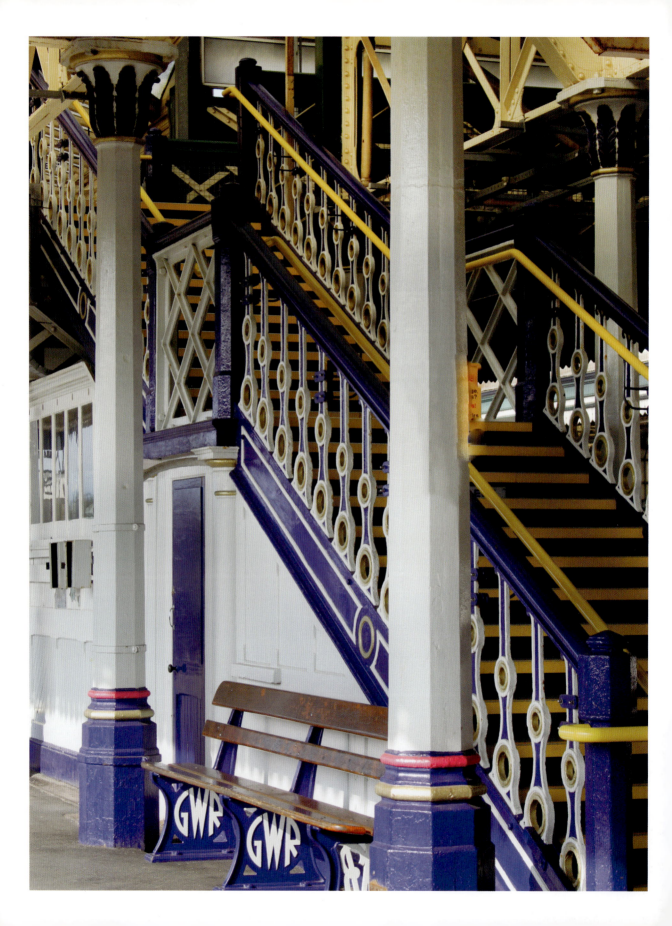

platform, as if on to a cottage garden. One is of the original waiting-room, the other the stationmaster's house. They are now private. Roses ramble and flowers spill from tubs. On a lazy summer afternoon, Eggesford is Devon's Adlestrop.

EXETER ST DAVID'S
★ ★

Exeter's original station was built by Brunel in 1844 for the Great Western Railway's (GWR) affiliated Bristol & Exeter line. There next appeared a rival service from London with the London & South Western (LSWR) arriving via Salisbury and Yeovil. In addition, there were lines from Crediton (the Exeter & Crediton Railway) and an extension to Plymouth via the South Devon Railway. To further confound confusion, some of the lines were standard and some broad gauge (see p. 141). To this day, passengers can find different trains to London leaving the station in opposite directions, depending on whether they are heading for Paddington or Waterloo.

In the more accommodating 1860s, the companies collaborated and a new station was built by a Bristol architect, Henry Lloyd. A giant wall supported one of the widest shed roofs in England, built by Francis Fox, creator of Bristol Temple Meads. His shed was demolished in 1914 and replaced by the present conventional ridge-and-furrow canopies.

This story is impossible to understand from the forecourt. Most prominent here is a 1938 addition, a neo-Georgian façade in stone, with the GWR's initials on its parapet. The entrance and canopy below are uncomfortably off-centre, and the station name is BR corporate lettering at its crudest.

This building is framed, quite literally, by Lloyd's inelegant attempt at baroque. As at Bournemouth, Exeter seems to be more wall than station, here without any crowning shed roof to support. The original wall, behind the 1930s addition, is composed of two storeys of neo-renaissance arches and an elaborate cornice. All this is in soft Devon stone with Bath stone dressings. It has the faded dignity of a Roman folly that has lost its purpose.

The removal of Fox's roof left a confusion of space on the platform side. An attic of wooden offices above the shed roof survived the roof's demolition, but is without a floor. It hovers above the platform like a clerestory, full of pigeons. The footbridge, tiled with GWR ceramics, has towers that echo the façade of the main station. In 1992, a local artist, Bridget Green, decorated the footbridge with murals of local characters in the style of Michelangelo's Sistine Chapel. They are an improvement on most railway art, to a programme well conceived and competently executed. I hope they survive.

It was at Exeter's station bookstall in 1934 that the publisher Allen Lane was awaiting a train after visiting Agatha Christie at her house, Greenway, on the River Dart. He was so dismayed at the quality of the books on offer that he decided to produce ones in paper covers for ease of reading on a train. Exeter St David's can thus claim to have inspired the paperback – and the publishers of this book. A plaque on the station honours this event.

above: **Sistine Chapel on the Exe**
opposite: **Exeter: stylish Great Western**

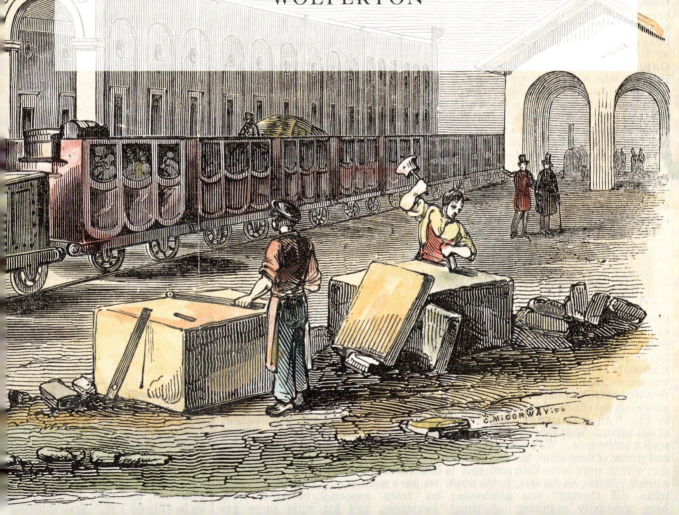

EAST ANGLIA

BURY ST EDMUNDS · CAMBRIDGE
CHAPPEL & WAKES COLNE
HERTFORD EAST · INGATESTONE
NEEDHAM MARKET · NORWICH
STAMFORD · STOWMARKET
WOLFERTON

EAST ANGLIA

Nowhere was the 1840s Mania (see p. 7) more manic than in East Anglia. At its height, thirty-two railways were under construction, most of them built to transport agricultural produce to the nearest port. Norwich found itself with four termini. Not until 1862 did company amalgamation yield the Great Eastern Railway, a *de facto* monopoly operating from Liverpool Street. By then the shambolic Eastern Counties Railway had built some of Britain's most eccentric stations, including a series by Sancton Wood and Frederick Barnes on the Ipswich & Bury line. Late-Victorian flair came from William Ashbee at Norwich, Chappel and Wolferton. The region was devastated by Beeching in the 1960s but, as a result, it has been fruitful territory for heritage railways.

BURY ST EDMUNDS

★ ★ ★

In 1845, the short-lived Ipswich & Bury Railway held a competition to design its new stations, intended to out-dazzle any competition. The termini at each end went to a 29-year-old London architect, Sancton Wood, while the intermediate ones went to Ipswich's Frederick Barnes. Both had worked in the London office of the classicist Robert Smirke, to whom Wood was helpfully related.

These were wild days on the railway, and the two men clearly felt free to design as they chose, with little thought for cost. The stations are without equal for their time, the more remarkable as East Anglia was thinly populated. Four of them, Bury St Edmunds, Stowmarket, Thurston and Needham Market, survive in recognisable form.

Sancton Wood's Bury is so odd it is thought both he and Barnes may have had a hand in its design. The neo-Jacobean stationmaster's house – mansion would be a better word – is similar to Barnes's stations down the line. On the other hand, the main station, with blind arches and baroque towers, has Wood's scholarly signature.

An antiquarian with a prolific practice in London and Dublin, Wood was an enthusiastic art student and had visited Spain and Portugal. His 1886 obituary described him as 'of a somewhat nervous and excitable temperament . . . possessed of considerable vigour of mind, and great refinement and delicacy of feeling'. He designed in neo-gothic at Stamford, neo-renaissance at Cambridge and Newmarket, the latter wretchedly demolished in 1980, and railway buildings in Ireland. All were charming essays in the prevailing eclecticism.

Bury St Edmunds station opened in 1847, its platforms at first-floor level on a viaduct over the surrounding buildings. The entrance on the street below has a façade of three large arches flanked by baroque pavilions. The left-hand one forms the base of one of two vaguely 'Wrennish' towers, matching another on the far platform.

The station was initially a terminus with an overarching roof, before the line was later extended to Ely and Cambridge. Today the roof has gone and Wood's towers and supporting walls beckon across the Bury rooftops, like the ghost of some ruined baroque palace. They have been restored and convey a sense of how Victorian stations looked when new, delighting in the colour of red brick and buff stone. A platform waiting-room is furnished with desks, sofas and WiFi terminals, presumably for delayed passengers. Gas lamps hang outside.

This was all very grand for what was (and is) a modest market town. To the left of the entrance range is the stationmaster's house, possibly by Barnes. It suggests, says the historian David Lloyd (in Binney and Pearce), 'a Cambridge college master's lodgings'. The façade has two projecting wings with Dutch gables and decorative bull's-eye windows between floors. Its back wall is that of the platform above, with a brick screen continuing to its left. However imposing, it must have been noisy and smoky.

Despite various plans for its re-use, this part of the building was derelict at the time of writing, dangerously invaded by buddleia. It seems strange to have restored just half a station. The environs are scruffy, and trees, slopes and embankments cry out for landscaping. In 2000, Bury celebrated the millennium by completing its first cathedral. It now needs to complete its second.

opposite: **Wrennish baroque on the Ipswich & Bury line**

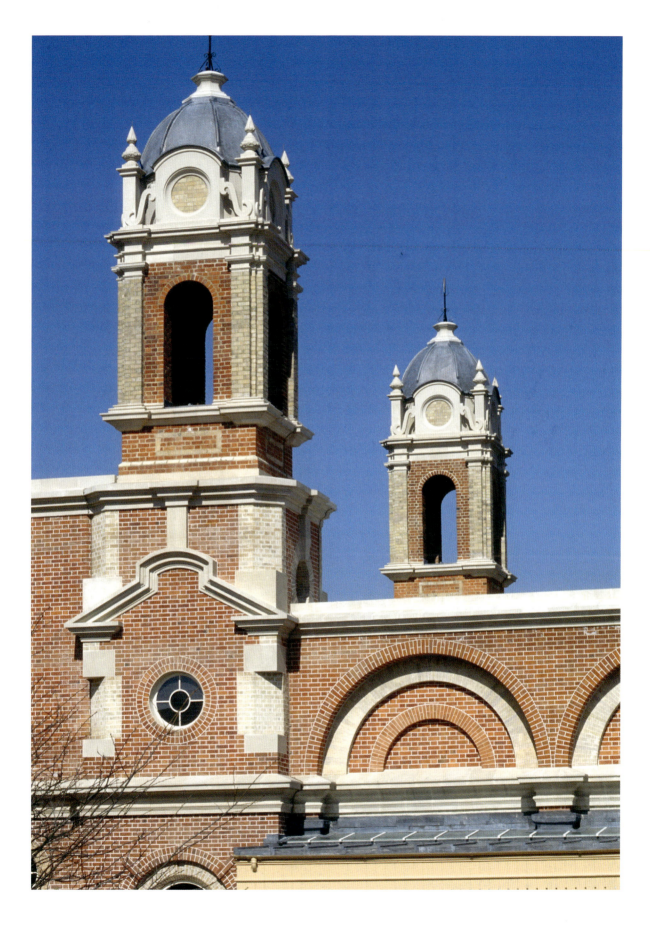

CAMBRIDGE

★

The early railway system was ostracised by academic institutions across Britain. Progress-hating dons wanted neither sight nor sound of so immoral a conveyance. The master of Cambridge's Magdalene College ordained that 'The coming of the railway to Cambridge would be highly displeasing both to God and myself.' There was no doubt whose opinion he regarded as decisive. College 'bulldogs' or security guards had to be given right of entry on to railway property to seek errant undergraduates, and a £5 fine was imposed on the Great Eastern Railway (GER) for any passenger conveyed to or from within three miles of the city between 10am and 5pm on a Sunday. Trains were duly banished to a station a mile away from the town centre in an inconvenient fenland meadow.

The GER hit back with a station façade that would have done credit to a Florentine piazza (see pp. 152–3). Its authorship is uncertain. Some attribute it to Francis Thompson (see p. 212) but others give it, more plausibly, to Sancton Wood (see p. 156).

The building was constructed in 1845 and, in early prints, appears as fronted by an open colonnade of fifteen arches. A lateral arch at each end greeted carriages into a long porte cochère, hung with large glass lanterns. The building was of pale East Anglian brick. Overhead was a smart Italianate cornice, with the coats of arms of Cambridge colleges in the spandrels. The railway would associate itself with the university, even if the university did not reciprocate.

The station platform was, at 500 yards, one of the longest in England and originally just one-sided. This meant it had to accommodate both leaving and arriving trains at the same time, with a scissors crossing in the middle. This now rare scissors crossing

Cambridge: dignity amid dross

survives, visible from the new, and hideous, foot-bridge. An island platform was not added until 2011.

As new railway companies arrived in Cambridge, extra platforms were added at the ends of the existing one, although this was impeded by the continued refusal of colleges to sell land for expansion. An 1889 history deplored the fact that 'four rival companies embrace a tangle of mutual inconvenience . . . owing to opposition of members of the university who by tradition take a blind side on railway matters'.

Cambridge station is not what it was. Its noble colonnade has been filled in, with brick footings and glass above. Horizontal bars in the arches spoil the vertical grace of the composition, exacerbated by filling one end with an M&S convenience store with garish window advertisements. A once great station is reduced to a cheap high street. The façade to the platform is more graceful, like a stucco terrace in Islington. I counted forty window and door bays facing the elongated platform. They are cluttered but still elegant.

The neighbourhood of the station is gateway to the new Cambridge, that of 'silicon fen' and the digital revolution. This revolution does not compare in architectural panache with its Victorian predecessor. The station's hinterland is a mess of unplanned estates with no attention given to the urban form of what is a new city. The station environs are given a square, but that is all. Only the ghost of the original structure retains a strange dignity.

Critically, the digital revolution seemed to think it could ignore the station. The result was a series of near riots in 2012, as commuters overwhelmed ticket barriers and platforms. Waits of forty minutes just to enter the station were reported. An urgent reordering reduced some of the chaos, but has left the station with the air of a refugee camp under siege. The university Science Park is to get a new station, but residual antagonism clearly continues. Platform signs announce Cambridge as 'home of Anglia Ruskin University', which must baffle any tourist.

CHAPPEL & WAKES COLNE
★

The modest branch line from Marks Tey to Sudbury was a lucky Beeching survivor. It has been rebranded confusingly as 'the Gainsborough Line on the edge of Constable country'. The station sits next to the Chappel viaduct which, at 355 yards over 32 arches, is the longest in East Anglia. The station was built against the side of an embankment, with a theatrical, very steep double flight of staircases from the street to the ticket office and platforms.

The station was designed by the Great Eastern's versatile William Ashbee and opened in 1891. It is now part of the East Anglian Railway Museum, but it is used by regular services to Sudbury. The building is a stern redbrick structure. Tall windows have keystones like surprised eyebrows and unusual brick skirts beneath them. There are store-rooms in the basement, rising to what appears to be a *piano nobile* above, containing museum displays. The stationmaster's house is in one wing. The canopies over the stairs have gone, but one remains on the footbridge.

Chappel has the period charm of a heritage station. The canopy brackets contain wheel motifs. Offices and waiting-rooms are furnished with old sofas, fireplaces and pictures, and the ticket office includes an early W. H. Smith's, monopoly supplier of news and books to the early railway passengers (see p. 19).

Across the track is a delightful shambles of old engines, carriages, wagons and signal-boxes, the customary wonderland of steam. I was standing here early one morning, lost in the past and with not a soul in sight, when the quiet was suddenly broken by the whoosh of a passing diesel. It intensified the subsequent silence.

EAST ANGLIA

opposite: **The wonderland of steam**

HERTFORD EAST

★

In a town blighted by road engineers, Hertford's station shows that transport can care about style. It is not just a station but a terminus, a spur built in 1888 from the Great Eastern Railway's Cambridge line. It was built by the company's architect, William Ashbee, who knew how to combine flair with a sense of place.

The station is a miniature essay in Elizabethan renaissance, an echo of the nearby palace of Hatfield. In front is a dominant porte cochère, with two arches on each of its three sides, similar to the much grander one at Norwich built by Ashbee a few years earlier. This is flanked by two Dutch gabled wings and majestic panelled chimneys. A second porte cochère, more modestly decorated, is round to one side.

Hertford has an architectural enrichment rare in stations. The walls are of fine red bricks, with York stone dressings to doorways and windows. The two front doors are divided by a carved pilaster that might have been borrowed from Hatfield. No expense was spared in the treatment of the window pediments and door over-mantels. These are of strapwork, in stone and terracotta, mostly displaying floral and animal motifs.

The interior is equally elegant. The ticket office ceiling is coffered, the panels filled with intricate plasterwork, again reminiscent of Ashbee's Norwich. The platforms have canopies with intricate brackets and elaborate column capitals. It is as if nothing but the best ironwork would do. Since the station is a terminus, its buffers reach almost to the concourse, their stop-lamps on delicate fluted columns. They are now so valued as to be 'listed' in their own right.

INGATESTONE

★

Ingatestone illustrates the desire of the early railway to reassure passengers that it was safe and un-revolutionary, indeed a traditional part of the landscape. Trains were like horses and carriages, just a bit faster, and stations like inns or tollbooths. Today, the station sits comfortably in its surroundings, as if nothing so indelicate as an engine would come near it.

There was another reason for this. Permission for a station in the village had been obtained by the Eastern Counties Railway as early as 1836. Litigation dragged on with the obstructive but influential local landowner, Lord Petre, leading to extensive delay. It was not until 1846 that the present building opened, with the company forced to accede to Petre's demand for a design in the style of his Tudor Ingatestone Hall.

The station today could pass for a gatehouse to the Hall. It is neo-Tudor with an entrance wing and cross-range for the stationmaster's house. The asymmetry is well balanced. The walls, restored in the 1990s, are in bright red brick with black diapering and creamy dressings. The chimney stacks answer the hollyhocks in the flower beds.

The up platform across the tracks was designed in an echoing style by the Great Eastern Railway in 1885, by the company's William Ashbee (see p. 165). Like so many railway architects, he was happy to show deference to the existing station. The shelter has a fine canopy with deep ogival valances. The peculiar joy of Ingatestone is to walk to the end of this platform on a summer's day, and gaze out over green-belt meadows to distant farms. If ever the green belt needed an advertisement, this is it. How can anyone tear themselves away from this scene for a City office?

NEEDHAM MARKET
★ ★

Most railway architects of the 1840s sought to slot their stations into the neighbouring architecture. Frederick Barnes (see p. 156) clearly felt the need to signify the arrival of the Ipswich & Bury Railway in Needham Market with a touch of class. The station building could pass for a mayoral mansion. It sits, self-important, overlooking a courtyard at the end of the town.

Built in 1846, the building is grand but a stylistic hodge-podge. A weak central bay with a pedimented gable is flanked by larger side bays, carrying gables and with projecting Tudor windows on ground and first floors. For some reason, Barnes then decided his composition needed medieval corner towers, complete with battlements. Was this an afterthought, as though the house were insufficiently grand, or was he just rustling through his pattern book looking for devices?

The entrance door has a rusticated surround, and the walls are diapered with black bricks. The side façade leading to the platform is altogether more poised. It might be that of a Dutch townhouse. One side was for the stationmaster, the other for a lucky head porter.

Like many of East Anglia's oversized stations – and many of its churches – Needham fell into neglect and is now a modest halt. The original building was eventually rescued with the help of the Railway Heritage Trust and is now privately occupied as offices. It still looks rather disjointed, with cars parked where there should be a front garden. Here is a former station straining after a new civic purpose fit for its dignity.

The platform side of the old building is decorous, canopied with slender columns and fine valances. The far platform gives on to woods and open fields. This is Suffolk at its most peaceful.

NORWICH

★ ★ ★ ★

Below its cathedral enclave, the city of Norwich slides downhill towards the river, and heads for open country. Across the river, it briefly returns to life with a magnificent station. Norwich, once Norwich Thorpe, was a gesture of victory by the Great Eastern Railway (GER) after its absorption of the Eastern Counties and Eastern Union in 1862. It was the culmination of East Anglia's twenty-year-old railway wars (see p. 155).

The town's railway age had begun with George and Robert Stephenson, father and son, recruited to build Norfolk's first line, from Great Yarmouth to Norwich. This was projected in 1843 and opened just a year later with twenty miles of track. There followed the usual rivalry, with the city blessed, or cursed, with termini at Thorpe, City, Trowse and Victoria. Not until 1886 was the GER able to concentrate on Thorpe, with a new terminus built by the in-house team of John Wilson as engineer and William Ashbee as architect.

East Anglia's early railways had espoused a tradition of domestic architecture from the 17th century, neo-Jacobean with vaguely Dutch features. By the 1880s, such tradition no longer dominated. Ashbee, for many years a practitioner of 'new Essex' Jacobean, here turned to fully-fledged French Renaissance. It was a style briefly but fiercely fashionable across southern England, as at Slough (see p. 127), Portsmouth (see p. 123) and Denmark Hill (see p. 97).

Ashbee's façade at Norwich is spectacular, a shotgun marriage of French nobleman to Russian princess, part Loire, part Hermitage. The four central bays rise over a massive porte cochère to a first floor of pilasters and window pediments. The building has a convex domed roof covered in scaled tiles of zinc. A central cupola is fronted by a clock within a pediment, guarded by four tall chimney stacks and a parapet with urns.

On either side of this central pavilion stretch two-storey wings of eight bays, their windows alternately triangular and segmental. The ground floor has elliptical arches, some above doors, some above windows. These have carved tympanums, with elaborate classical motifs. The whole composition is executed in red brick with stone dressings. Well restored, it beams confidently over its forecourt, a sophisticated work of its period.

The interior is no disappointment. The ticket hall hints at a Versailles ballroom. Fluted Ionic pilasters rise to a plasterwork cornice of swags and coffered ceiling, all in yellow and cream wash. To buy a ticket here is a privilege. The concourse beyond is no less grand, a fitting terminus for a railway that begins at magnificent Liverpool Street. Its roof, on long elliptical girders, takes the form of four ridge-and-furrow naves and two side aisles, enclosed by handsome brick walls. The only solecism is the tacky, plastic-roofed shops that flank the concourse. Ashbee would turn in his grave.

Where the roof ends, its function is assumed by conventional platform canopies, leading away in a graceful avenue of columns and brackets.

opposite: **Tudor grandeur at Needham Market**
pages 166–7: **Norwich: France meets Russian princess**

STAMFORD

★ ★

Aristocrats were as nervous as bishops and academics when faced with the coming of the railway. They saw it as dirty, noisy and alarmingly democratic. Only when they found trains rather useful for getting up to town did some of them change their view, and then they wanted stations of their own. The Marquess of Exeter, with his palatial mansion at Burghley on the outskirts of Stamford, was no exception. When the Midland Railway's Peterborough line sought access to the old market town in 1848, the marquess insisted that the line pass through the town centre in a tunnel and the new station be kept out of sight. When the marquess later regretted his decision and wanted a station of his own, he had to pay for a link to the Great Northern Railway. Built in 1856 in a neo-Elizabethan style, this station is now closed and is a house in Water Street.

The Midland's station, on the other hand, designed by Sancton Wood (see p. 156), is set in a modern estate next to the river and is a charming small-town station of the 1840s. It comprises a station house of two storeys, linked by a crenellated gothic arcade to a double-gabled booking hall with tower and bellcote. One façade has an arch enclosing two others. Peter Burman sees 'an echo of the Abbot's Kitchen at Glastonbury and elements of 18th-century Hawksmoor gothic'. Wood must have enjoyed this commission. The building material is the honey limestone used throughout this exquisite town.

Stamford's footbridge perfectly complements the station. It curves over the tracks with a mass of latticework, framed by the sight of the marquess's tunnel beyond. On my visit, a volunteer was quietly weeding the platform garden, intrigued that a stranger should find her beloved station so remarkable. 'It's just a station,' she said.

Touch of Glastonbury at Stamford

STOWMARKET

★ ★

Stowmarket is the star of the short-lived Ipswich & Bury Railway company, and was by Frederick Barnes at his most bravura. Where his Needham Market (see p. 164) is eccentric and rather squeezed, Stow-market is expansive and polished. The station sits on the edge of the town, a civic building in its own right. The reason for this appears to be parish pride. The town was keen to show a welcome to the new railway and made it an offer of a low-interest loan for the station, as well as voting the enormous sum of £1,000 for a new road to its forecourt. The only sadness is that they did not provide a lawn in front, to add to its manorial dignity.

Completed in 1849, the building is composed of a central pavilion and two wings, each a variant on that East Anglian foible, the Dutch gable. The central entrance block is an extraordinary building, its roof essentially four giant gables with a single chimney. The frontage has two side bays thrust forward, with rusticated pilasters and arched windows. On either side of this centre block are single-storey ranges linked to side pavilions, again Dutch gabled and flanked by three-storey polygonal turrets. This is a sophisticated articulation of an extended façade, for which the Dutch style seems ideally suited. In front of the side ranges are small front gardens with ornamental screens.

The buildings are now mostly sub-let. The plat-forms to the rear are unexciting, although the flat awnings are original. On my last visit, the day was so exceptionally hot the station staff were handing out free ice-creams to delayed passengers. A block of bland modern flats across the forecourt makes a nod in Barnes's direction. It has three brick gables on its façade.

WOLFERTON
★

The closure in 1969 of the line from King's Lynn to Hunstanton deprived the royal estate at Sandringham of its railway. Since the family had not used it since 1966, this was no great hardship, and the Queen declined an offer to take the local station of Wolferton into her guardianship. The halt was left marooned, part museum, part private property. The mooted reopening of the Hunstanton line allows me to include it in my list.

The initial station was built in 1862 for the use of the Prince of Wales (later Edward VII) after the purchase of Sandringham. The Norfolk landscape apparently reminded his homesick wife, Alexandra, of her native Denmark. The entrance to the royal waiting-room is duly adorned with the Prince of Wales's *fleur de lis*, not the monarch's coat of arms.

The station was rebuilt in 1876 and then enlarged by the Great Eastern Railway's William Ashbee in 1898. Ashbee here revelled in his favourite neo-Tudor, the style of most of the Sandringham estate. It must have irked him that the royal train had to travel from St Pancras (and the Midland Railway) rather than the GER's Liverpool Street, which he was also rebuilding. By tradition, the royal family could not enter the City of London except by invitation on ceremonial occasions.

Over time, the number of buildings expanded on both sides of the track, giving Wolferton the feel of a town station. Photographs show royal guests mounting carriages for the journey to the house, with guards of honour on parade. The museum records 'Kings and Queens, Emperors and Empresses and all the high society of the day disembarked here . . . the drive ablaze with scarlet uniforms and aloud with music of military bands.'

Wolferton was the scene of one of the best-known railway anecdotes. Edward VII and Tsar Nicholas of Russia, having abandoned their guards, went walking in the Sandringham woods and became lost. Hitching a lift to a neighbouring station, they boarded the train for Wolferton, and were duly asked for their tickets. 'But I am the King of England and this is the Tsar of Russia,' said the king. 'Glad to meet you,' said the ticket collector, 'and I am the Archbishop of Canterbury. Tickets, please.'

After closure, the station was acquired by a railway buff, Eric Walker, as residence and museum. It languished after his death until it was bought in 2001 by Richard Brown, another enthusiast worthy of the place. The main buildings are private houses, but the rest of the station has been restored and opened to visitors.

The station is reached from the main road along a lane through the Sandringham estate, lined by banks of rhododendron. The platform buildings flank the former track bed, which is currently filled with a garden. Railway trolleys and baggage fill the passages. Signs, lights and signals are in place, proudly boasting the GER 'at Her Majesty's service'. The gas lamps are topped with royal crowns. If the Hunstanton line does reopen, intrepid engineers will have to cut through a wall of forest heading north. All strength to their arm.

opposite: Stowmarket: Holland comes to East Anglia
above: Ashbee's regal Gents
pages 172–3: Sandringham Tudor for arrivals of State

MIDLANDS

BIRMINGHAM NEW STREET
CROMFORD · GOBOWEN · GREAT
MALVERN · HEREFORD · LEAMINGTON
SPA · LEICESTER · LOUGHBOROUGH
CENTRAL · NOTTINGHAM
SHREWSBURY · STOKE
WELLINGBOROUGH · WORKSOP

MIDLANDS

The Midlands was the battlefield of the early railway. First into the charge was Robert Stephenson's early London & Birmingham which, as early as 1846, merged with the Grand Junction to form the stately London & North Western (LNWR), with its principal works at Crewe. Of the LNWR's original Birmingham stations, only the forlorn Curzon Street arch remains.

A plethora of companies fought for business down the west Midlands and Welsh Marches, leaving fine stations at Chester and Shrewsbury. The Potteries had the North Staffordshire Railway all to itself, with headquarters at Stoke-on-Trent. To the east lay the legacy of George Hudson's mighty Midland Railway based at Derby. It competed over much of its territory with the Great Northern, a company famously more interested in speed than architecture. Matters were complicated at the end of the century by the arrival of Sir Edward Watkin's abortive Great Central company.

The post-war losses of Birmingham New Street and Derby were almost on a par with that of Euston (see p. 24). The region's best surviving stations are the late-Victorian baroque façades of Leicester and Nottingham. Charming smaller ones remain at Great Malvern and Wellingborough. In the 1930s, the Great Western put in an appearance at art deco Leamington Spa. The Midlands has something for everyone.

BIRMINGHAM
NEW STREET

★

There have been three versions of New Street
station, the first majestic, the second hideous, the
third controversial. Meanwhile Curzon Street,
the classical terminus of the world's first intercity
railway, the London & Birmingham, stands like a
folly in a derelict wasteland a mile away. It closed in
1966 and awaits the possible arrival of High Speed 2,
once again dividing custom across the city.

The first New Street station boasted one of the
finest early shed roofs. Bombed but not destroyed, it
was replaced in 1967 by what Steven Parissien rightly
calls a 'Stygian gloom . . . [a] breathtaking vapidity . . .
[a] depressing underground bunker'. In 2003, *Country
Life* readers voted New Street the second worst
eyesore in the country (after wind turbines).

In 2008, a third New Street emerged, or at least a
branch of the John Lewis Partnership with platforms
in its basement. The ticket barriers are subordinated
to a shopping mall. The platforms are the old ones,
still emphatically 'below stairs', and no more dignified than before. The new concourse atrium is
Birmingham 'bling' at is most promiscuous.

The original design of Alejandro Zaera-Polo of
Foreign Office Architects was for an undulating
stainless steel reptile, snaking round the entire site,
with screens in its jaws for train information. Now
substantially modified and much defiled by advertisements, where it survives it is certainly eye-catching.

More dramatic is the interior atrium surrounding
the John Lewis store, puckishly called Grand Central.
Here three domes are linked by swirling white
membranes, like the innards not of a snake but a
shark. The treatment of this post-modernist space was
the subject of so much argument between architect
and client that Zaera-Polo walked away from the
project. What amounts to a giant shopping centre
makes an impressive overture to a once great station,
and a vast improvement on its predecessor.

**Birmingham bling: New Street's
Grand Central**

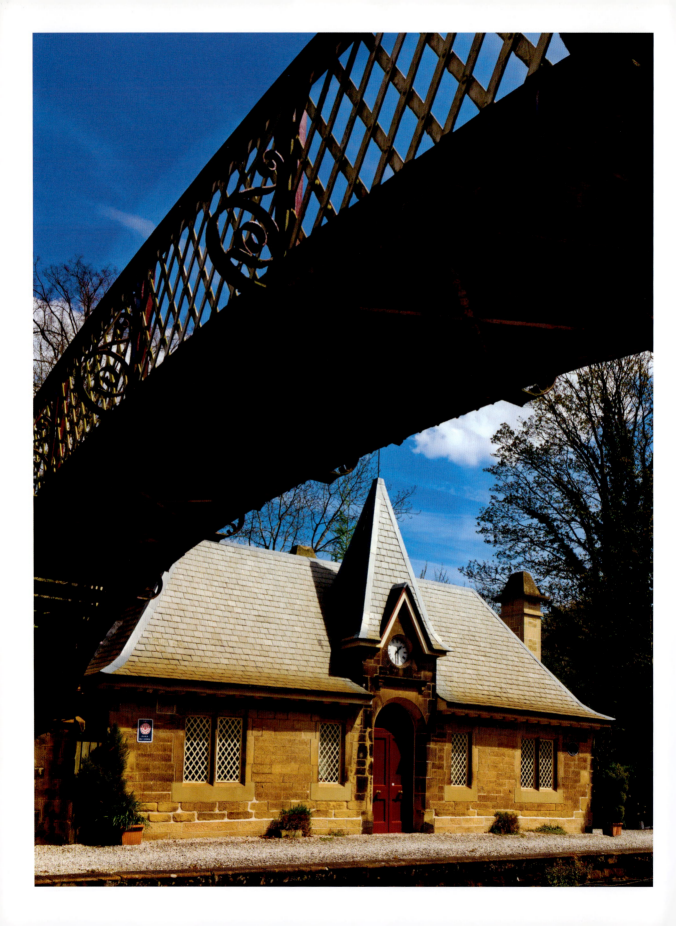

CROMFORD
★ ★

A climb is needed to reach this Derbyshire gem, nestling in the woods over the Derwent valley, a mile to the north-east of the old village. Cromford was the site of Richard Arkwright's first water-powered spinning mill in 1771, and thus claims the title (with others) of being the cradle of the Industrial Revolution. The arrival of the railway and its tunnel to Matlock came in 1849. A stationmaster's house overlooking the tunnel entrance followed in 1855, with the present station in 1860.

The builder was Joseph Paxton's assistant (and son-in-law), George Stokes. At the time, Paxton was working on the Rothschild mansion of Mentmore in Buckinghamshire, in a high French Renaissance style. Hence, perhaps, the hints of France about the station. It may also explain the grandeur of the stationmaster's house, possibly intended by Stokes and Paxton as an entrance lodge to the surrounding Willersley estate owned by the Arkwright family. It is an example of stationmaster's houses aspiring to the status of rectories.

Stokes' original waiting-room sits on the far up-side of the tracks from the present entrance, like something out of a fairy tale, an impression enhanced by the dark entrance to the Willersley tunnel beyond. The picturesque building has steeply pitched roofs with a curious, steeple-like central turret and gable. The windows are filled with lattice tracery and the walls are of creamy Derbyshire stone.

In 2010, the building was restored as a holiday cottage and is inaccessible. Its restoration was celebrated on the cover of the Oasis single *Some Might Say*, with its line, 'I've been standing on the station In need of education in the rain.' The Gallagher brothers can be seen on the footbridge, one with a watering can, while a homeless man asks, 'Education please.' The clock has been replaced in the gable. All that is lacking are the original iron finials on the roof ridges.

A later station building erected by the Midland Railway on the down platform is in the same style but plainer. Over the platform is a deep canopy with white valances above Midland columns. This building is now unstaffed and is let as offices. The whole enclave is buried in delicious greenery.

GOBOWEN
★

Historians of station architecture love Gobowen. With the closure of Oswestry's other station in 1966, it is the main halt for the town three miles away. The old building looks as if it were transplanted from Nash's Regent's Park. When restored in the 1980s, it shone resplendent, but on my last visit the building, let out to a firm of lawyers, was down at heel and much in need of decoration.

opposite and above: Cromford's *cottage orné* picturesque, plus album sleeve

The station was one of many designed in 1846 for the Shrewsbury & Chester Railway (later, the Great Western) by Thomas Penson, member of the Penson surveyors' family of Oswestry. He designed Shrewsbury station (see p. 194) and was responsible for much of the neo-Tudor rebuilding of medieval Chester (see p. 212). Even for a Victorian, his eclecticism was impressive. At Gobowen, he abandoned Tudor in favour of an essay in late-Regency Italianate.

The plan is asymmetrical, two-storey with a three-storey Italianate tower, round-arched upper floor windows and a bow window looking out over the level crossing. Most distinctive are the deep eaves and slate roof with, tucked beneath it, elaborate console brackets on a red background. On the platform elevation is a frieze with strapwork panels. For its date, it is novel only in being a railway station.

A pharmacy now occupies the pretty keeper's cottage next to the level crossing.

The present station building opposite is later, in the same style as the original but lacking stucco render. Its dull brick exterior shows what a difference comes from a splash of white. The original platform canopies have been moved further along the platform, with segmental roofs and valances. The station still has its semaphore signals, while its original name board, 'Gobowen for Oswestry', is 'listed' for preservation.

The station is rare in being run not by a railway company but by volunteers of the not-for-profit Severn Dee Travel agency. Facing closure in 1992, the ticket office was taken over as a project by a local girls' school, Moreton Hall, and its enthusiastic geography master, David Lloyd. The then doomed British Rail challenged the girls of 'Moreton Hall

Travel' to take £10,000 in tickets in the first year, which they did. They never looked back. In 1995, the operation became Severn Dee under Lloyd's management, and continues in being since his death. It is a model of community enterprise.

GREAT MALVERN
★ ★ ★

Victorian Malvern espoused one industry, that of retirement. It was an upland Torquay, spread along the soft slopes of the Malvern Hills. As such, it offered much scope for ambitious architects such as Edmund Elmslie, from a local family rich on West Indian sugar. In 1861–2, he snapped up commissions for both the station and the adjacent Imperial Hotel. The station, on the Worcester to Hereford line, had opened in 1860.

Elmslie was designing at the height of the battle of styles. His Great Malvern station was an essay in neo-romanesque – known as trecento. In grey-green sandstone with limestone dressings and slate roofs, the building sits low against the hillside. A charming (but anachronistic) gothic tower was sadly demolished in the 1960s and has yet to be rebuilt.

Great Malvern's romanesque is chiefly manifest in the doors and windows, which are round-arched, some with attached columns and foliated capitals – all faintly monastic. The most celebrated features are on its platforms, where Elmslie's canopies rest on iron columns and brackets bursting with delicate quatrefoils. The capitals on these columns are the most remarkable ironwork on the Victorian railway. They were the creation of a local sculptor, William Forsyth, in 1863 and are in the form of bunches of flowers, brilliantly painted. Each is different, borrowed from the adjacent Malvern Hills. Such manifestations of nature must have been uplifting for those arriving to seek relief from the ailments of life. They are a vivid echo of the 13th-century leaf capitals of Southwell Minster in Nottinghamshire, so evocative that Pevsner gave them an entire book to themselves (*The Leaves of Southwell*).

At the west end of platform 2 is a mysterious locked door under a stern romanesque arch. This is the entrance to 'the Worm', a twisting subterranean passage built to take first-class passengers uphill to Elmslie's Imperial Hotel. The hotel became St James's girls' school (now Malvern St James) in 1919 and the Worm is listed as historic. It is accessible only on 'open' days.

Lady Foley's Tea Room on platform 1 was the private waiting-room of Lady Emily Foley, daughter of the 3rd Duke of Montrose, on whose land the station was built. She clearly wished to avoid contact with ordinary mortals. Today, it is a haven of home-baked cakes, whisky and free newspapers, surrounded by photographs from *Brief Encounter* and other railway impedimenta. It compensated me for a cancelled train to Worcester.

above and pages 184–5: **The leaves of Malvern brought to life**

HEREFORD

★ ★

Here is another Marches town once under siege from railway speculators. At one point it was targeted by the Newport, Abergavenny & Hereford, the Shrewsbury & Hereford, the Hereford, Ross & Gloucester and the Oxford, Worcester & Wolverhampton. In the 1850s, this led to it being blessed, or cursed, with two stations. It tried to build a third 'joint' station, plans for which survive with a Venetian colonnade and campanile. In the event, the Shrewsbury & Hereford won with a building by the company's architect, Thomas Penson (see p. 182).

Just as Penson had earlier designed Shrewsbury to match the adjacent castle, so he appears to have given Hereford the appearance of a bishop's palace, presumably in deference to its cathedral city host. Certainly he allowed his imagination, and the company's expense, to run wild. The frontage is exceptionally elegant, an extended two-storey composition in Tudor gothic, with a multitude of paired lancet windows. There are six steep-gabled bays, two of them thrust forward and two at each end. The gables have stone finials and the chimneys are also dressed in stone. The only concession to the building's function is a fine clock attached to the central gable.

The platforms maintain the clerical theme, again with paired gothic windows with trefoil tops. The canopies have unusually slender columns, with pretty gothic tracery in their end gables. Valances are all in place. Particularly handsome is the restored foot-bridge, brightly painted in navy and white and with twin lift towers, wooden on a brick base and with pyramidal caps. It proves these structures do not have to be as ugly as they so often are.

Penson's episcopal gothic

LEAMINGTON SPA

★

Few stations were built between the world wars and fewer still in the art deco style of the 1930s. At Leamington the Great Western Railway (GWR) competed fiercely with the London & North Western, but after the 1923 Grouping, the two lines gradually merged until a new joint station was built by the GWR's ubiquitous Percy Culverhouse. This was in 1938 in a last burst of corporate pride before nationalisation.

The main entrance façade is handsome, of three storeys in Culverhouse's cross-over style from neo-Georgian to Modernism (see p. 281). The central block is of nine bays with extensive wings, and is covered in white stone panels with metal windows. The metal lamps have survived. The ensemble is reminiscent of a factory on London's Great West Road.

Although the building was awaiting urgent restoration at the time of writing, the structure and most of the original interiors remain. The ticket windows still have their wood surrounds and the subways are lined with yellow tiles, imaginatively decorated with interwar posters. Most remarkable are the waiting-rooms and buffet, restored in 2008 with a grant from the Railway Heritage Trust. Fireplaces, benches, door fittings, mirrors, railings and parquet all date – or are reproduced – from the 1930s, in clean art deco. A vigorous group, the Friends of Leamington Station, has ensured that these are

Leamington's art deco

matched, as in the subways, with posters of the period.

The Friends' activity is also evident in a most enterprising station garden. This is no apology for a municipal flower bed, but a fully fledged herbaceous border, heavy with rye grass, lawns, trees and shrubs. Two name boards with Victorian lettering have been installed at the platform ends. They look curiously old-fashioned, but the place names are large enough to be visible to passing trains, a convenience for transient passengers that the railway usually neglects.

The waiting-room interior restored

LEICESTER
★★★

Baroque Leicester or baroque Nottingham? The two East Midlands cities rival each other in the splendour of their stations, both built for the Midland Railway at the end of the 19th century. Central Leicester has little architecture to admire, so the more precious is the station, rebuilt in 1895 by the Midland's chief architect and maestro of baroque revival, Charles Trubshaw.

The station is the survivor of what, at the height of the Mania (see p. 7), were no fewer than seven stations in Leicester, Leicester North Road being at the middle of what were a dozen cross-cutting regional routes. The former Midland Counties Railway station in London Road was a magnificent classical building, of which two Egyptian-style gateposts still stand in a rear

car park. Of the others, only the battered façade of the closed Leicester Central still stands in Great Central Street, awaiting restoration of sorts.

Mercifully, it was London Road that survived, or at least its façade did. This lies sleek in stone and terracotta on a sloping bridge over the railway tracks below, displaying the Victorian talent for walls with character. The façade is essentially a baroque screen to a giant porte cochère. It is composed of large arched openings, two for arrivals and two for departures, with Wren-style windows in between. These are balanced by a clock tower at one end, and a graceful turn to a side street at the other. The brightly restored red and white stonework looks exceptionally rich.

The entrances, dressed in terracotta, show Trubshaw's sense of fun, the two arrival arches are crowned with enriched pediments, with the word

ARRIVAL set on golden mosaics between pediment and arch. Departures were felt to be less worthy of recognition and are more modest, just arches with the words set into the balustrade. Panels offer variations on the company's initials MR and the words IN and OUT. This is repeated on the parapet of the bridge across the road.

The domed clock tower has a faintly Indian appearance and contains what is apparently England's last station clock wound by hand. At its foot is an amiable statue of Thomas Cook, founder of the mass travel industry. It was from Leicester in July 1841 that Cook, a Baptist preacher, led his first railway excursion, ten miles north to Loughborough. The journey was intended to promote temperance. Simon Bradley records '500 sober but happy

Leicester arrives in style

189

travellers' journeying to a lunch at which 'dancing, speeches and other diversions were provided in the private park of a wealthy supporter'. Cook urged the crowd to give 'One cheer more for Teetotalism and Railwayism!'

Within four years, Cook was running profitable tours to Liverpool, Snowdonia and the Great Exhibition in London, and a global service industry was born. Born, too, was that horror of train managers ever since, the excursion special, its occupants rarely teetotal.

Leicester's porte cochère is now enclosed as a concourse, restored in 2012. The interior walls replicate the external arches. Beyond lies a former ticket hall, tiled in tones of burnt sugar and leading to what is the modern station below.

LOUGHBOROUGH CENTRAL
★ ★

Loughborough Central is the archetypal railway museum, the reincarnation of a main-line station of the 1950s. The line itself is a relic of Sir Edward Watkin's 1899 dream of bringing his new Great Central Railway south to Marylebone and, he hoped, the Continent via a channel tunnel (see p. 62). Watkin's base was the old Manchester, Sheffield & Lincolnshire Railway and the new company's tracks were even assigned as 'down' not 'up' to London.

Most of the line fell to Beeching in the 1960s, amid much protest, but fragments survive. Loughborough Central reopened in 1974 as part of the restored Great Central main-line heritage railway, and a private company now runs steam trains on a double track over eight miles and four stations between Loughborough and Leicester North Road. They draw some of the smartest Pullman cars I know.

The station is reached from a bridge and entrance building overlooking an island platform. It evokes in its entirety the final days of steam. The original nomenclature and details are carefully preserved. The café is a 'refreshment' room, the shop an 'emporium'. The ticket office is a wood-panelled 'booking hall'. A coal fire burns in the waiting-room. I even spied a typewriter in a rear office. Staff wear company uniforms, waistcoats and caps.

Apart from the passengers, everything is from the great age of steam: luggage trolleys are piled with steamer trunks, walls are lined with seaside posters. An early radio and an early television adorn the waiting-room. The smell of coal smoke hangs about the canopies. Signals rise and noisily fall, and jointed rails clank satisfyingly under passing trains. The bridge and entrance buildings remain coated in soot. Even the lavatories are still in use, the Gents being glass-roofed and splendidly tiled.

Beside the stairs down from the ticket office is a wooden ramp on which to slide parcels, an admirable facility. The platforms are protected from the weather by a fine glass, metal and wood canopy with deep valances, restored in 2013. At the end of one platform is a small museum of railway memorabilia, a museum within a museum.

MIDLANDS

opposite: Old times and news at Loughborough

NOTTINGHAM

★ ★ ★ ★

Nottingham after the Second World War was a fine city on a hill, and blessed with four of England's best provincial stations, the Midland, Victoria and two in London Road. The neo-renaissance Victoria was built in 1900 for the new Great Central Railway by a local civic architect, Albert Lambert. This was smashed to the ground for a shopping centre in the devastation of central Nottingham in the 1960s and 1970s, only its clock tower surviving. Of the London Road stations, one has gone and the other, Dutch revival in style, is a health club.

The Midland remains in its original glory. The company's adherence to the classical tradition followed the evolution of that tradition over the 19th century, passing from Greek revival under George Hudson in the 1840s, through Italian Renaissance to full-blown baroque revival. Unlike its effete Renaissance companion at Leicester, of ten years earlier, Nottingham is vulgar baroque through and through. It was built in 1904 in place of its predecessor, a stern Tuscan structure, to avert the threat from the newly arrived Great Central's Victoria station. It sits confident in the centre of town, a monument to the last great flourish of the Edwardian railway.

The station is on a bridge over its tracks, with spacious stairs down to island platforms, but its power lies in its entrance block on to Carrington Street. This is in heavy railway baroque, on a bombastic par with London's Victoria and Waterloo stations. The stone was once coal-black but is now dark pink, bold and loud. The frontage consists of the grandest of porte cochères, with a giant arch at each end and five arches along the front. Those at each end and two in the middle have pediments breaking through the bold cornice. The arches drip with terracotta swags and heavy rustication.

The centrepiece of the frontage is a large clock tower worthy of Vanbrugh, with heavy coping and a domed cap. This is truly an entrance to rank with Newcastle Central. It clearly overawed the rival Great Central and even deterred Nottingham's council, as it razed much of its post-war city to the ground.

The porte cochère's interior has been sensitively converted into the inevitable enclosed concourse, but divided between a taxi drop-off and shops. At the drop-off end, the original art nouveau ironwork has mercifully survived and is some of the finest I have seen on the railway. Nor is that all: the concourse's inner wall is treated with the same baroque stylishness as the exterior, again with arches in sandstone and terracotta. One segmental pediment displays superb arts and crafts flair.

above: **Nottingham's railway art nouveau**
opposite: **East Midlands Vanbrugh-style**

MIDLANDS

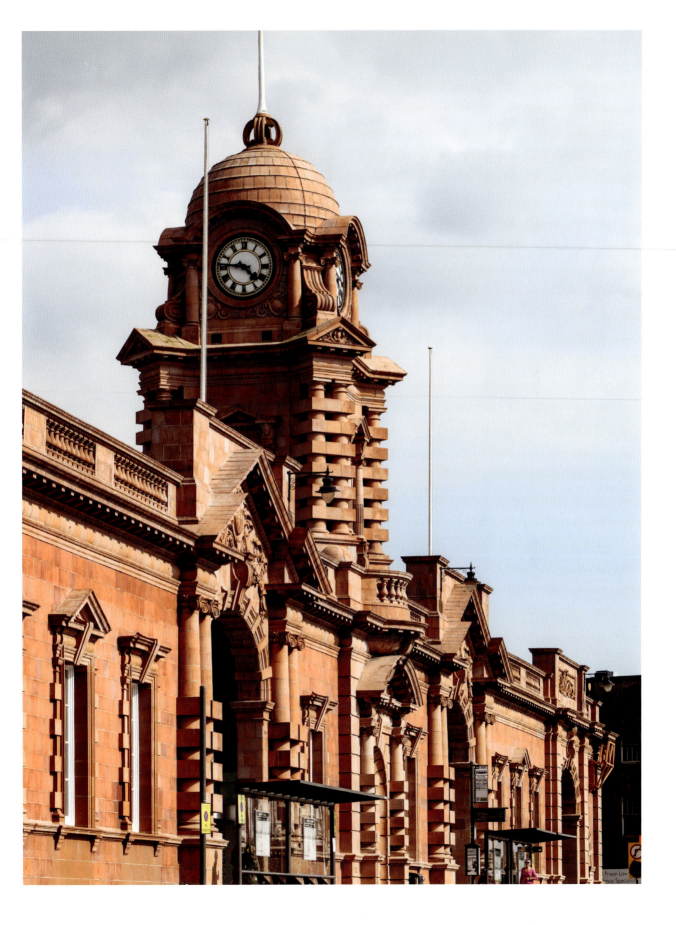

Nottingham then has a second spectacle, the ticket hall beyond. It is of similar proportions to the porte cochère and could be a dance hall or gallery. Here the classicism is closer to Renaissance. The walls are in pale stone above a green-tiled dado, with arched windows surmounted by round ones, divided by paired pilasters. Overhead is a long central lantern letting light flood into the interior. Surely this gallery could be put to some imaginative use, perhaps by Nottingham Museum?

Beyond lie the two island platforms, continuing the sandstone and terracotta baroque of the main building. The old buffet has been restored, including its ceiling and fireplace. A new southern concourse links the station to the new tram system.

SHREWSBURY
★ ★ ★ ★

Shrewsbury was a town massively abused by the Mania (see p. 7). From the 1840s onwards, the Shrewsbury & Chester Railway (SCR), in alliance with the Shrewsbury & Birmingham and the Shropshire Union companies, smashed their way across the delicate isthmus in the bend of the River Severn. They crashed past the medieval castle, the Georgian prison and the Elizabethan school, wrecking the setting of them all. At one point, there were more railway lines into Shrewsbury than there were roads. Although time has softened the impact of this assault, its scars are still painful. Railway consumes an absurd amount of Shrewsbury's land.

As if in remorse, the Shrewsbury & Chester coated the new station façade in neo-gothic. The architect given this task in 1849 was Thomas Penson (see p. 182), deferring to the aggrieved castle with a design of Tudor windows, chimneys, battlements and an entrance tower. This made the composition lopsided. Penson later added an ungainly wing at right angles to the façade, creating a miniature St Pancras of the Marches, and rendering it even more lopsided.

In 1903, hard though it is to envisage, the station forecourt was excavated and a third storey was inserted actually beneath the other two. What had

Apologetic gothic: Penson's Shrewsbury façade

been an attractive castle square with a central obelisk became today's scruffy car park. Is there no landscape architect on the railway?

Penson's façade is picturesque, especially when lit at night, its grey limestone an emphatic contrast with the red brick and stone of Shrewsbury's other buildings. Medieval windows carry corbel heads of men and monsters. A canopy across the façade has brackets with quatrefoils, in white, red and green. The panelled Edwardian ticket office might be the foyer of a comfortable hotel.

The rest of the station merits drastic restoring. Even on the platforms, Penson adhered to medieval. The rear of the main building over platform 1 has an attractive upper storey of cottagey windows, floating on a river of ridge-and-furrow canopies. The remaining façades are in red brick, with elaborate stone dressings, arch spandrels and corbel heads. Looming

overhead is the dark stone of the old castle, while on the far side of the tracks is the former prison, the 18th-century Dana Gaol. From here, Housman's condemned Shropshire Lad could hear 'the trains all night groan on the rail'.

To the south is the best feature of the station, the view created by what it had destroyed. The platforms were later extended over the bridge crossing the Severn, where the tracks of the former railway companies can be seen swerving back and forth across the old goods yards. Beyond stand the town's two great monuments, gothic Shrewsbury Abbey and the Severn Bridge Junction signal-box. On any but the finest day, they seem gaunt and isolated, surrounded by a swirl of tracks and car parks, clinging to each other for companionship.

Last of the greats: the 180-lever signal-box

The signal-box is England's most famous. It was built by the London & North Western in 1903 and is perched 35 feet high on three storeys of brickwork. The 180 levers make it not just the biggest mechanical box still in use in Britain but, since the closure of the 191-lever box in Melbourne, Australia, the biggest in the world. In an electronic age, it is hard to appreciate the importance of these landlocked lighthouses to the early railway. They were its nerve-centres, critical to its safe operation and manned by men of skill and lonely comradeship.

The phasing-out of Britain's last mechanical boxes is not expected until well into the 2020s. We can only hope that, by then, someone has taken Shrewsbury in hand and made it the fine station it could yet be, hovering over the splendours of the Severn valley.

STOKE-ON-TRENT
★ ★ ★

Their most ardent fans would accept that the towns of the Potteries are no beauties. Their failure to modernise their staple industry, ceramics, was accompanied by the destruction of their industrial heritage of old kilns and factories. As in the Welsh valleys, history's one legacy, a distinctive architectural personality, vanished in what, to Pevsner, was 'an urban tragedy'. Most of the old potteries were simply smashed to the ground. The more blessed is Stoke station, centre of a most attractive group of Victorian buildings and well preserved.

The North Staffordshire Railway retained a proud and separate existence until the 1923 Grouping, running trains between Crewe, Stafford and Derby. Its office headquarters, principal station and hotel, all in Winton Square, were built by Sir Henry Hunt, the company's civil engineer as well as site surveyor to the Palace of Westminster and the Great Exhibition. Living from 1810 to 1889, Hunt was one of those rocks on which the Victorian age was built.

At Stoke in 1848, he produced a masterpiece of station architecture. It is in the Jacobean style, of two storeys with three widely spaced Dutch gables and gabled wings, all in wine-coloured Staffordshire brick. The roof is punctuated by Tudor chimneys and covered in two colours of hand-made local tiles. In front of the façade is an arcaded loggia of seven arched bays and Tuscan columns. The balcony above looks as if it were designed for members of the board to address the shareholders in the forecourt below.

The ticket hall seems largely intact, with a bold memorial arch leading to the platforms. These echo the Jacobean of the entrance building, with a ridge-and-furrow glass roof overhead. The station offices are now used by Stoke-on-Trent University, a fitting replacement of one civic institution by another. A smaller but equally handsome building forms a second entrance to the far platform. Again, it has an arched loggia in matching Jacobean style.

Winton Square was an entire company development. It is flanked by terraces and townhouses for railway staff, each gabled and dignified. Facing the station is Hunt's North Stafford Hotel, a stylistic complement to the station itself, three-storeyed on an E-shaped plan. It has strapwork dressings to the windows and diapered brickwork on the upper storeys. For some reason, the planners have allowed a modern porch to be slapped across the hotel entrance arch, marring the façade. The square is shaded by plane trees and a fine statue of the patron of Stoke's greatness, Josiah Wedgwood.

pages 198-9: Potteries Jacobean: the Winton Square façade

WELLINGBOROUGH
★ ★

Approached from the town, the station is an apparition, a gingerbread house by the master of mid-Victorian eclecticism, Charles Driver (see p. 90) Its defining characteristic is polychrome brick, once blighted by decades of soot but now restored. It is the embodiment of 1850s railway picturesque.

The main building is a neo-Tudor stationmaster's house with a low entrance extension. Its red brick, is enlivened with blind arches, doors and window surrounds in contrasting white and blue brick, but horribly polluted by signs and posters. The steep roof eaves have elaborate, almost voluptuous, bargeboards to both front and side elevations. There are lozenge glazing bars in the windows.

This basic design is replicated on the platform façade. Here is a transverse ridge-and-furrow canopy, resting on Driver's signature iron columns and coloured brackets, crowded with foliage. From the north end of the platform, the bargeboards form a lovely undulating pattern. Above all, Driver's architecture was intended to be fun. A platform shelter has been converted into a pub, the Little R'Ale House.

The modern footbridge is a lumbering affair, dominating the south end of the station, in tawny local ironstone with two-tone blue woodwork. It is dramatic but emphatically not the Driver style. Adjacent to it lies a curiosity, a derelict goods shed in the same polychrome brick as the station and for some reason saved from the wrecker's ball. Inside lurk a former platform and two rusting cranes, like ghosts of the railway past, in a haze of decayed antiquity. Surely it will soon be a museum.

WORKSOP

★

A station near a great house was often careful to take from it a stylistic cue – if only to apologise for the intrusion. Worksop was the station for the Dukeries, not one ducal estate but four stretched across north Nottinghamshire, mostly built on coal. It is uncommonly handsome, doubtless in consideration of its anticipated aristocratic patronage. In particular, Worksop was the station for the agoraphobic 4th Duke of Portland, who lived at Welbeck and travelled to London without leaving his carriage. It would be loaded by his staff on to his own flat-bed truck and, with the blinds drawn, would convey him to the capital.

The station was built by James Drabble for the Manchester, Sheffield & Lincolnshire Railway in 1849, with a variegated roofline in a rich Dutch mannerism. It is festooned with gables and chimneys in white local stone. Since the Duke of Newcastle's adjacent Clumber Park was classical, this part of the station can hardly have been designed with the duke in mind. The eastern continuation of the building was added in 1900 but in a matching style, with a flurry of gables.

The original entrance porch has an arch, pilasters and elaborate strapwork round the clock. The stationmaster's house is two-storey, again with pilasters and here a double-stepped gable. It is now the Mallard pub. The old waiting-room next door has a remarkable bay window with broken pediment.

The platform is graced with a pretty latticed footbridge, surviving with its valances intact. The nearby signal-box retains its bargeboards. It has all fared better than Clumber's house, pulled to the ground by its owner in 1938.

NORTH-WEST

BIRKENHEAD HAMILTON SQUARE
CARLISLE · CARNFORTH · CHESTER
GRANGE-OVER-SANDS
LIVERPOOL LIME STREET
MANCHESTER LIVERPOOL ROAD
MANCHESTER OXFORD ROAD
MANCHESTER VICTORIA · PENRITH
PRESTON · ULVERSTON

pages 202–3: Central Railway Station, Chester
by G. Hawkins, 1840

NORTH-WEST

The advent of the railway coincided with the sudden rise of the north-west as a centre of oceanic trade, based chiefly on the port of Liverpool and Lancashire's cotton industry, which took over from slaves as the source of Liverpool's wealth. In 1830, the world's first steam-hauled passenger line linked Liverpool and Manchester. In 1846, at the height of the Mania (see p. 7), this in turn joined the Grand Junction Railway and the London & Birmingham to form the spine of Britain's rail network, the mighty London & North Western Railway. Its rival in the north-west was the Lancashire & Yorkshire, which became one of the busiest railways in the country. The resulting stations in Liverpool and Manchester challenged the London termini for size.

To the north of the region, companies fighting for Scottish and trans-Pennine business literally did battle in the streets of Carlisle, until Sir William Tite, in full Tudor rig, built a union station for them all. Lesser lines serving coastal Lancashire and Cheshire competed round Preston and Chester, typifying the wasteful duplication of the Mania. At Ulverston, Grange-over-Sands and Penrith, Lake District tourism produced picturesque curiosities during the railway's most eclectic period.

BIRKENHEAD
HAMILTON SQUARE
★

For urban display, the centre of Birkenhead once rivalled Liverpool, its big sister across the Mersey. Today, Georgian Hamilton Square is magnificent, but the town's civic buildings, churches and warehouses stand like palaces of a lost empire in a dystopian wilderness. They must also endure the sight of the new Liverpool, rising over the water like the proverbial golden city on a hill. Presiding over the scene is Hamilton Square station. With the appearance of a church with a short-gabled nave, its station tower is second only to St Pancras in height.

Crossing the River Mersey was long a Birkenhead obsession. It was traditionally by ferry, but the coming of the railway focused attention on the possibility of a tunnel. One was often projected but not built until 1886, by the Mersey Railway company. It had to be 103 feet deep, given the depth of the river. Although there were steps, three hydraulic lifts were installed in 1898, capable of carrying 100 passengers each. In addition to the pumps required to operate the lifts, steam pumps were needed to remove seeping water and extract the near intolerable amounts of smoke from the engines. The last effort was in vain. Engine smoke made the journey so unpleasant that most commuters continued to use the ferry until the line was electrified in 1903.

The tower containing the hydraulic tanks for the lifts – now also electrified – is integral to the station and was designed by the Liverpool architect George Grayson. At 120 feet, it is higher than the tunnel is deep, vaguely Florentine in style and of dark-red brick

with terracotta dressings. It is of eight stages, with bold string-courses and windows. It demonstrates the flair of Victorian architects in giving visual character to a simple utilitarian structure.

The adjacent booking hall seems under-powered in comparison. It is top-lit and spacious, with bull's-eye windows and a generous entrance canopy. The interior is modernised but retains the white tiling with which the company tried initially to convince passengers that the trip would be clean – before dousing them in soot.

Another tower for the extraction pumps survives at a distance down Shore Street. It is a splendid work of industrial archaeology, a neo-Norman brick keep with blind arcading and small, almost slit windows. The original Giant Grasshopper pump lurks silent inside. The tower was opened as a museum in 1989, but it is a sign of Birkenhead's woes that it is closed for lack of custom. Below on Canning Street is the equally fine warehouse boasting the names of its joint users, the Great Northern, Great Central and Midland railway companies. This at least is restored as an office block, harbinger perhaps of a new Birkenhead.

CARLISLE
★ ★ ★ ★

The railway age brought Carlisle a significance it had not seen since Edward I's campaign against the Scots. It sat astride the west coast route to Scotland, and was the focus of early attempts at trans-Pennine travel. A line from Newcastle-on-Tyne reached Carlisle as early as 1838. Soon, no fewer than seven companies were beating on its gates, with three stations being erected.

By the time Carlisle's Citadel Station was built for the Lancaster & Carlisle (L&CR) company in 1847, rivalry was fierce. A mob of a hundred workers from the L&CR, armed with axes and sledge-hammers, descended on the Maryport & Carlisle Railway's Crown Street terminus and demolished it overnight. It took an act of parliament in 1861 to compel the seven companies to collaborate. The arrival of the Midland Railway in 1876 led to the concentration of all traffic at the Citadel, which was more convenient

opposite: Florentine Renaissance at Hamilton Square
pages 208–9: Tite's Citadel: a first for railway gothic

but turned the station into a feuding shambles of rival trains, offices, staff and passengers.

The architect was the distinguished Sir William Tite whose railway buildings stretched from Southampton to Perth. At Carlisle, he took his theme from the adjacent Tudor citadel, which had been rebuilt as law courts by Robert Smirke in 1810. Its bold twin keeps continue to form a distinguished entry to the town.

Tite's deference to this medieval context was explicit. He wrote: 'I believe I was the first man who attempted to make a gothic railway station . . . it suited what I may call the genius loci.' The station is collegiate in appearance, of two storeys with square windows divided by buttresses and punctuated by an octagonal bell-tower. This is crenellated and has a stone cap. The range to the right has shapely white dormer windows, the range to the left is fronted by a wide porte cochère, glazed and strongly buttressed. Its battlements carry the coats of arms of the companies Tite hoped would share the station, with spaces still vacant for those who initially declined the offer.

Further to the left is an elaborate one-storey extension, still medieval in style. It contains the former first-class waiting-room in the form of a baronial hall. Rising behind the composition, a row of gable ends reveals the much-extended train shed roof erected in 1880. The ends have exaggerated caps to let out the smoke, termed a 'repeated greenhouse' feature. The whole façade has great presence, in keeping with Smirke's law courts opposite.

The station interior was much altered, mostly in the 1880s expansion, as other companies came to share it. The shed roof, an extension of Tite's original, remains spacious, despite the loss of its end screens in 1958. It retains unusual traceried brackets, composed of circles and struts. An original arched footbridge has picturesque lattice panels.

Carlisle is undergoing comprehensive restoration at the time of writing. It has a peculiar sense of grandeur, which seems to derive from Tite's talent in fusing medieval architecture to 19th-century engineering. To Matthew Hyde (in Pevsner), it embodies the romance of the northern railway, 'especially on a winter's night when rain-streaked trains rumble in from the outer darkness, pause briefly in the great lighted room and, after a short space, vanish out of sight'.

CARNFORTH
★ ★ ★

Carnforth is where trains to the Lake District part company with the main line to Scotland. Today, its fame is more as the setting, indeed the museum, of the most celebrated of railway films, David Lean's *Brief Encounter*. The film, starring Celia Johnson and Trevor Howard, depicted two lives tossed together by chance, victims of the twin tyrants of trains and time. Their love was measured in minutes, culminating in genteel heartbreak as the lovers returned to normality. Foreigners found the film's asexuality and dying fall inexplicable, but it struck an extraordinary chord in war-weary Britain (see p. 35)

Although the interior scenes were filmed in a studio in Denham, wartime Carnforth supplied platforms, steam trains and the ever ominous clock, which audiences prayed would stop. Filming took

Howard and Johnson's brief encounter

place in February 1945, mostly from two to four in the morning when the tracks were not in use. Carnforth was chosen as being far from German bombing activity and therefore the need for blackout.

Today, the Denham sets have been re-created on the island platform, including the famously bleak café. It carefully serves wartime buns and tea, in addition to modern designer beers. Visitors can sit by the stationmaster's stove, where Celia Johnson warmed her hands during freezing nocturnal shoots. The stationmaster, she wrote home, 'was such a gentleman, and always tipped his cap to me when we passed'. Indeed she found 'everyone awfully nice', given that they were filming at two in the morning.

No cineaste's stone is left unturned. There is a room where addicts can watch the complete film on continuous loop. There is a David Lean exhibition, with clips of his other work. The opportunity has

also been taken for a more general railway exhibition, with the usual heritage clutter of a 1940s ticket office, luggage, signs and advertisements, and some rather sad bunting.

None of this came easily. The handsome main station building was designed in 1846 by Sir William Tite for the Lancashire & Carlisle Railway. By the 1990s, a combination of Beeching cuts and British Rail neglect had reduced it to dereliction. Only Herculean efforts by the Carnforth Railway Trust brought it and the island platform back to life, and equipped a museum. The Carnforth Station Heritage Centre opened in 2003, with another film telling the story of this, more protracted, encounter. An unusual stone signal-box at the end of the down platform,

Carnforth: the ominous clock

211

designed in 1870 to match Tite's station, has also been restored.

In 1939, the London, Midland & Scottish Railway unfortunately rebuilt the far platform with what was at the time the longest unsupported concrete roof on the railway – its sole claim to fame. It blocks the view from the museum to the adjacent Carnforth Engine Works, a former repair and marshalling yard that lingered on after the demise of steam, to be revived by steam enthusiasts. It was a sort of railway Purgatory, where old engines came to die.

With the growth of heritage lines (see p. 42), it became a centre for engine restoration and a 'steam-town' museum, dominated by two giant 'drop' towers. One lifted coal wagons into the air and emptied their contents via a giant hopper into waiting engines. The other reversed the process, removing coal ash from engines and dropping it into disposal wagons. They are the only ones of such a size to survive.

The Steamtown Museum has closed but the works live on, feeding the world's voracious demand for reconditioned steam engines. Carnforth is no brief encounter. It is part of the railway's future.

CHESTER
★ ★ ★

While medieval Chester was a bastion of the northern Marches, Victorian Chester was a bastion of the Marches railway. The opening of a railway line from London to Liverpool in 1838 led to the Irish Mail abandoning Telford's coach road across Wales to the port of Holyhead on Anglesey. Replacing that road with a railway to seize back the traffic became an urgent and potentially lucrative prospect.

Two lines reached Chester in 1840 and a new company was formed, with Robert Stephenson as engineer, to drive on to Holyhead. However, a railway along the north Wales coast, including bridges across the Conway and Menai Straits, proved expensive. The new Chester & Holyhead line was not completed until 1850, under the auspices of the London & North Western, by which time five companies were laying siege to Chester's ancient walls.

The result was chaos. Gordon Biddle records a fight in 1849 between the LNWR and the Shrewsbury & Chester, when the S&C 'had their booking clerk dragged out of his office and his tickets thrown after him'. Arrivals would be timed so passengers would miss connections to a rival company. When relief bus services were provided, staff barred their entry to competing stations. By the 1850s, the Irish Mail had returned to Holyhead, and this business was supplemented by Lancashire holiday-makers colonising the Welsh coast from Rhyl to Llandudno. Chester's five companies were still fighting in 1903.

The city's principal station, Chester General, was completed in 1848 by Francis Thompson, here working alongside Stephenson as engineer. Thompson was a Derby tailor who turned to architecture in the railway booms of the 1830s and 1840s. Sometime after 1840, he was sacked by the Midland after designing the majestic (now destroyed) Derby station, and went to work for the Chester &

Holyhead. He later moved to the Great Eastern. Even assiduous railway historians have failed to trace his elusive career.

At Chester, Thompson had to accommodate each of the different companies demanding their own entrances, ticket desks and waiting-rooms, not to mention platforms and sidings. The contractor was Thomas Brassey, a native of Chester, whose building firm was responsible for an estimated one-third of all the mid-Victorian railways. There is a magnificent memorial to him in Chester cathedral.

Pevsner describes Chester as 'one of the most splendid of the early railway stations'. It is certainly one of the longest. The central façade of fifteen bays is painfully featureless, flanked by two promin-ent five-bay pavilions. Windows in the central range are adorned with curious pediment carvings, Hindu in character. The pavilions have Venetian windows, pierced balustrades and twin towers. The

frontage then drifts off into further offices, goods yards and eventually train sheds. The building material is purple-pink bricks with grey stone dressings.

The original curtilage of the forecourt is intact, with two hotels facing the entrance. One of these, the Queen, was for first-class passengers and the other, the Albion (now the Town Crier), was for 'other ranks'. Chester is a rare survivor of the railway's social ecology.

The platform area is much altered, although still the hub of the five spokes to Chester's railway wheel, including commuter lines to Liverpool and Manchester. In 2008, a rather desperate effort was made to 'upgrade' the platforms, with catering pods of copper sheeting. They look uncomfortable, an example of what happens when today's railway architects seek to outsmart rather than respect their Victorian forebears.

GRANGE-OVER-SANDS
★ ★

North of Lancaster, the Furness line goes briefly into wilderness as it skirts the salt marshes and sandbanks of Morecambe Bay. To the east rise the Pennines, ahead is the Cartmel peninsula and the hills of the Lake District. For a while, the railway seems to float on water, only reaching dry land at Grange. This is a railway-age settlement of stout Victorian villas for stout Mancunian families. The station clings to the coastline, like Dawlish in Devon. It is a sublime location.

The building is by the prominent Lancashire architect, Edward Paley (see p. 232), and was built in 1864. It takes its cue from the surrounding villas, a low, single-storey building of grey stone with a wide-hipped slate roof. The forecourt is landscaped, with gardens, copper beeches and an impressive monkey-puzzle tree. It is hard at first sight to believe it is a station.

The platform is shielded by glass canopies on ironwork columns and ornamental brackets, all in white, green and red and dripping with flower pots. It could be a conservatory. The main canopy is replicated on the down platform opposite. Here the backdrop is not the wooded hills beyond Grange but the expanse of Morecambe Bay, glimpsed through arched windows. To the left of the view is a small private island, Holme Island, which once belonged to the engineer of the Furness Railway and is reached by a short causeway.

Morecambe Bay from Grange

It was at Grange in 1876 that a journey by John Ruskin from Ulverston to north Wales began to degenerate. His diary records the arrival in his first-class compartment of 'two young coxcombs who reclined themselves on the opposite cushions . . . talking yacht and regatta listlessly'. To Ruskin's fury, neither they nor another passenger reading a newspaper 'ever looked out of the window at sea or shore where the tide lay smooth and silent along the sands melancholy in absolute pause of motion'. This philistinism was to continue with one passenger after another during Ruskin's entire, increasingly infuriated journey to Barmouth. I wonder what he would make of today's travellers, glued to their mobiles.

Ruskin would at least approve of the small building at the end of Grange's down platform, which now houses the splendid Over-Sands second-hand bookshop. On the wall outside is an original Furness Railway lamp bracket.

LIVERPOOL LIME STREET

★ ★ ★ ★ ★

Liverpool ranks high in the story of the railway. It was here that George Stephenson in 1830 opened the world's first steam-hauled passenger service, between Liverpool and Manchester, his engine *Rocket* having won the Rainhill trials the previous year. The Liverpool terminus was in the suburb of Edge Hill, from where winding engines winched carriages through cuttings down to the city centre and docks.

When the steam-hauled line was extended to Lime Street in 1836, two matching station buildings were erected at Edge Hill. These remain standing, Georgian pavilions in red sandstone with, next to them, one of the original winding towers. Although the station is operational, on my visits the place has been locked and sad, despite the valiant efforts of a resident arts group to keep it alive. This wilderness of cuttings, sidings and tunnel portals, overgrown with vegetation, should be a magnet to train enthusiasts the world over, not empty and mostly inaccessible.

Meanwhile the arrival of the Liverpool & Manchester (L&MR) in the city centre was the source of much civic pride. The corporation commissioned its own architect, John Foster, to design an appropriate façade looking out over the site of what was to be St George's Hall, with the Mersey beyond. Growth in demand led to Lime Street being twice expanded and rebuilt, notably with magnificent shed roofs.

The first of these was erected in 1867 by the London & North Western company's engineer, William Baker. A second adjacent span, an exact copy, was added in 1879. At 212 feet, Baker's span was the widest in the world, until beaten by William Barlow's 243 feet at St Pancras, Jersey City and others. The station buildings were smothered in 1871 by Alfred Waterhouse's massive North Western Hotel and then by later buildings to its side.

By then Liverpool was a global metropolis, not just a port on the Mersey but the departure point from the Continent of Europe for refugees and emigrants to the New World. The historians Jeffrey Richards and John M. Mackenzie describe a Lime Street 'where may be found groups of Germans, Swedes, Poles, of men, women and children of nearly every European nationality, surrounded by curious luggage and, in railway porters' opinion, "jabbering a lot of nice lingo"'. Many had crossed England after landing from the Continent at Hull (see p. 250) and now had to troop downhill to the harbour for their last hazardous voyage.

Lime Street languished through the 20th century in relative squalor. Outside its gates we can still see the remains of the disaster that was Liverpool development in the 1960s under its ardently Socialist chief planner, Graeme Shankland. His slash-and-burn approach to urban renewal took the form of destroying historic buildings and erecting an excruciating shopping centre facing the station, which even he later regretted.

The area degenerated until, in 2008, the buildings in front of Lime Street were demolished to reveal at least part of the original terminus to the square. The impact is sensational. Today, the pillared frontage can at last gaze down on the Grecian masterpiece of St George's Hall opposite, although it is still elbowed aside by Waterhouse's ponderous hotel – now a student residence – next door. Hotel and station offer a provincial echo of London's stylistic duo of St Pancras and King's Cross.

The gable end facing the square is the best station façade in Britain, and indeed puts King's Cross in the shade. A wide segmental screen is filled with thin mullions and crowned with a miniature pediment. This is visually permeable, allowing views through into the train shed beyond and giving the composition an almost floating levity. The screen rests on a Doric arcade of nine bays, again with views through

pages 216-17: Liverpool's battle of the styles

into the station. The front curves slightly, giving it an added sense of thrust.

Lime Street's interior, like London's Paddington, is essentially a station of two roofs, the one a facsimile of the other. The chief feature of Baker's roof is its graceful curve to a screen at the far end over the tracks, where it resolves itself into a beautiful sickle-shaped arch. This repeats those throughout the station. Each arch has a subordinate rib beneath it, forming a sequence of spidery membranes curving into the distance.

The arches are enlivened by their supporting Doric columns. These clearly repeat the four close-spaced columns next to platform 1, surviving from a railway bridge of 1846 over a side street. All are painted red. Along the divide between the two roofs, the columns are repeated but doubled and banded in white. It creates a pop-art effect, very Liverpool.

MANCHESTER LIVERPOOL ROAD
★ ★

The Liverpool & Manchester Railway (L&MR) opened in 1830 and its route would, in most countries, today be a major tourist destination. Visitors would chug along George Stephenson's sacred way, past the scene of the 1829 Rainhill trials and end at Edge Hill station in Liverpool (see p. 215), where there is a potential theme park of industrial archaeology.

Manchester does at least make an effort in Stephenson's honour. His first station, non-operational since 1975 but occasionally open for excursions, is buried within the sprawling enclave of Manchester's Science and Industry Museum. Trains came in on a viaduct from the west, with the passenger entrance below on Liverpool Road (thus rivalling Baltimore in the USA as the world's oldest surviving station). The station could pass as the townhouse of a Mancunian merchant. Built in 1830, it shows how eager this first railway was to give its venture a townscape façade of respectability.

The house is ashlar-fronted, in the late-Georgian style of Sir John Soane. The first-class ticket office is a five-bay house, while facilities for second-class travellers are behind a single-bay façade next door, as if through a tradesmen's entrance. The railway was so keen to attract genteel travellers that it even offered flat trucks on to which private coaches could be loaded, occupants, horses and all. Passengers thus segregated would enter, pay and go upstairs as if to bedrooms, but in fact to their respective waiting-rooms on the platform above.

These buildings owe their miraculous survival to the L&MR's 1846 merger with the Grand Junction and the London & Birmingham to form the London & North Western. It duly sent its trains round the northern city perimeter to Victoria station, thus ending the passenger service at London Road. What is sad is that Liverpool Road Station can no longer be accessed from the street outside, but must be entered from the platform above by a laborious route through the museum.

None the less, the platforms above are still in place and from here the railway's original path can be seen snaking across the city. A fine warehouse of the same date fills the other side of the track, and is now part of the museum. This whole group seems in the grip of educational officers and school trips. It has the bloodlessness that comes from a desperation to 'engage' young children. It needs the buzz of a heritage railway, a touch of Carnforth magic (see p. 210) – which children really love.

above: The oldest station platform in the world
pages 220–21: Railway respectability: Liverpool Road façade

MANCHESTER
OXFORD ROAD

★

The old industrial enclave of Little Ireland has long gone, but southern Manchester between the university quarter and the former Central Station (now G-Mex) is a flurry of industrial relics. Every vista seems closed by a railway bridge, a canal basin, a viaduct or a warehouse, treasures increasingly precious amid the swift renewal of the city centre.

Oxford Road station is something of a cult among modernists. Its 1840 predecessor was the metropolitan end of the posh Manchester, South Junction & Altrincham commuter railway (MSJAR), rare for a railway in having a favourable nickname: 'Many Short Journeys and Absolute Reliability'. The station was rebuilt in 1960 by two architects working for British Rail's London Midland Region, W. R. Headley and Max Glendinning. Their task was not easy, to deliver a small station on a triangular site off Whitworth Street, with tracks running through the city on a weakened viaduct.

Their solution was ingenious, a series of three overlapping wooden cones or 'conoids', with side 'flaps' as platform canopies. The design was clearly borrowed from the architectural sensation of the day, Jørn Utzon's Sydney Opera House, then emerging in a blaze of controversy. For a modest British station in the 1960s, Oxford Road was daringly unusual.

Of the cones, one contains the ticket hall and another the concourse. The wider end facing the car park is like the cowl of a monk's habit. Indeed, when seen from above it is three monks' habits. In order to lighten the load on the viaduct below, the entire structure is of wood, as are the platform canopies. The ticket windows and shopping arcades are also of wood, lending a breezy informality to the interior.

Wood may be easy on the eye but it ages badly. Like many modernist buildings, the structure was

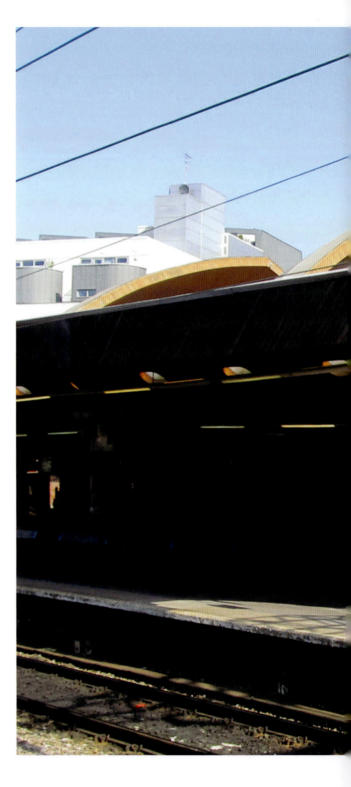

Oxford Road's daring conoids

leaking within ten years and has required two repairs. But it remains a station of class, holding its own in a wilderness of high-rise flats. It is faced across the road by an enclave of old Manchester, the baroque tower of the Palace Theatre and adjacent Palace Hotel, both welcome reminders of the city's architecturally virile past.

MANCHESTER VICTORIA

★ ★ ★

Manchester's second station (after bland Piccadilly) long held the distinction of being regularly voted 'Britain's worst'. Bloggers deluged it with abuse, as the embodiment of depressed post-industrial Lancashire. In 2010, the coalition government adopted Victoria as the terminus of a new trans-Pennine high-speed link and figurehead of the 'northern powerhouse'. From being a symbol of Mancunian decay, it has become the symbol of recovery, although there is much still to be done.

The concept of linking Manchester across the Pennines with industrial Yorkshire, other than by toll roads and canals, was commercially magnetic. It was first mooted by George Stephenson at the time of the Stockton to Darlington Railway back in 1825. The Manchester & Leeds Railway was incorporated in the first railway boom in 1836, the trains eventually running into an 1844 station shared with the old Liverpool & Manchester line. This was built controversially on once-consecrated land near Manchester cathedral. By 1847, four lines fed into Victoria, making it one of the busiest termini in Britain.

Manchester in the late 19th century was both immensely rich and desperately poor, inspiring the writings of Marx and Engels. The old Victoria station was overwhelmed by commuters from the sprawling suburbs of the Lancashire plain. Its custom soared with the cheap third-class services ordained by statute as compensation when railways cleared slums for their stations. Such was the confusion of companies pouring into Victoria that the London & North Western Railway built itself a new station,

Manchester Exchange, across Ducie Street a hundred yards to the west.

In 1909, William Dawes was commissioned to upgrade the façade on to what is now Victoria Station Approach, although a fragment of the old 1844 station was left at the angle of Hunt's Bank to the north. It now looks like a gentle townhouse, forlorn among the box architecture of modern Manchester. Dawes' new wing extends at right angles to it.

At a time when Edwardian stations were flowering into the baroque glories of Leicester, Nottingham and London's Victoria, Dawes' effort was sadly lifeless. It is a long, un-articulated façade culminating in a cupola, worthy of little more than a branch insurance company. The only uplift comes from the vaguely art nouveau red ironwork on the canopy, carrying the names of the destinations served within – Blackpool, Hull and even Belgium. These places are also recorded inside the entrance on one of the Lancashire & Yorkshire's celebrated tiled mural maps.

The new station was to serve commuters on expresses from burgeoning resorts up the Lancashire coast, Southport, Lytham St Anne's, as far as Blackpool. These trains were running faster in 1900, so it is said, than they were in 2000. After the 1923 Grouping, Manchester's Victoria and Exchange stations were merged, producing a joint platform of 746 yards across the Ducie Street bridge. It was reputedly the longest in Europe, although nothing on the scale of India's mile-long monsters.

None of this improved the station's image. In 1970, Marcus Binney and David Pearce dismissed Victoria as 'a mess and hardly important enough to warrant description'. Revival did not come until 2010, when George Osborne offered £44m to renovate the building. 'Please bear with us while we make Victoria posh' said a station poster with some desperation.

opposite: Manchester Victoria: the art nouveau canopy

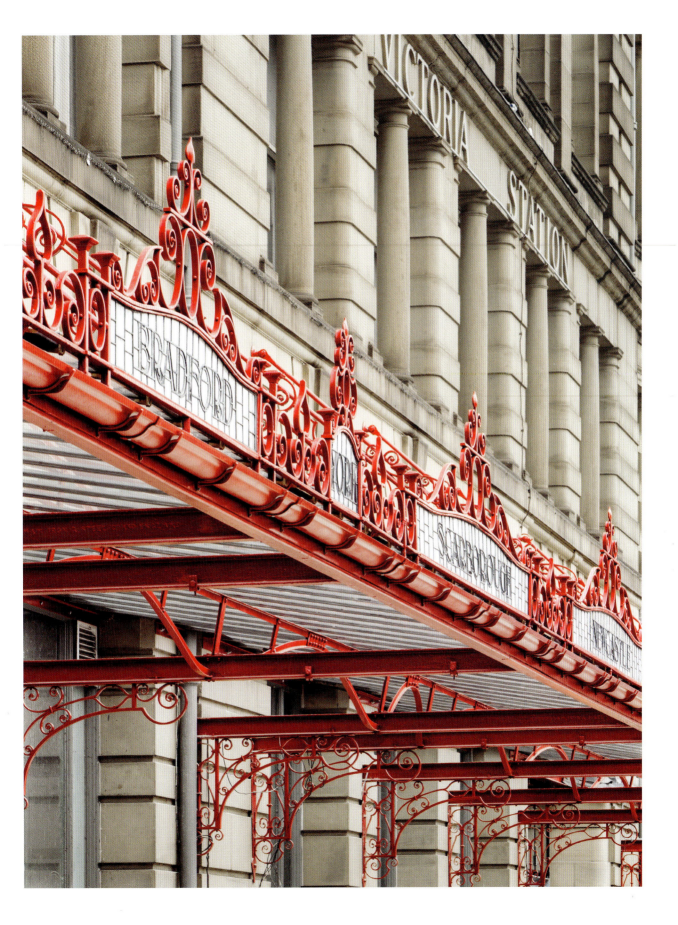

The result is undeniably dramatic. Although the exterior remains dull, the impact of the interior is immediate. The renovation of the concourse involved the insertion of an L-shaped, arched and glazed roof, designed by Peter Jenkins of BDP. The roof soars and dives in a whirl of parabolic arches, cleverly fastened to the insides of Dawes' frontage. Here the ghosts of the old ridge-and-furrow gables are visible in the brickwork, picked out with strip lighting at night.

Across the concourse and beneath the parabolic arches threads an overhead walkway, linking the station to the city's Arena sports and exhibition centre to the north. On the south side is the Metrolink light rail station. The space is airy and exciting and ranks with John McAslan's new King's Cross (see p. 56) among the most impressive sheds of the modern railway.

Dawes' original Edwardian designs, well restored, still grace the concourse. The tiling of the walls in cream and maroon is a gallery of art nouveau. So, too, are signs for the old tea shop, grill room and book-stall, mostly in elaborate lettering on a sky-blue background. The cafeteria, formerly the first-class dining-room, is delightfully extravagant.

Off the concourse is the 'soldiers' gate' through which thousands of Mancunian soldiers passed on their way to the Great War. The gate is now a sheet of metal, punctured with holes representing that conflict's cemeteries. To the north are Victoria's old through-platforms, now lurking beneath the new arena. They are a sad sight, much in need of imaginative renewal.

The cafeteria: Mancunian neo-baroque

226

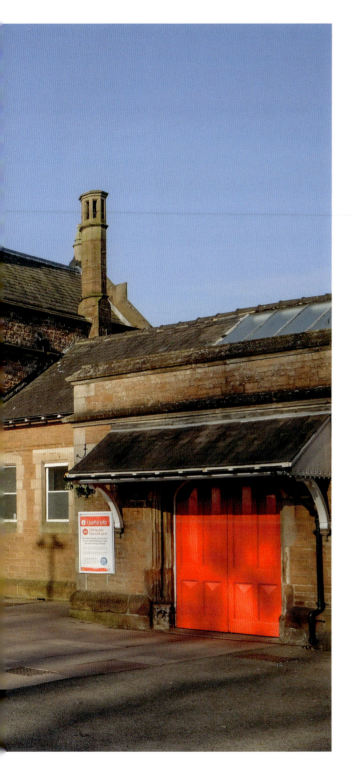

PENRITH

★

Penrith is a handsome little town but 'doughnutted' by bad planning and, as yet, with nothing to reinvigorate its centre. The station retains its dignity, looking not so much a railway as a rural manor. It was built in 1846 by Sir William Tite for the Lancaster & Carlisle, in collusion with the Cockermouth, Keswick & Penrith and, later, the North Western. Thus did the coming of a railway make an isolated town into a substantial interchange.

Tite would turn his hand to Italianate, baronial or gothic at will. At Penrith, he took his lead from the castle ruin in the park opposite, designing an Elizabethan stationmaster's house with a modest entrance next to it and then a waiting-room wing. This is in the style of a Tudor great hall with a large window looking out over the forecourt. The chimneys are exotic. The building is of comforting red sandstone with pink stone dressings. The gables are stepped, the dormers friendly. We sense a serious architect having some weekend fun.

A measure of Penrith's importance is the second building across the tracks. This is also in neo-Tudor style, with an elaborate canopy and iron columns painted red and white. These have long arched brackets with circles in their spandrels. Gordon Biddle claims these were based on designs by Robert Stephenson for the original Euston in London. The station is well maintained as the gateway to the northern Lakes.

Tudor manorial at Penrith

PRESTON

★ ★ ★

Preston's prosperity grew on the Victorian cotton boom and its associated docks. These brought it no fewer than nine railways during the Mania boom of the 1840s (see p. 7), with five separate companies and five stations. The waste of space and investment was prodigious. Not until 1879 were five stations merged into one, and even then the Lancashire & Yorkshire Railway (L&YR) declined to use the London & North Western's entrance. It had a building of its own on the far side of the tracks in Butler Street, with a separate stationmaster and staff. As a result, Preston once boasted fifteen platforms.

Today the entrance building sits uncomfortably on an island at the foot of a ramp down from Fishergate bridge. Seen from the bridge, it can look like a gothic horror house, with the roof gables flapping like bats' wings on either side. Yet it is a building of charm. Designed by the little-known J. Crosbie Dawson, it is in the Italianate/French style much in vogue during the 1880s. The lower floor is of five Tuscan bays, while the roof is crowned with a French mansard roof, prominent dormers, chimneys and much ornamental ironwork.

The interior comprises a small ticket hall and sloping ramp down to the central island platform. Here Preston takes on a more distinctive character. In the days before restaurant cars, trains on long trips would break their journey for half an hour so passengers could purchase refreshment. Preston was the chief stop-over on the west-coast main line from London to Scotland.

These breaks came to be regarded as a national disgrace. Hundreds of passengers would rush to the buffet, desperate for food and drink in the time available, often leading to a near riot. Simon Bradley quotes a newspaper complaint that trying to secure a

cup of scalding soup or gristly pie was 'enough to chafe the patience of a saint and impair the digestion of an ostrich'. Another accusation was that the tea was so hot it could not be drunk in time and contents left by departing passengers were poured back into the tea-urn.

Either way, the island concourse was designed for crowds. The central buildings are palatial. Numerous waiting-rooms and cafés have tall, round-headed windows with a classical cornice above, features repeated on the station's outer walls. In one waiting-room is a memorial to the ladies who served 'free tea and comfort' to soldiers passing through on their way to the Great War. The old L&YR entrance remains, shockingly altered, in Butler Street, for those passengers determinedly loyal to the good old days.

above: Colour enlivens architecture
opposite: Preston: place of 'tea and comfort'

ULVERSTON

★

The Lancaster architectural practice of Paley and Austin embodied northern solidity. It produced churches, houses, and civic and industrial buildings across the north-west in the late-Victorian era. They were eclectic in style, mostly in stone, heavy and stern. One of the partners, Edward Paley, designed in manorial Tudor at Grange-over-Sands. At Ulverston in 1873, his firm supplied the Furness Railway company with an early Italianate palazzo. The station served the southern Lakes and was Ruskin's departure point on his dire journey to north Wales (see p. 215).

The main building is long and low, culminating in a three-bay Italianate façade of two storeys. The windows are round-arched and paired, the roof French-style with ornamental ironwork round its crown. Above rises a four-stage clock tower, square with ball finials. This tower might serve for a parish church were it not for the intrusion of a chimney. The whole composition is in the firm's favourite pink stone, which ages a dour black unless ruthlessly cleaned.

The platform exchanges corporate solemnity for holiday levity. The platform floors are red. The canopies are glazed ridge-and-furrow, their columns in white and green, their brackets picked out in red. The island platform once served a branch line to Windermere and has a double arcade of columns, exceptionally graceful. That line fell to Beeching's axe and the track became a road, wretchedly forbidding reopening.

At the east end of the main platform is an extraordinary building, like a large garden gazebo.

232

Ulverston: corporate formality and holiday levity

It is of two storeys in soft red sandstone with cream ashlar dressings, Italianate windows and a strong cornice. It was apparently the original Gents. The Railway Heritage Trust, which has paid for its restoration, believes the spacious upper chamber may have been for a water tank, for engine boilers and toilets alike. It is now reborn as a café and bike store. Ulverston station is a casket of wonders.

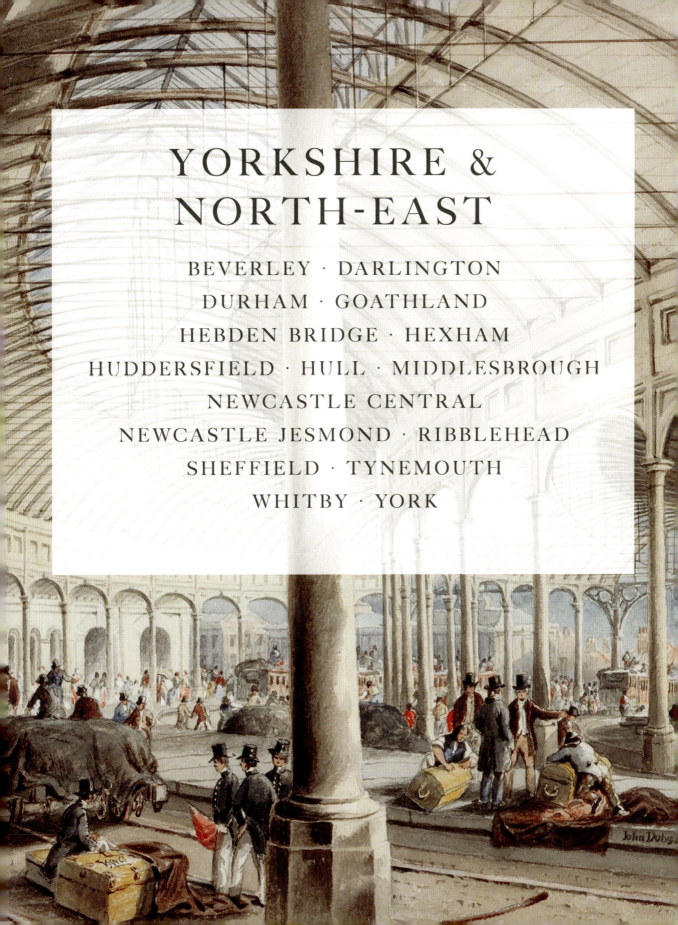

YORKSHIRE & NORTH-EAST

BEVERLEY · DARLINGTON
DURHAM · GOATHLAND
HEBDEN BRIDGE · HEXHAM
HUDDERSFIELD · HULL · MIDDLESBROUGH
NEWCASTLE CENTRAL
NEWCASTLE JESMOND · RIBBLEHEAD
SHEFFIELD · TYNEMOUTH
WHITBY · YORK

YORKSHIRE & NORTH-EAST

This is rich territory for railways. Not only did it see the original Stockton to Darlington line in 1825 but also Robert Stephenson's first engine works at Newcastle. During the Mania (see p. 7), the 'Railway King', George Hudson, ran his empire from bases at York then Derby, commissioning mostly classical stations from his architect friend George Andrews, notably at Hull, Beverley and Whitby.

Hudson's legacy did not die with his fall in 1849 (see p. 265). His successors at the North Eastern Railway continued his tradition, with two master-pieces – John Dobson's Newcastle and John Prosser's shed at York. The company broadened its range, with a rare instance of civic gothic at Middlesbrough and, later, with William Bell's decorative art nouveau at York, Darlington and Hull.

In south Yorkshire, the 1840s saw the London & North Western and the Lancashire & Yorkshire reach Huddersfield over the Pennines in spectacular style. Ordered by that town's estate-owner to show appropriate respect, they built what remains England's handsomest small station.

Towards the end of the century, the Midland sought its own route to Scotland over the Settle–Carlisle line, with the loneliest of halts along the way. Further north, the Newcastle & Carlisle is today the last main line on the network still largely Victorian in appearance and working methods. Its stations are minor gems of railway vernacular architecture. The Tyne and Wear Metro is the only urban network outside London to pay serious attention to the design of its stations.

BEVERLEY
★ ★

Beverley ranks high among my favourite market towns. Rich from wool, rich in churches, it is also blessed in its station. This was designed in 1846 by George Andrews for George Hudson, and was completed shortly before their joint fall in 1849 (see p. 265). The station remains virtually as built, intended, as Gordon Biddle says of all Hudson's stations, 'to please and to endure'.

Andrews' stations belied the hectic spirit of the Mania period (see p. 7). They were calm and restrained, Regency classical rather than Victorian, with elegant windows and hipped roofs. Only when Andrews was designing in dramatic settings did he become eclectic – as in episcopal Durham. Beverley is firmly classical.

The main building is single-storey, its walls red brick with rusticated stone dressings. A seven-bay pavilion has a portico entrance, with the elegance of a magistrates' court, flanked by recessed wings. The tower of Beverley Minster watches over the scene from the south. The setting is marred only by the replacement in 1908 of Andrews' double-span roof with a taller single span.

The station interior is entrancing. Here the shed is no longer overpowering. Its hipped ends cover two platforms on either side of the track. The walls have tall Georgian windows, and the space has an uncluttered austerity, a case of a listed building shown a respect rare among old stations. When I was last

Yorkshire demure: Beverley's footbridge

there, a scattering of passengers were sitting quietly on the green benches looking across the tracks at each other. It was like a Quaker meeting house, waiting for someone to speak.

Outside the west end of the shed is Beverley's charming footbridge, a wood-panelled structure with arched entrances and unusual cornices. One of the panels is removed to enable the signal-man in the neighbouring signal-box a clear view down into the platform. It is a reminder that, on the railway, the signalman was always the most import-ant person in sight.

DARLINGTON
★ ★ ★

Every schoolchild should know that, in 1825, the world's first steam train ran twenty-six miles from Stockton to Darlington, and that its presiding genius was a self-taught Northumberland engineer called George Stephenson. The train was drawn by his celebrated engine, *Locomotion*.

Less well known is that for eight years, from 1825 to 1833, *Locomotion* drew only freight wagons. Passengers on the line were drawn more gently at four miles per hour by horses. Steam was still a novelty and dangerous, and investors were waiting to see if it would pay. As a result, the prize for the first

Darlington's two stations in one

regular steam-hauled passenger service went to the Liverpool & Manchester line in 1830, also operated by Stephenson.

The Stockton end of the line has gone, but Darlington's early North Road station survives as a railway museum, still with an adjacent platform in operational use. It was built in 1842 and is a two-storey Regency villa in white stucco, with single-storey wings and a veranda. It stands at the end of a tree-lined drive, looking like an ante-bellum mansion in the American South. The museum includes the original *Locomotion*, as well as the old station footbridge and an early North Eastern Railway (NER) ticket office.

Today's Darlington station, formerly known as Bank Top, is some distance away in the centre of town. It dates from a later age, that of the NER's William Bell in 1887, working with the company's engineer, Thomas Harrison. Bell was an architect who straddled neo-baroque and art nouveau, with work at York, Hull and Tynemouth.

The station is two in one, reflecting the merger of the NER with the old Stockton & Darlington. The former wanted a modern station with buildings on an island between the tracks while the latter insisted on a baroque frontage facing the town. It has a split personality that is confusing to this day.

Bell's frontage building has four wide arches to a porte cochère in red brick with stone dressings. The interior is, in effect, a grand hall, with tall Dutch gable ends. It is crowned with an extraordinary tower, with pilasters, arched windows, a clock and finally a steeple. This Wren pastiche above a Frenchified roof is typical of late-Victorian eclecticism.

Decorative iron railings lead from this entrance to the second one, which is from a bridge over the tracks and down a ramp on to the central island. Overhead is a fine roof of three broad spans, over 300 yards long and slightly curved at one end. They are closed by semi-circular glazed lunettes, in an excellent state of preservation. The echo of York is clear. The spans rest on brick walls on the outside and sturdy iron columns on the island. These are fluted and painted in an elegant blue and grey. The brackets contain the shields of Darlington (a train), Durham (a cross) and Newcastle (three castles).

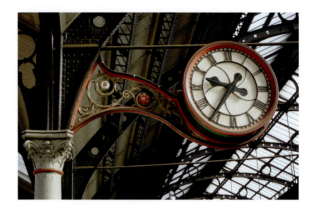

The island service block is substantial, of blood-red brick, but lacks the baroque flair of the frontage building. The platform area has lost its steam-age exhibits, notably *Locomotion*, to the museum at North Road station, a pity. Pot plants in tubs are no substitute.

On platform 4 hangs a prominent and magnificent railway clock on a cast-iron bracket. These clocks were vital station furnishings, when trains had to run 'on time' and local watches might vary. The company's clock man would travel the railway every week to check and wind the platform clocks. Only later did people come to describe time in simple numerals. Dickens ridiculed a railway child who 'hasn't time to say twenty minutes to twelve, but . . . jerks out, like a little Bradshaw, "eleven forty"'.

YORKSHIRE & NORTH-EAST

above: Railway time
opposite: Durham's festive down platform

DURHAM

★

One of England's great spectacles is the sight of Durham's cathedral from its station. It rises on its promontory, surrounded by the gorge of the River Wear, ablaze with floodlights at night. It was a view that made John Betjeman long for the job of station-master (as he said of many stations).

The station sits at the end of an eleven-arched viaduct overlooking the town. The access road is a steep climb from the river, on a site riddled with steps and tunnels. Opened in 1857, the station's Tudor-gothic appearance has been much restored, giving its sandstone surface a patchwork appearance. The stepped gables and buttressed porch are a clear echo of cathedral architecture.

The station is attributed to Thomas Prosser, chief architect to the North Eastern (NER) at the time, but since Prosser did nothing else like it, Gordon Biddle suggests it might have been from a design by George Andrews, surviving from his and Hudson's downfall in 1849 (see p. 265): 'with perhaps the dean and chapter's hostility to the coming of the railway the reason for choosing Tudor-gothic'. The dean had certainly demanded an exorbitant price for the land, the issue clearly being financial rather than spiritual. One wonders whether gothic appeased him.

The main up platform has been heavily rebuilt, with a glassed-in retail area. A second entrance on the opposite down platform is quite different. Added in 1872, it is open, generous and looking as if prepared for a flower show. Its hipped canopy has iron columns and gothic perforations to the girders and gable ends.

Enthusiasts should visit this station in winter, when the tree cover recedes and the cathedral can be seen from the platforms in all its glory. With luck, your train will be delayed.

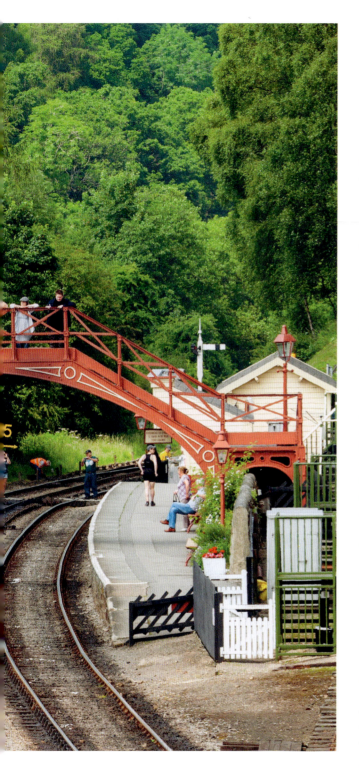

Viewing Hogwarts from Goathland bridge

GOATHLAND

★

Many of the earliest railways were built for freight, not passengers, and then chiefly for the transport of heavy minerals. When the minerals were exhausted, so was the railway, often leaving disused lines in wild and scenic places. One such was the Whitby & Pickering line (now North York Moors Railway, NYMR), planned as early as 1831 and opened in 1836 by George Stephenson. It was operated by horses to get stone and other materials to the port of Whitby. It was soon taken up by George Hudson and equipped for steam, although it was never a success.

The line was axed by Beeching in 1965 and reopened as a heritage line eight years later. Its stations are curiously 'themed' by periods of 20th-century railway history. Goathland was allocated the 1920s slot. The station was perfectly cast as the set for 'Hogsmeade' on Harry Potter's Hogwarts Express (having previously featured in the television series *Heartbeat*). This celebrity has earned the line much profit. The NYRM claims the most passengers of the heritage sector and 'maybe the busiest steam heritage line in the world'.

The station, built in 1865, is buried in a ravine next to its remote village high on the moors. It lies alongside a small tributary of the River Esk. Moorland presses on every side, with steps directly up to the hills from the platform. Nearby, the line's single track broadens out into a depot, rest home for ancient rolling stock. There was no need to refashion Goathland as a film set. It is one.

The station building might be a Brontë rectory. It was designed for the North Eastern company by Thomas Prosser, author of many stations on the Esk Valley line to Middlesbrough. Stern limestone walls and slate roofs enclose solid doors and windows. A scatter of sheds and warehouses are also in stone. Nothing seems to have changed for a century.

The station is overlooked by a delightful rust-coloured footbridge. Its soft curve, elegant with lattice panels, is a model Victorian work, a lesson to all who feel modern bridges should be made of straight lines and boxes. The bridge appears in the final scene of the first Potter movie (with CGI-added Hogwarts turrets), although later films in the series curiously locate the station at various points of the compass round the notional school buildings. What Beeching killed, Potter's wand brings to life.

HEBDEN BRIDGE
★ ★

The station is as self-conscious as the town it serves. Notices proclaim the home to 'five hundred years of creativity'. It is the 'year-round Glastonbury of the North', magnet to artists, foodies, gays, lesbians and writers (including Ted Hughes' ghost). In 2005, a poll voted it 'fourth funkiest town in the world'. I forget the other three.

After the Second World War, Hebden Bridge's mills closed and the familiar northern morbidity threatened. The town was doomed to join others in obliterating the monuments of their past, before realising that they might hold the key to their future. Somehow it restrained itself. Old mills, warehouses, canals and bridges were the new textiles. Local historian Paul Barker says Hebden Bridge went from manufacturing corduroy to manufacturing lifestyle, and found it sold well. The rest of Calderdale can only look on in envy, and complain of gentrification.

The station is perched on the side of the valley above the Rochdale Canal, and is a modest showcase for the town. The line over the Pennines from Manchester to Leeds was authorised in the first rail boom in 1836. Opening in 1841, it had five trains a day. The impact on cloth production in these steep valleys with their fast-churning water mills was dramatic. The town boomed. A large warehouse for the station once stood on the site of the present car park.

The two-storey limestone station, rebuilt in 1893, is set behind a neat forecourt. Platform canopies have curious, perhaps sawn-off, valances. The columns are in two shades of pink. The globe lights are original and other heritage features survive or have been replaced, including a signal-box, lamp room and a second platform 'staggered' some way along the opposite track.

Hebden Bridge is a fine advertisement for station

'friends'. Its group was formed in 2007 and is responsible for the gardens, flower baskets, library, piano, photographic display and general tidiness. It is a true community centre. The station's most celebrated attribute is the original signs, restored in the 1990s. Thick sanserif lettering, white on black, is visible everywhere, from the station identification boards to the toilets. This being Hebden Bridge, the lettering is already marketed as a font, known as Hebden. It shows how small things matter in station design.

Banished to the far end of the platform is a quaint solecism. The current operator, MetroTrains, has a sign in its own house-style lettering, like a dog marking out its territory. It is dire, but will one day doubtless be revered as historic.

**Calderdale: architecture
meets calligraphy**

HEXHAM

★

The original Newcastle & Carlisle Railway (N&CR) was one of England's earliest 'main lines' – a full fifty miles – and the first to cross the Pennines. It was a product of the first railway boom, completed in 1838. According to Gordon Biddle, it is today 'the nearest we have to a working Victorian main line' in something like its early form, including semaphore signalling. The line from Newcastle clatters along the bank of the River Tyne amid rolling hills and gentle meadows. It is a delight.

Choosing between its stations is not easy since the early railway's *cottage orné* is everywhere in evidence, with gabled roofs and Tudor windows and chimneys. Biddle regards twelve of the line's twenty stations as original and suggests their designer was the Newcastle & Berwick company's Benjamin Green. Most have the

N&CR's 'signature', arched footbridges with lattice-sided handrails and white and maroon paintwork. Some also retain distinctive signal-boxes, set high on gantries with clear views up and down the line.

The most substantial station is Hexham, isolated some distance from the centre of the ancient town, with its abbey and crypt. The station has been extended but in keeping with the original. Platforms line the tracks on both sides, beneath pitched and hipped roofs, with a double row of columns on the entrance side and a single row on the other. The buildings are in a creamy limestone. Everything has the sunny appearance of a greenhouse. The adjacent station restaurant claims a bizarre affinity to the Indus Valley.

An elevated signal-box with an unusually tall semaphore can be seen down the track from the footbridge, painted in the old North Eastern maroon and cream. The line is now called the Hadrian's Wall line.

HUDDERSFIELD

★ ★ ★ ★

Nowhere is British railway architecture so honoured as in Huddersfield, one of the few stations fit to rank with the great union termini of the Continent. Pevsner ranked it 'among the best' of stations, and Betjeman declared it 'the most splendid façade in England'. The main entrance presides over St George's Square with a princely confidence, focus of what is a rare survivor of a north-country commercial town plan. The square and the streets round it are ghosts of former offices, banks and hotels in honey-coloured stone. Among the fountains stands a statue of Huddersfield's son, Harold Wilson, looking as if anxious to catch a train. He replaced one of Sir Robert Peel.

For all this there was a reason. Huddersfield was built on land owned since the 16th century by the Ramsden family and their trustees, and not released to the local corporation until 1920. The coming of the railway in the 1840s saw the Ramsdens demand that it signify its presence with appropriate pomp. The two companies, the London & North Western and the Lancashire & Yorkshire, agreed on a joint station. The Ramsden trustees included Earl Fitzwilliam, owner of South Yorkshire's grandest Palladian mansion, Wentworth Woodhouse. He insisted his architects, James Pritchett and his son, also James, be appointed to design the new station, while Sir William Tite laid out the square.

opposite: Hexham gantry: a Victorian original
above: South Yorkshire's Palladian splendour

Pritchett's design of 1847 echoes Wentworth, at least in splendour. It boasts a central pavilion, colonnaded wings and corner pavilions. The portico dominates the square. Its six Corinthian columns are crowned with a pediment and flanked by three pilastered bays on either side. These are then extended by lengthy colonnades leading to the corner pavilions. These were to accommodate offices for the two rival companies, including separate ticket halls, apparently as far apart as possible. The centre block was for a hotel, which the companies were prepared to share. Only a clock in the pediment gives away that this is a railway rather than a grandee's mansion.

The hotel appears to have been short-lived and is now council offices. The pavilions are homes to two smart pubs, one The Head of Steam, the other the King's Head. The whole façade has been shown the respect due to a grade 1 listed building. Its soft sandstone is undefiled by signage, with even the British Rail logo hidden behind the portico in sober silver.

Entering under the portico, we expect Huddersfield's celebrated choral society to be incanting a march from *Aida*. Instead, we are presented with what is in truth rather a modest station interior. The ticket hall is plain and, until late in the 19th century, there was just one unroofed platform. Across the tracks looms a listed 1880s warehouse, a citadel of commerce in brown and purple vitreous brick. It makes the old station look like a stage set.

As for Huddersfield's current celebrity, I can only quote Wikipedia. 'Felix joined the staff as a nine-week-old kitten in 2011. Since then, she has patrolled the station to keep it free from rodents, and even has her own cat-flap to bypass the ticket barriers. In 2016, Felix was promoted to Senior Pest Controller, and has her own hi-vis jacket and name badge.' She has over 100,000 followers on Facebook.

opposite: Hull: Larkin 'getting away' at Whitsun

HULL
★ ★ ★ ★

I am torn between lauding Hull Paragon as an unsung masterpiece of the railway age, and pleading for it to be rescued from its owners and taken into care. Of all the damage inflicted on this proud city since the Second World War, few examples were more botched than the 2007 rebranding of its station as a bus and rail interchange. But like much of the railway's walking wounded, the damage is rectifiable. My four stars for Hull are stars of hope.

The original building of 1848 is second only to Huddersfield as a survivor of the great age of station classicism. It was built for George Hudson by George Andrews, and was the last of their collaborations. Today, it lies desperately forlorn to the rear of the present building. Its centre is a two-storey range with a porte cochère, whose Doric arcades have been filled in. Flanking wings lead to corner pavilions, one of two storeys, the other of three. Façades are pilastered, windows pedimented, eaves corniced and roofs hipped. It has the presence of a mayoral residence, but it looks unused, gazing out over a bleak car park (which should surely have formed the bus station).

Andrews also built Hudson an Italianate hotel, the Royal, blocking the station from the main road, known as Ferensway. This is of five central bays with deep, arched windows and flanking pavilions, all beneath a roof heavy with eaves and cornices. It has been much extended and altered.

The station's interior was rebuilt at the end of the century, and is the work of William Bell. He arrived in Hull in the 1900s as architect to the North Eastern Railway (see pp. 240 and 262) and rebuilt the train shed and a new concourse. Bell's roof has five arched spans with semi-circular end screens. Two transverse spans cover the concourse. These roofs are exceptional: long,

low vaults in brown and green, glazed at the apex and lightened by the terrazzo floor beneath. On the concourse, Bell erected wooden kiosks for shops in a vaguely Queen Anne style.

This station was adapted in 2007 by architects Wilkinson Eyre to serve as a transport interchange. The right-hand span now serves as access to the bus station, its former walls opened up as brick arches with market stalls. The ambition was admirable, as was removing an ugly office block next to the hotel in front, but replacing it with a bland modern canopy was crude. All station architects should be forced to visit London's Liverpool Street (see p. 58) to see how to respect a Victorian station.

Back on the train concourse, the various shops have been replaced by a series of bland structures intended to honour Hull's status as 2017 'City of Culture'. A new travel centre is a valiant but frigid affair, raised on a plinth and surrounded by plants.

Worse is the fate that befell Bell's masterpiece, the former art nouveau booking hall, ranking with that of St Pancras (see p. 71) as among the finest in Britain. It is tiled in green, cream and brown faience, with four decorated skylights overhead. Rich terracotta openings supply windows on to the street on one side and the concourse on the other. In the centre is the former carved oak ticket office, with Ionic pilasters flanking twelve (boarded-up) ticket windows. Finding a way to re-use this hall defeated the architects. It is currently used as a bicycle store and has plastic cubicles for 'small businesses'.

On the concourse next to the hotel is a statue of Hull's modern celebrity, Philip Larkin. He is shown dashing from the hotel bar as if enacting the first line of his poem, *The Whitsun Weddings*: 'That Whitsun I was late, getting away.' Set into the floor are other Larkin lines, like those by Betjeman in the floor at St Pancras.

To the south-west of the main shed in a siding off Anlaby Road is a single-storey warehouse, now housing a football supporters' club. This was the Immigrants' Building, used to process refugees fleeing eastern Europe at the turn of the 20th century. They were isolated here so that any diseases might be contained. In 1906 alone, 75,000 refugees were recorded passing through the building before travelling on to Liverpool Docks and North America. It is a nondescript place to encompass so much despair and so much hope.

MIDDLESBROUGH
★ ★ ★

Middlesbrough is a town struggling to recover its spirits. The central area round the handsome Exchange Square remains blighted by the elevated A66 roaring above it at first-floor level. Railway bridges respect city buildings, road ones seem to crush them. This has stripped the neighbourhood of all dignity and, with its associated office blocks, left downtown Middlesbrough gasping for revival.

A heavy responsibility duly rests on the restoration of the adjacent station. At the time of its construction by the North Eastern company in 1877, the town was described by Gladstone as 'an infant Hercules'. The building was designed by the Yorkshire architect William Peachey, in a gothic style unusual in the north of England.

Peachey brilliantly handled a complex, two-sided corner site with neighbouring Albert railway bridge and viaduct, by creating what is a group of buildings. They make no grand statement but carefully relate to the surrounding streetscape. Peachey had to elevate his entrance building on the side street to run parallel

above: Hull art nouveau: the booking hall
opposite: Railway medieval: entrance building

with the railway track. He did this with a long ramp, with undercroft and shops beneath, mimicking London's St Pancras (see p. 71) which was being built at the same time.

At the top of this ramp is a free-standing building for the entrance and ticket office, in the form of a medieval hall. It is a picturesque mix of round and pointed arches, crowned with a steep roof and two enormous gothic dormers. These have plate tracery in their windows. It is a building that would do credit to a Hanseatic League town hall.

Round the corner on Exchange Place, Peachey designed a separate office building, linked by stairs to the ticket hall, which again is in handsome gothic, here possibly a Hanseatic merchant's house. On the far side of the tracks, a third building completes the enclave, linked to the ticket hall by a palatial tiled underpass.

The interior of the ticket hall is in keeping, with a hammerbeam roof and tall gothic windows. Screens to the ticket office windows and the café are of harmonious dark wood. There is a delicate frieze of tiles. Round-arched doorways give on to a platform concourse, surrounded on three sides by the neo-romanesque façades of Peachey's platform building.

The platforms were once covered by a miniature St Pancras train shed. This was partly destroyed in the war and later demolished. The replacement canopies are 1950s stock issue but, to the east over Albert Bridge, are survivors of old canopies with richly coloured bases and capitals with elaborate brackets. At the time of writing, most of the station was under scaffolding, but the future for this crucial corner of tomorrow's Middlesbrough seems bright.

Middlesbrough's Victorian Hanseatic

NEWCASTLE CENTRAL
★ ★ ★ ★ ★

This is the grandest of provincial stations, if not the most lovable. It stands at the hub of the city centre, gathering the bridges over the Tyne into one pathway and turning them along the foot of the hill before bending them away again. The street façade, concourse, train shed and curving tracks offer some of the finest views in British architecture.

The Regency developer Richard Grainger projected a new suburb for old Newcastle in the 1820s, at the same time as Nash's Regent Street in London and with an eye to Edinburgh's earlier New Town. The development was fuelled by the port's sudden wealth from shipping coal, and was designed by an outstanding local architect, John Dobson, much of whose work was tragically destroyed in the 1960s and 1970s. What survives remains the most handsome city centre in the north.

Dobson also designed the station, which enjoyed a narrow escape from demolition. Its insertion at the junction of Grainger's new district and the old town dictated the character of his design, and required much ingenuity. Tyneside was already being described as 'the native land of railways'. George Stephenson was born on the banks of the Tyne and the city was home to his son Robert's engineering works. George Hudson's Newcastle & Berwick railway was part of his projected London to Scotland railway, authorised by parliament in 1845.

above: The great shed: Dobson's 'distinctive aesthetic'
pages 254-5: Palladio-on-Tyne: Prosser's porte cochère

The line was to enter the city from the south over the Tyne on the High Level Bridge, which was opened by Robert Stephenson in 1849. This required the destruction, drastic even for those days, of half of medieval Newcastle, including some 800 dwellings. Even the castle was not spared, sliced through by bridges, viaducts and tracks.

Dobson's first design was published in 1848 and showed one of the grandest neo-classical buildings of its day in Europe. He turned for inspiration to his hero, Sir John Vanbrugh, whose magnificent palace for the Delaval family, Seaton Delaval, close to the Northumberland coast, he later restored. Vanbrugh's style of baroque seemed ideally suited to so grand a project, despite being out of fashion at the time. Dobson's plan was for a long colonnaded frontage, with a projecting portico of attached columns and a tower looking out over the town. Work on the original project fell foul of Hudson's downfall in 1849 (see p. 265) and a consequent lack of money.

Hudson's successors, the North Eastern Railway (NER), resumed work on the station in 1850 to altered designs by the company's Thomas Prosser. The chief casualty was Dobson's portico. This was replaced by Prosser's gigantic porte cochère, formed of grand arches flanked by Doric pilasters in soft Northumberland stone. Wings on either side culminate in Dobson's original pavilions, truly Vanbrughian baroque, with rusticated office entrances. Dobson lived to see Prosser's dilution of his original design but, said his obituarist, was mortified and died in 'grief and disappointment'.

The railway historian Christian Barman called Dobson 'the greatest of all railway architects', and Newcastle 'the highest moment of functional adventure and discovery'. This was not enough to stop British Rail trying to demolish it in the 1970s, prevented only by statutory listing. We may miss Dobson's portico but Prosser's porte cochère remains magnificent, flanking the view along Neville Street, from Pugin's Catholic cathedral in the west to the Anglican cathedral in the east.

A second, albeit less drastic, disaster came in 2013 with Network Rail's thoughtless glazing of the porte cochère to form a 'retail concourse'. This not only prevented vehicle access under cover, but filled Prosser's openings with plastic reinforced glass that discoloured and became opaque. This lost the contrast of light and depth so important to a classical façade. The interior was filled with insipid cabins and kiosks. What had been epic became anaemic.

Yet the station interior is breathtaking. While Dobson's street frontage is straight, in line with the road, his interior frontage is curved in line with the bend of the tracks. It might be the façade of one of Bath's sublime circuses. The soft grey limestone admirably fuses with the grey of the ironwork and the terrazzo floor. The footbridge over the tracks is original.

Overhead rises Dobson's shed, built in the 1840s barely a decade after Brunel's at Bristol. It was the first of the curved roofs that contributed a distinctive aesthetic to British station design. To engineer his curve, Dobson visited ironworks and then devised a new type of rolled iron girder to support his three roof spans. The vertical lines drift into the distance, described by Jeffrey Richards and John M. Mackenzie as a 'formal beauty of line and curve, facilitating constantly changing patterns of light, shade and steam'. It is a glory of the Mania age. The diminutive steam engines shown in early railway prints seem lost amid such grandeur.

The station was enhanced in the 1890s by the NER's William Bell, with his distinctive art nouveau touches. He added a new span to the shed roof and canopied extensions to the platforms. The Centurion pub of 1893, probably by him, is a sensational neo-baroque confection of coffee-coloured faience tiles. In the 1960s, British Rail police used it for overnight cells, taking sledgehammers to the walls to insert partitions. Its subsequent restoration has been immaculate. Smart post-modernist waiting-rooms on the outer platforms are a mercifully subtle modern insertion.

opposite: Jesmond: Mies on the Metro

NEWCASTLE JESMOND
★

This is a surprise. Sandwiched between a submerged urban carriageway and a John Dobson church is a small garden with, lurking in its midst, a miniature homage to the modernist architect Mies van der Rohe. To the rear is (usually) a small sculpture display.

The Tyne and Wear Metro is second only to the London Underground in urban transit design. The electrification of Newcastle's suburban services goes back to the North Eastern Railway in 1904. The Metro emerged in its modern form in 1970 with the planning of a sixty-station local network, stretching from Whitley Bay in the north to Sunderland and its suburbs in the south. Attention was paid to station design to a degree rare on such networks outside London.

The Metro's Haymarket station has four parabolic arches over its ticket office and an escalator worthy of Charles Holden (see p. 22). Other striking stations are at Four Lane Ends, Pelaw, St Peter's and Northumberland Park. Jesmond is the most satisfying, in a modern movement idiom, well suited to its sylvan setting.

The station, which was opened in 1980, is by the local firm of L. J. Couves and is a rectangular box with an open courtyard at the back. It is simple, each side composed of panels of black glass with plain glass round the middle, allowing light to flood the interior. From inside, there is an all-round view of the surrounding trees, with stair access to the platforms below. The ceiling is composed of wooden slatted ridge-and-furrow, a vernacular theme throughout the Metro. One wall has a dramatic abstract mural by Simon Butler.

The front entrance has two doorways, both marked by a bright yellow station sign. Filling the view out to the rear is an ornamental garden, guarded by a row of obelisks flanking a rusticated antique arch with a fleur de lis on top. It is all faintly surreal – and like most modern buildings in need of regular upkeep.

RIBBLEHEAD
★

If there is a wilder spot in England I don't know it – though Rannoch in Scotland runs it close. Ribblehead sits high and lonely on a Pennine plateau, guarding that great work of Victorian engineering, the 24-arch viaduct over the upper River Ribble. The scene is dominated by the twin summits of Ingleborough and Whernside, with Blea Moor to the east. The plateau has four times the rainfall of London.

Apart from the small Railway Inn under the shadow of the viaduct, the landscape is devoid of settlement. There are few trees, just a clutch of ash, some fields and sheep. The line was virtually a vanity project by the ever-expansionist Midland Railway in the 1870s, hoping to compete with the east- and west-coast main lines to Scotland. Engineered by the Midland's surveyor, John Crossley, over the hostile Pennine contours, it was the last line built by manual labour. Its constant viaducts and tunnels required 6,000 navvies, with a hundred dying in the construction of Ribblehead viaduct alone. The station's waiting-room was used for regular church services, its harmonium coming from the old mission chapel in the navvy village under the viaduct.

The Settle–Carlisle Railway opened for passengers in 1876, never made money and survived successive attempts at closure only by the efforts of a vigorous preservation lobby. The final battle occurred in the mid-1980s, fought by myself and others, within as well as outside British Rail. The chief bone of contention was the cost of viaduct repairs. I remember walking the track with a local contractor who complained that the £7.5m price for Ribblehead's repair was grossly inflated by BR, intent on closure. One workman said he could solve its leaks for

High in the Pennines: the wildest halt in England

twenty-five years with a barrow-load of tarmac. It was eventually restored for half the original estimate.

Most of the stations on the line were designed by Crossley, in two sizes of near identical neo-Tudor. Ribblehead, however, is attributed to the company's John Holloway Sanders. Twin-gabled cross wings enclose a small loggia between them. This loggia is sensibly glazed. Every roof eave is decorated with ornamental bargeboards and the building is both cheery and uncommonly handsome for somewhere that was never likely to be much patronised.

A small museum fills the booking office and there are stained-glass company roundels in the windows. The old stationmaster house, which is now a holiday cottage, stands to the north. Until the 1950s this doubled as a meteorological station, its occupant sending reports to the Air Ministry. It must often have consisted of one word, rain. Like many such lines, it depends heavily on the support of volunteers, here the Friends of the Settle–Carlisle line. Their Trust takes on even such main-line tasks as station refurbishment – and thank goodness.

At the end of March 2017, special events were held to celebrate the reopening of the line following a land-slip. This included a special excursion, crammed with railway enthusiasts, hauled by the *Flying Scotsman*.

opposite: **Roman pomp in Sheaf Square**

SHEFFIELD
★ ★ ★

Nowhere is Sheffield's hesitant renaissance more evident that in the former Midland Railway station in Sheaf Square. At night, its environs recede into the darkness and careful lighting picks out Charles Trubshaw's twelve-arched screen. For a brief moment, Sheffield becomes the Rome of the North, with the Baths of Caracalla and the Trevi Fountain in the foreground.

Sheffield was subjected to much attention during the Mania (see p. 7), assailed by the Manchester, Sheffield & Lincoln Railway, the London & North Western and the Midland, all pushing viaducts, bridges and tunnels across its steep hills and valleys. The Midland was the tardiest, with a branch line from Rotherham and a station built in 1870.

It was the Midland that survived, to be extended by Charles Trubshaw in 1904 as part of the company's response to the arrival on the scene of Sir Edward Watkin's extravagant Great Central Railway to London. As with his Leicester frontage (see p. 188), Trubshaw did not hold back. He was a master of railway baroque and delivered a screen of gabled arches to the porte cochère, concealing a beautiful internal wall to the station proper.

The screen is an exceptional work. Each of the elliptical arches is boldly rusticated and divided by stumpy pilasters. Instead of the expected strong classical cornice, there is a series of pedimented gables reflecting the ridge-and-furrow of the roof behind. It is as if something were missing, a tower or central portico. Yet the composition sustains itself, with turrets between the gables and a cluster of four turrets at the corners. The arches are now glazed and the interior has become a covered concourse.

Facing this screen is the new Sheaf Square, which slopes down to the railway from the town centre.

One side of the square is a wall of Sheffield steel, guiding a cascade of water. On the other is a rococo curve of steps, with fountains at its foot. It is an accomplished celebration of Sheffield's most famous product, and commendably uncluttered. In front of the station façade is a pedestrian piazza with café tables. Even the British Rail logo and station notices are demoted to a free-standing pillar. Here, for once, is a forecourt that works, with taxi access banished to a surviving bay of the old station to the right.

The interior concourse is airy and smart. The grey slate paving of the square outside becomes shimmering white terrazzo. The arches outside are matched by internal ones to the platforms, with baroque rustication, art nouveau reliefs in the spandrels and ornamented fanlights. The pediments above the arches and below the ridge-and-furrow roof are curiously stepped. The retail kiosks are designed with exposed steel roofs.

Beyond the concourse is the old ticket hall, with three clerestory lanterns. It is dominated by a double stairway up to the platform bridge. Here Sheffield reflects the gutting of its insides in 1957. Its overall shed was lost and replaced with modern platform buildings and canopies. However, on platform 1 is a Trubshaw period first-class waiting-room, now the Sheffield Tap, its Edwardian fittings intact. When I asked a member of staff the whereabouts of 'the historic platform pub', he said he did not know, but I had better ask 'in the Tap'. The platform canopy valances are in a decorative grey and white. They make a happy contrast with the brutalist palisades of the Park Hill housing estate looming from the hillside overhead.

TYNEMOUTH

★ ★ ★

Tynemouth and Whitley Bay developed from the boom in seaside holidays in the late 19th century, as working-class northerners were liberated to spend Sundays and Bank Holidays by the sea. Acres of coastline were duly given over to amusement arcades and boarding houses. The railways needed to handle 'excursion' traffic, and the stations became their advertisement and their welcome. Fashion in holidays has moved on, and the station now services a gentler trade of Tyneside commuters and retirement estates.

The first station, by Benjamin Green, survives as a modest stone house with a blue plaque in neighbouring Oxford Street. Today's Tynemouth was built by the North Eastern Railway's William Bell in the 1880s. For his entrance building of 1882, Bell chose neo-romanesque. A long, low, single-storey façade has round-arched windows with pretty columns and capitals, and some grotesque corbel heads. Above the entrance canopy is a sweeping slate roof, with French-style ironwork along its ridge.

None of this prepares us for Tynemouth's interior. The concourse, clearly designed to marshal crowds of holidaymakers, is a winter garden wonderland, a feast of Victorian ironwork. One hundred columns march into the distance beneath a rolling canopy of ridge-and-furrow roofs. These columns, painted green and white, support lattice girders on ornate brackets, each a swirl of rococo iron. Mock-Ionic capitals are painted lurid colours, festooned with spilling flower baskets. The girders in turn support ribs with elongated spandrels, again much ornamented.

Directly facing the entrance is a double staircase to a curved footbridge over the tracks. Here the valances on the canopies have curious keyhole perforations. Fancy railings once guided the crowds

Tynemouth's holiday welcome

262

round the platforms. Today they stand ghostly and slightly forlorn.

The station is no longer on the main network but on the Tyne and Wear Metro. It seems largely deserted and its old waiting-rooms and shops house those concomitants of modern travel, wine bars, hairdressers and physiotherapists. A wide entrance arch includes a tile wall map of the NER's domain, and works by local artists. At weekends, Tynemouth takes on an alternative life, given over to antiques and book fairs, farmers' markets and much bunting. It becomes what every good station should be, the life and soul of its community.

Whitby's seaside Italianate

WHITBY
★ ★

I have a soft spot for Whitby. The train journey from Middlesbrough down the Esk Valley, courtesy of its not-for-profit community rail partnership, is, at least in fine weather, one of the glories of the North. Soft vales cut into high moorland. Ash and alder shade tumbling rivers as they tease the railway to leap from left bank to right, from one bridge to another.

The port of Whitby is laid out casually round its harbour, where George Stephenson's station claimed early prominence near the quayside. Tourists are today as grateful as once were fishermen, leaving the station entrance to find themselves beside the harbour with, high on the cliff opposite, the magnificent ruins of Whitby's abbey and, further along, the fine parish church. The town periodically celebrates the landfall there of Count Dracula. The resulting 'goth' festivals have brought it a new prosperity.

The station was designed by George Andrews in 1845. He would have no truck with seaside quaintness, rather the decorum of an Italianate villa. Peter Burman (in Binney and Pearce) is justifiably over the top. Whitby station is 'an evocation of the Renaissance, with a nod in the direction of the Loggia dei Lanzi in Florence'. It is single-storey in soft limestone, fronted by a five-bay portico, with a two-bay portico at the side entrance.

The interior offices have been converted into a restaurant and a pub, or at least a 'micro-pub'. It is confusingly named The Waiting Room, which means it needs a prominent notice pleading with passengers not to use it as such but to buy a drink if they wish to enter. There is an NER tile map on the platform wall. In 1900, the company authorised the installation of these maps at twenty-five of its stations. Whitby is one of the nine with its map *in situ*, the others being at Beverley, Hartlepool, Middlesbrough, Morpeth, Saltburn, Scarborough, Tynemouth and York.

The platforms are much blighted by seagulls and have had their view of the harbour unkindly blocked by a supermarket in the old goods yard. It is a small price to pay for so splendid a location.

YORK
★ ★ ★ ★ ★

In railways, as in bishops, York has long been England's 'second city'. I said of Newcastle that it was the grandest of provincial stations but not the most lovable. That title surely goes to York. Its informality and sense of mild chaos would never pass muster on the Continent. Yet it is a station of personality, in which the architecture is an overture to the grandeur of its roof, another station to benefit from a curve. Its track appears to have swerved away from its intended route for our personal convenience, before resuming its natural inclination to straightness.

Early Victorian York was in thrall to the 'Railway King', George Hudson. A local draper who inherited a minor fortune from a relative, he founded the York & North Midland company in the first railway boom in the 1830s, and went on to dominate the second, the 1840s Mania (see p. 7). His ambition was to 'mak all t'railways cum t'York', which he saw as equidistant between Britain's north and south.

At the height of the Mania in 1844, Hudson abandoned that motto and moved his company headquarters south to Derby. Whereas most of the new railways were formed to build lines, he grew by acquisition and amalgamation. Soon he was pushing north towards Scotland and south as far as Bristol. In 1845, he merged with the ailing Eastern Counties and conquered East Anglia. He became Lord Mayor of York, MP for Sunderland and owner of a palace in Knightsbridge, although parliament baulked at allowing him a terminus in London.

Hudson was the Icarus of the Mania. He soon made enemies among his competitors, and a Great Northern company was founded in 1846, specifically to challenge his virtual monopoly. Rivalry became intense, and Hudson was eventually accused of every kind of financial irregularity, fairly and unfairly. In

pages 266-7: York's sinuous perspective

Way out ⬆ 🏃Fire exit

Platforms 1 - 3 & 5 - 11

Toilets

Gentlemen

1849, he faced prosecution and fled the country. He later said his inheritance had been 'the very worst thing that could have happened to me. It let me into the railways.'

In 1841, Hudson had been allowed (with the help of George Andrews, City sheriff and Hudson's company architect) to smash through York's ancient walls and bring his terminus, shed and hotel inside the medieval city. The site soon proved inadequate. Through trains had to enter the terminus and then reverse out to continue on their way.

It was not until 1873 that the present station was begun by the inheritors of Hudson's empire, the North Eastern Railway (NER). The new site was outside the city and, to reach it, the line had to make a tight curve. As at Bristol and Newcastle, this accident of geography was to give York's shed roof its elegance. The architect was that of Newcastle's great porte cochère, Thomas Prosser, and the station was completed in 1877.

York revels in the title of 'gentleman among stations,' but its exterior is anything but special. The entrance of nine arches is in plain Yorkshire brick and distinctly workaday. Its chief virtue is in giving arriving visitors a first glimpse of the city walls and the Minster in the distance.

York's modest ticket hall leads directly on to the concourse. An outcry greeted a proposal to erect a barrier of ticket machines across this entrance, and it was duly dropped. As a result, York is the only big station with open platforms. The concourse has three sides of warm yellow-brick walls, forming a pleasantly casual meeting point. But where the fourth side should be open and reveal the vista of the shed roof, there is an obstruction.

Plumb at the apex of the station curve stands an old two-storey signal-box clad in wood. Its location was to give the signalmen a clear line of vision north and south round the bending platforms. Somehow the box has survived and is now a coffee bar with a bookstall beneath. Fastened to its far side is York's famous three-faced clock, above the footbridge to the far platforms.

Beyond the signal-box we can finally see York at its most splendid. The shed was built by Thomas Harrison to accompany Prosser's station, and ranks with those of St Pancras and Paddington as masterpieces of Victorian engineering. There are three spans of differing dimensions, with a fourth shorter span added to one side. The glazed roof is supported on classical columns, with colourful Corinthian capitals. The brackets contain spandrels depicting the white rose of York and the NER's coat of arms. The roof ribs are thick at first, then taper gracefully and are pierced to reduce their weight.

The pronounced bend gives the roof a subtly diminishing perspective when viewed from almost every angle, best from the central footbridge. The aesthetic of engineering seems to crave a curve. Each shed end is closed by a glazed screen, its tracery looking like scimitars. By keeping the bottom transom as a curved arch rather than a horizontal crossbar, Harrison gave his sinuous composition a crowning elegance. At night, York takes on an additional magic, as the lighting throws the arches into relief, their warmth contrasting with the darkness outside.

The station is busy with detail. Platforms extending beyond the shed roofs have canopies thick with valances. A redundant semaphore signal adorns a platform. Lights are in their original globes.

Tucked in beside the porte cochère is Tearoom Square, guarded by a 1906 pub, the York Tap, designed in 1906 by William Bell (also responsible for the Centurion Bar in Newcastle). The pub's façade to the platform has swirling art nouveau windows, echoing the curves of the roof above.

Next to the pub in Tearoom Square is a picturesque canopy over the carriage entrance, with a side door into the adjacent hotel. The homely scene is overlooked by the end screen of the side platform. It is one of those informal corners that make wandering about English stations so rewarding.

York station stands next to that Mecca for train enthusiasts, the National Railway Museum. This is located in the former locomotive shed, once the heart of Hudson's envisaged national railway hub. We can occasionally see thoroughbred engines being taken out to show their paces, in honour of the heritage railway revival.

opposite: The three-faced clock

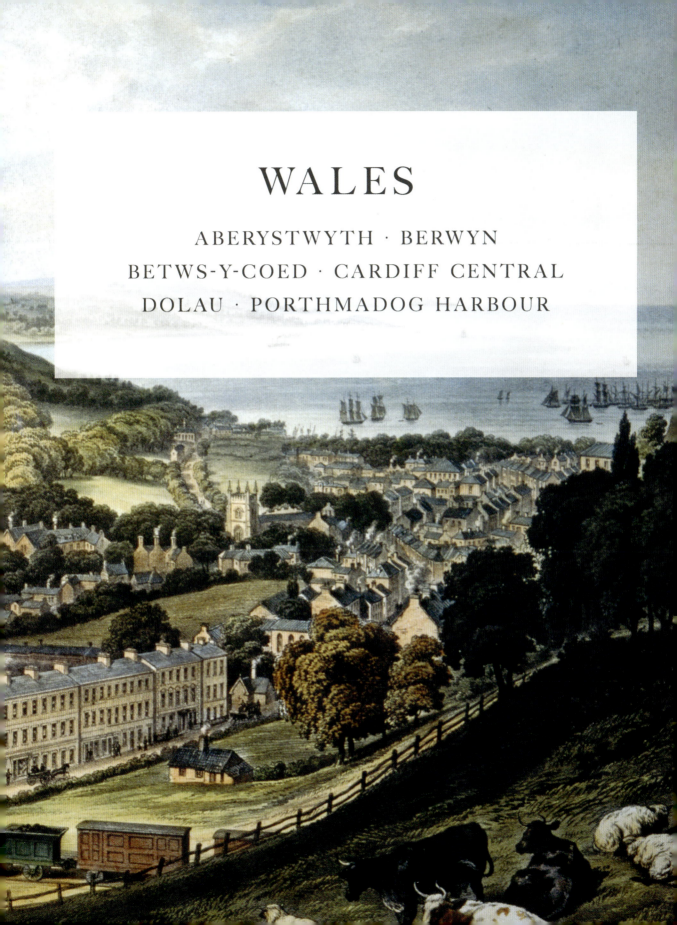

WALES

ABERYSTWYTH · BERWYN
BETWS-Y-COED · CARDIFF CENTRAL
DOLAU · PORTHMADOG HARBOUR

WALES

Wales claimed its place in railway history when Richard Trevithick's 1804 steam locomotive was the first to draw wagons on iron rails. It proved too heavy and the rails broke. Subsequent lines in South Wales were dominated by the transportation of coal and iron from the Glamorganshire valleys to the coastal ports. The iron settlement of Dowlais had nine 'stations' between the two world wars. Virtually all this heritage, was swept away before and during the Devastation (see p. 24). As a result, precious little of Glamorgan's industrial archaeology survives.

Passenger railways in the south were dominated by the Great Western Railway. The company continued to build new stations into the 20th century, including those at Cardiff, Swansea and Aberystwyth. Mid- and north Wales saw extensive investment in railways serving the slate quarries, while the north coast saw a race to bring the Irish Mail to Holyhead. This was reinforced by the growth of holiday traffic along the coast from Merseyside (see p. 212).

Closures and assiduous conservation made Wales fertile ground for heritage railways. The Great Little Trains of Wales group comprises eleven services, with a similar number of lesser enterprises. They include Britain's longest heritage line, the now merged Ffestiniog & Welsh Highland Railway. The tourist trade has also brought prosperity to picturesque Betws-y-Coed and Berwyn.

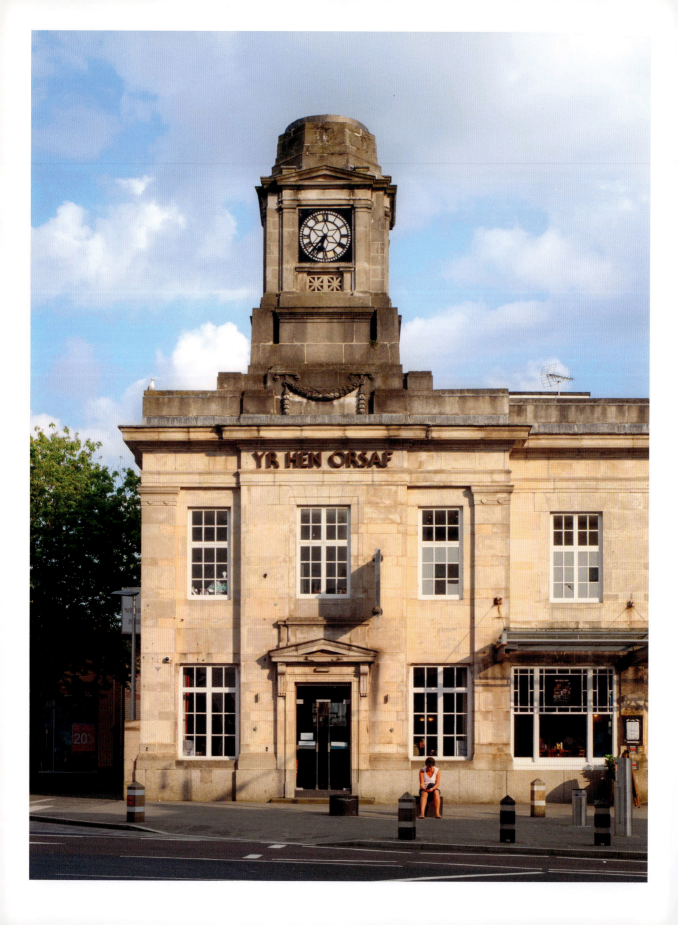

ABERYSTWYTH

★

Travellers on the Cambrian Line across mid-Wales might wonder what justified the impressive terminus at Aberystwyth. A sequence of modest stations up the Severn valley and down the Dyfi ends in a miniature version of Cardiff Central. The answer is that in 1911, the Great Western Railway (GWR) had recklessly taken over the debt-ridden Manchester & Milford Railway, an eccentric venture hoping to profit by carrying freight traffic down the Welsh coast from Lancashire to Milford Haven Docks. It had opened in 1867.

The GWR thought Aberystwyth would make an ideal holiday resort for south Wales. It did not. The section of the line from Carmarthen to Aberystwyth made heavy losses, and was an easy target for Beeching in 1964. Its closure to passenger services is commemorated in the Lord Beechings pub opposite the station entrance.

The terminus is just one platform and the new entrance is to one side of the GWR's imposing stone-fronted office building. The building dates from 1925, and is possibly by the GWR's house architect, Percy Culverhouse. If so, its neo-Georgian is an interesting foretaste of his later flirting with art deco at Cardiff (see p. 281) and Leamington Spa (see p. 187). Of two storeys in dull grey ashlar, it has end pavilions of three bays, with pilasters and swags. Above the left-hand pavilion is an apology for a clock tower.

The main 1920s building has long been out of use, but has been converted into a Wetherspoons pub, Yr Hen Orsaf (The Old Station), with admirable results. The restaurants and bars spill out to the rear, bringing the old station concourse to life. This is covered by a glass canopy, which serves as a winter garden. To its left is the former platform 1, now converted as part of the adjacent shopping centre and rather deadening that side of the station.

Opposite is the remaining Victorian platform, excellently restored. It is flanked by the original brick-built offices, with stone surrounds to the doors and windows. The canopy supports are exceptional, comprising rows of diminishing gothic arches, each with a vigorous quatrefoil in its spandrel, a design I have seen nowhere else. The platform is brightly painted and cheerful. The station entrance is now to the rear of this building, with a dramatic modern canopy.

Down the track to the south is the terminus of the narrow-gauge Vale of Rheidol Railway that runs for nearly 12 miles to Devil's Bridge. When London's London Bridge station was recently being demolished, its old shed roof was, somewhat implausibly, offered to the Vale of Rheidol for possible reuse, perhaps as part of a new museum. It still lies in pieces in a yard.

BERWYN

★

The gorges of the upper River Dee are among the most dramatic in Britain. Undaunted, the Llangollen & Corwen Railway, built by the Great Western in 1865, wound its way from Llangollen into Snowdonia through a series of hair-raising bends, tunnels and bridges. The line closed in 1965, but was reopened by the dogged Llangollen Railway Society in 1981. It well illustrates the debt the Welsh tourist industry owes to Wales's industrial past.

Berwyn station, the first halt west from Llangollen, is perched precipitously on a platform between the Dee gorge and the A5. It was designed in the 1860s, probably by the doyen of Marches stations, Thomas Penson of Oswestry (see p. 181). The style is the same black-and-white Tudor he employed in rebuilding much of the city of Chester. The station-master's house is of three lofty storeys, steeply gabled, with one gable looking out over the gorge. This is now available as a holiday let for those with a head for heights.

opposite: Cardiff classicism comes north
pages 276–7: Chester Tudor on the Dee gorges

Attached to one side of this building is the old booking office. It was locked when I was there, but I could see it stacked with old trunks, laundry baskets, milk churns, coal for the fire and a somnolent cat. Season tickets apparently cost 10/6d, plus a hefty 2/8d for a dog. To stand on the platform, with only the track between oneself and the cliff edge, is to see the upper Dee at its most Alpine.

The river beneath is crossed by the Llantysilio chain bridge to the Chainbridge Hotel, as black and white as the station.

BETWS-Y-COED
★ ★

Driving railways through Snowdonia was no mean task. The initial purpose was to move slate and tin to the coast, but tourism soon followed as visitors began to appreciate the drama of the Llanberis and Aberglaslyn passes. Railways followed through even the steepest ravines. Betws lies on the A5 at the gateway to the Snowdon massif. Its buildings snake along the valley floor in dark grey stone, the colour of Welsh rain.

The station, built by the London & North Western Railway in 1868, sits on the outskirts of the town, surrounded by looming slopes thick with conifers. It was clearly designed to cope with crowds, and is of two gabled storeys of rough, undressed stone. Triple windows are surrounded by yellow bricks, the only concession to style being that some are Venetian. The builder was a local man, Gethin Jones. The gables on the platform side are surmounted by fierce Welsh dragons.

The platforms are thick with flowers, which also spill on to the tracks, a landscape indulgence rare on today's network. The canopy brackets are elaborate and the gas lamps are original. When I was last there, a lamp in the entrance passage had been colonised by a bird's nest. The station, which is now run by Arriva's Conwy Valley line, is an unstaffed halt, but the buildings behind form a busy row of tourist shops and cafés. The adjacent bus station has 'Sherpa' shuttles to the foot of Snowdon.

Opposite the platform is a small railway museum. It runs a miniature children's train which, when seen from the main track, looks eerily Lilliputian.

Betws: harmony of brick and stone

Eclectic art deco: Cardiff's concourse

CARDIFF CENTRAL
★ ★ ★

There was a brief moment in the Edwardian period when Cardiff, Wales's capital, aspired to the grandeur of another Edinburgh. It had expansive docks and a wide harbour. It had a castle enclave and, proudest of all, a sequence of grand, neo-baroque civic buildings erected on the revenues of Glamorgan coal. But the city lacked strong planning and, at the end of the 20th century, crippled itself with unsightly projects. It blighted its downtown area with a rebuilt rugby stadium – arenas are empty holes in town centres – and banished Wales's dramatic new opera house and Senedd, the National Assembly building, to the docks. Cardiff was split in two.

The railway is left serving the older part of the city. Brunel's broad-gauge line had arrived in 1850, after diverting the adjacent River Taff to the west to make room for it. His original wooden station was extended in the 1880s and rebuilt completely in 1934 by the Great Western's architect, Percy Culverhouse. The style is that of the clean, confident 1930s. Cardiff Central is a rarity among stations, a complete work of proto-art deco.

The main front to the north is handsome, capturing the moment when neo-Georgian was flirting with new decorative forms. It is a long, low building of stone, with corner pavilions dressed with pilasters, pediments and large arched windows with Georgian glazing bars. The station entrance is in the centre of the façade, the latter being fronted by an aggressive canopy, spoiling its classical verticality. Above, in extraordinary prominence, is the name of the Great Western Railway in stone relief, below a modest cupola containing a clock.

Cardiff's finest feature is inside. The main concourse is a superb display of modulated art deco. The ceiling is vaguely Tudor, panelled and supported along the sides on broad elliptical arches with marbled pilasters. The space is lit by a superb sequence of hanging art deco lights.

The platforms, which are above street level, are painted white and GWR green. A new southern entrance has been added to handle crowds to the adjacent stadium on match days. Fanlights from the Victorian station have been installed on the wall of the new entrance hall. There are plans drastically to redevelop the station, possibly submerging it in a modern retail centre as at Birmingham New Street. We must hope the original façade and interiors are safe.

DOLAU

★

Small is beautiful at Dolau, styled the Welsh Adlestrop. In the 1960s, the old Heart of Wales line from Shrewsbury to Swansea was a prime candidate for Beeching. The line's survival was famously due not to its passengers, of whom there were few, but to its number of marginal constituencies. Even then, the case for a station at Dolau was hard to sustain. Lost in idyllic Radnorshire, the tiny settlement did not merit such a facility, and in 1983 closure was again inevitable.

What happened next was all too rare in railway sociology. Rather than just howl at the government, a group of local people formed the Dolau Station Action Group. They took over the station and demanded that it survive as an unmanned request stop. It was similar local activism that saved Gobowen (see p. 181). There is clearly life in the Welsh Marches.

After the station buildings had been demolished, the action group erected a small shelter and turned the verge of the single-line platform into an extended garden. The station name is written in clipped box and there are paintings by local people displayed among the flowers. The station was visited by the Queen in her Golden Jubilee year of 2002, commemorated with two flags, the Union Jack and the Welsh Dragon, still flying on the platform.

What is most remarkable about Dolau is the adjacent house whose owners have kindly made their garden accessible to waiting passengers. Trees and shrubs are dotted about with fragments of semaphore signals. This merging of station into a semi-private domain evokes the shared space of a traditional Welsh village.

The new shelter, with barely room for two people to stand, is coated with plaques and certificates won by the action group, variously for best, smallest, best-kept, most in bloom and most improved station. A selection of railway poetry is pinned to the wall, with works by Robert Louis Stevenson, Wilfred Owen, Aldous Huxley, Edmund Blunden and Siegfried Sassoon. Edward Thomas's *Adlestrop* is there, enlivened by a parody by Simon Rae. 'Yes, I remember Adlestrop. / Boy, do I remember Adlestrop. / That's the bare platform where my train / Came to an unwonted stop . . . no one yet had stumped up cash / For the franchise.'

The setting is exquisite. At either end, the track curves off into the tight contours of the Radnor hills. A sleepy by-road crosses the line, but there are neither trains nor cars enough to cause trouble. Dolau station is the only one I know that has a visitors' book. Rarely have I signed one so willingly.

PORTHMADOG HARBOUR
★★★

Porthmadog high street offers the most surreal of railway spectacles. Looking south towards the Traeth Mawr estuary, we see a cluster of buildings round the old harbour station. Suddenly a steam engine appears from their midst, as if from nowhere, and chugs down the main street in a cloud of smoke, followed devotedly by twelve coaches. They snake along rails in the middle of the road, before turning right and heading up the valley towards Snowdonia. Beautifully polished, with coaches in maroon and cream livery, it is like a ceremonial lion in an oriental parade.

In 1810, William Madocks built a cob wall and new town, Tremadog, on the estuary to develop its agriculture and slate industry. Porthmadog, on the sea side of the Cob, was its harbour, fed by narrow-gauge railways from the slate quarries of the interior. The train that makes its way down Porthmadog high street is a survivor of those railways, linking the Welsh Highway and the Ffestiniog lines in what is Britain's longest heritage railway, running some forty miles from Caernarvon to Blaenau Ffestiniog.

The final stage of the Welsh Highland's rebuilding in 2011, with aid from the Heritage Lottery Fund, was the most ambitious project in the heritage railway revival (see p. 30). The line runs through the most beautiful but also the most difficult valleys of the Snowdonia National Park, linking what was a maze of slate railways. For its part, the Ffestiniog climbs up the Ffestiniog valley through precipitous forests by means of loops reminiscent of India's Darjeeling Line.

When the connecting of the Ffestiniog and Welsh Highland lines was completed in 2011, Porthmadog Harbour became the terminus. The F&WHR's engineering works across the estuary at Boston

Lodge is now the largest steam railway workshop in Britain. Such enterprises should not be termed 'heritage' but, rather, thoroughly modern.

Porthmadog Harbour station sits between the quayside and the Cob causeway. The buildings are formed from the old goods shed and station building, incorporating the stationmaster's house. They sit immaculate in this setting, canopies brightly painted, flowers in order, posters not too evident, white paint offsetting grey slate walls. Round about is the paraphernalia of steam, signal-boxes, semaphores, sidings and hissing engines.

The walk to the end of the station platform and on to the Cob offers an incomparable panorama of Cardigan Bay to the south-west and Snowdonia inland. The backdrop is that of the Snowdon massif and the spike of Cnicht, the 'Matterhorn of Wales'. To the west are the Traeth Mawr estuary and Harlech. Today, the landscape is dotted with puffs of white smoke, that of an ever-busier railway in the throes of recovery.

pages 284–5: Semaphores to Snowdonia
opposite: Porthmadog's immaculate heritage

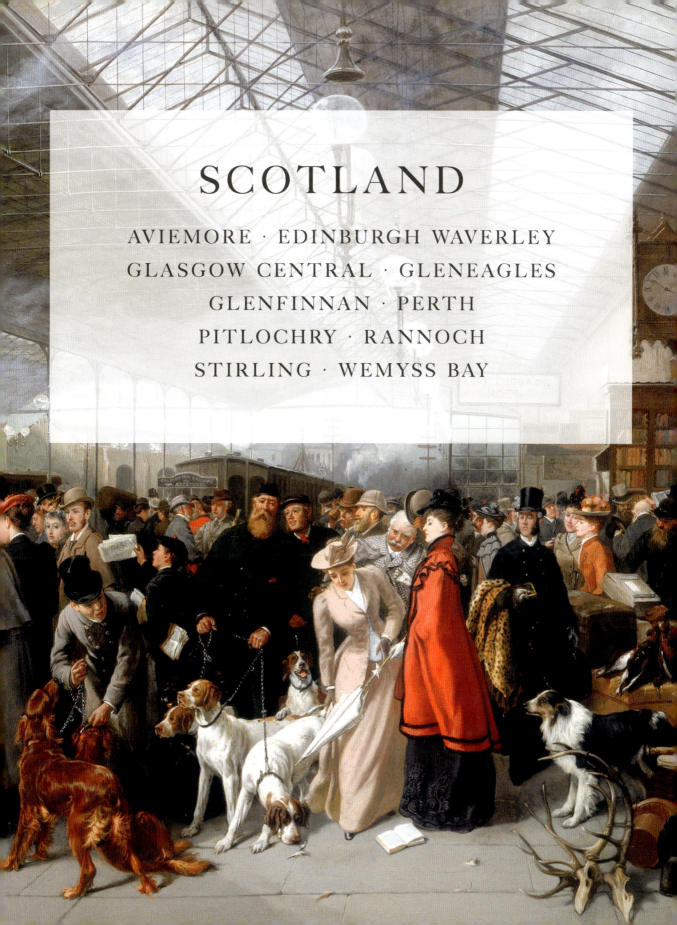

SCOTLAND

AVIEMORE · EDINBURGH WAVERLEY
GLASGOW CENTRAL · GLENEAGLES
GLENFINNAN · PERTH
PITLOCHRY · RANNOCH
STIRLING · WEMYSS BAY

SCOTLAND

Scotland did not escape the fierce competition that accompanied the coming of railways to England. It saw a two-pronged rivalry between the North British Railway based in Edinburgh and the Caledonian Railway in Glasgow. Rivalry was intense, producing the same, often chaotic, route configurations. The Lowland lines were on the whole profitable and produced fine stations, notably in Glasgow and Perth, while the Highland ones, promoted for tourism towards the end of the 19th century, found investment less easy and often took many years to complete.

One name dominates Scottish station architecture, that of the Glasgow architect James Miller. He began working for the Caledonian in the 1880s and, with his colleague Donald Matheson, the company's engineer and then general manager, enjoyed an extraordinary range of domestic and commercial clients. His contacts were unrivalled – and resented by rivals – but his buildings were outstanding.

Miller and his contemporaries were designing at a time when station style was emerging from the eclectic naïveté of the mid-Victorian period into a more confident revivalism. This ranged from a baronial baroque for large buildings to a widespread use of a Queen Anne vernacular for smaller projects, topped, in Miller's case, by virtuoso roofs at Wemyss Bay and Stirling. Their joyful levity is hard to marry to his reputation as a dour, rather tetchy individual.

The survival of many so-called chalet stations on the Highland lines is a particular pleasure, perhaps the outcome of their promoters' wish to present the region as a Scottish Switzerland. Their predominant woodwork offered a rich palette of colours, notably the Caledonian's shades of brown and cream, known as 'duck's foot', and the Highland's dark red, known as cinnamon.

AVIEMORE

★ ★

This is an exemplary case of station rescue. The revival was undertaken in 1998 to aid the promotion of Aviemore as a ski resort, the earlier station having been rebuilt in 1898 to serve what was already an embryonic holiday centre. Today, it might be a set for a Hollywood winter sports musical. Spreading roofs ensure that not a single flake of snow descends on alighting passengers. Cottagey façades and bright colours hint at Zermatt or Val d'Isère. Wide platforms leave uncluttered space for skis and luggage. In the distance hover the snowy uplands of the Cairngorms, the nearest the British Isles get to Alps.

As completed, the station is handsome. It was designed by the Highland Railway's engineer, William Roberts, and comprises two long wooden buildings in Highland chalet style. Waiting-room bay windows give views down the platforms, like rows of up-market tea shops. The roofs extend outwards into giant canopies with, at each end, a gable containing a semi-circular lunette, although one end has panelled windows with lancet tracery. All have valances and bargeboards of intricate fretwork.

The platform canopies rest on cast-iron columns, their capitals variants on Ionic and Corinthian designs. The spandrels carry unusual wheel motifs and scrolls. The paintwork is in the Highland Railway's cinnamon and white. From a distance, the impression is closer to Tibet than Scotland.

The east side of the station is now occupied by the heritage Strathspey railway, which runs to the delightfully named Boat of Garten station. To be at Aviemore when a steam excursion is departing is to get a lesson in the relative appeal of steam and diesel haulage. The far platform is reached over a delicate arched footbridge with lattice panels. Why do modern footbridges have to be so heavy and blundering when Aviemore's seems to float on air?

EDINBURGH WAVERLEY

★ ★

Waverley is a nervous breakdown of a station. From the arrival of the North British Railway in Scotland's capital in 1846, the line's occupation of the ravine beneath the castle walls appalled Edinburgh's citizens, since it wiped out most of the public gardens between the old city and New Town. With each expansion, more land was seized and tunnels were dug under the site of the present Scottish National Gallery. Naming the station after one of Sir Walter Scott's novels was no comfort. One of the finest ancient cities in Europe was divided by a pit of smoke and noise. It is as if the Great Western railway in London had come crashing south from Paddington, across Hyde Park and Green Park to reach Charing Cross.

The railway never turned this bullying presence to advantage. Its face to the city was always hesitant and apologetic. What claims to be the largest station in Britain after London's Waterloo (19 or 21 platforms, depending on definition) remains squeezed uncomfortably between two hillsides, so that all we see from outside is a rolling field of glass roof under Waverley Bridge. More impressive is the edifice of the 1902 North British (now Balmoral) Hotel towering over it. In a Scottish baronial style and among the most majestic of railway company hotels, it has all the bravado the station lacks. Its clock is still set three minutes fast to help passengers catch their trains on time.

opposite: Aviemore: a touch of Tibet in the Highlands
above: A station dividing a city

The station concourse is reached down steps, escalators and ramps from Princes Street, Market Street and Waverley Bridge. The resulting maze of galleries and walkways gives the approach to Waverley a mildly Piranesian touch. Restoration of the honey-coloured stone and painting of the shed roof has lifted much of the former gloom. The best is being made of a bad job.

The most distinguished feature of the station remains its only real work of architecture, the central waiting-hall and surrounding offices. This is in a solid baroque revival by the North British company engineer, James Bell, as part of the final 1892 rebuilding of the station. The interior of the hall has a grand domed skylight, surrounded by side-lights adorned with swags and foliage, all very late-Victorian. In the centre of Bell's composition was the actual ticket office, a free-standing wooden edifice in Queen Anne style with pilasters and a balustraded cornice.

During the 1970s Devastation (see p. 24), British Rail decided to cut off Waverley's nose to spite its face. In the cause of modernisation, it demolished Bell's ticket office in favour of, successively, a travel centre, a shopping kiosk and then a Costa Coffee stall. This was removed, and in its place is now nothing but rows of metal seats. Walter Scott himself could not tell a grimmer saga.

One day, the solution for Waverley is for the railway to build a raft and create over it a park or a piazza, extending the restored fragment of Princes Street Gardens as public space. It would atone for past wrongs and give the denizens of this great city somewhere central in which to breathe.

GLASGOW CENTRAL
★ ★ ★ ★ ★

Edinburgh may be the finer city, but Glasgow takes pride of place for stations. St Enoch's has gone and Queen Street is decent enough, but Central is custodian of the city's soul. For over a century, its sweeping roof has looked down on tear-stained moments of expatriate departure, whether via the docks to the outside world, or to seek fame and fortune south in England.

Central began life as replacement for a typical post-Mania mess of rival termini, cramped by the closeness of the River Clyde. Not until 1879 could the Caledonian Railway build a new bridge and station on the present site, and not until 1900 could something approaching the present capacity be reached, with a new bridge, platforms and concourse planned by Donald Matheson as chief engineer and James Miller as architect (see p. 291).

There is a vigorous, rather American feel to this part of the city, with a grid of cavernous streets and beefy Victorian buildings. The station lacks an impressive frontage, relying on the façade of the old company hotel, the Grand Central, in Gordon Street. It was built by Robert Anderson in 1884 in a style I have found described as Scottish 17th-century, Queen Anne, Italianate or even Swedish. It looks late romanesque to me. Its most distinctive feature is a lovely ironwork porte cochère, made by the cathedral screen designer Skidmore of Coventry. Arrangements for traffic movement are huddled and chaotic.

Where the station crosses Argyle Street is the 'Hielanman's Umbrella' (Highlandman's bridge) where

opposite: Miller's conservatory bridge over the 'Hielanman's Umbrella'

GLASGOW CENTRAL STATION

Gaelic-speaking migrants from the north would once congregate and exchange news out of the rain. The bridge is like a whale, beached across the street, except for Miller's ability to lighten a blank wall with stylish, classically detailed and arched windows. They offer a glimpse of the interior roof and make the bridge seem almost lightweight.

Central's interior is dramatic. Matheson's 1905 expansion turned the previous train shed into a concourse and then extended over his platforms what is reputedly the largest glazed roof in the world. The shallow-arched steel trusses seem to vanish into the distance, divided by fan-shaped lunettes. Modernisation in 1998 and subsequently has reglazed the roofs and laid white terrazzo tiles on the floor, turning what was a dark, deeply atmospheric, place into one of uplifting brightness.

Since trains had to enter at first-floor level to get over the Clyde bridge, passengers must reach the concourse up a slope from Gordon Street, which means emerging from darkness into light. A feature of Matheson's (or Miller's) planning was spatial curvature. Matheson, who had studied crowd control in America, wrote of 'the tendency of a stream of people to spread out like flowing water and travel along the line of least resistance'.

The station walls are flanked by curved façades, billowing forward in dark wood panelling, fronting ticket offices, shops and cafés. The original oval ticket office, known as the Torpedo Building, is now a restaurant, a two-storey structure in Queen Anne style, once festooned with train information placards

The 'moderne' gates at the Union Street entrance

frantically changed by hand. Two favourite concourse meeting points were traditionally 'under the clock' or 'by the shell', the latter a howitzer shell used for charity donations; this has now sadly been moved into a corner to prevent people stumbling over it.

Miller's mastery in the handling of walls is demonstrated on the Hope Street side, where his flanking windows march firmly down the platforms and out over the city. They reach a final classical gateway – beyond the reach of all but the most inquisitive passengers – welcoming trains, if not people, to the station. The windows are surmounted by semi-circular panes with Venetian tracery, as in a smart conservatory.

The station has an extensive vaulted undercroft which, along with parts of the roof, is open to guided tours. When the first 100 tickets went on sale in 2013, they were swamped with a reported 83,500 applications. Such is the appeal of today's railway station.

The Torpedo Building

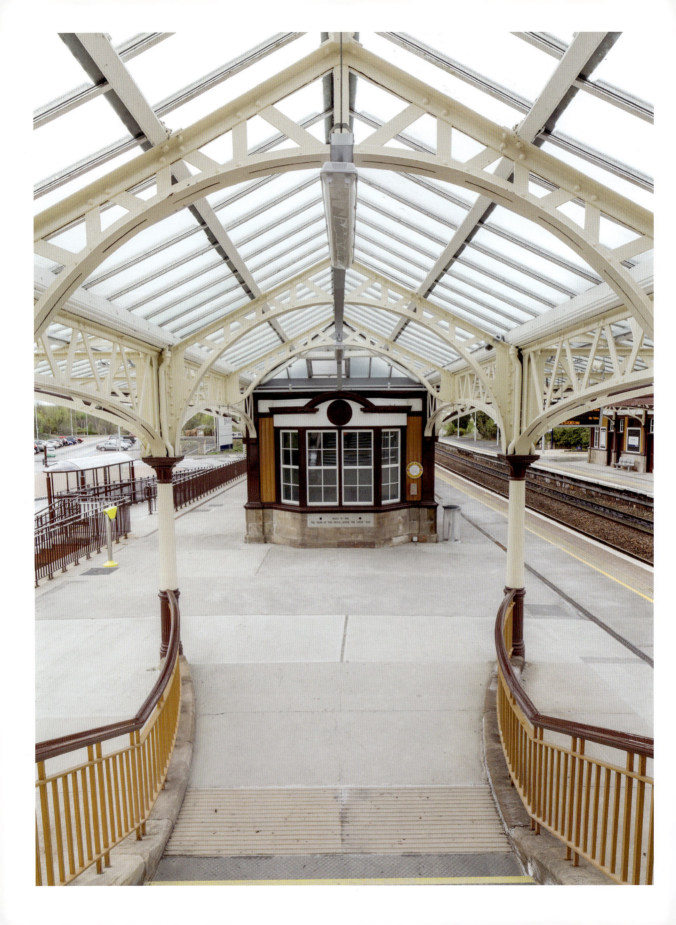

GLENEAGLES
★ ★

The station was built to serve Scotland's most celebrated hotel and golf course. It was drastically restored in 2014 when the course hosted the Ryder Cup. Although now deserted much of the time, it still has an atmosphere of expecting the arrival of someone more important than oneself. Rock gardens are trim. Rhododendron and conifers are smartly on parade, and the surrounding hills have been kept free of Scotland's pestilential wind turbines. Even the birds seem to be singing in unison. It is smart but, on my visits, eerily empty. The waiting-room merely lists the station's passing VIPs.

The hotel was well placed at Auchterarder, south of Perth, with trains from Glasgow and Edinburgh. It was built in 1919 and opened in 1924 by the Caledonian's golf-loving manager, Donald Matheson, who commissioned James Miller (see p. 291) to design and rebuild the station. The latter decayed over the years as guests preferred to arrive by car. Eventually it became an unmanned halt, its rooms boarded up and its platforms dejected. It was rescued first for the G8 Summit in 2005 and then, comprehensively, for the Ryder Cup. A small museum displaying the history of Scotland was installed in 2015.

The station has Miller's characteristic touches. Deep canopies swoop over wood-panelled pavilions with Queen Anne-style windows, some with little baroque pediments over them. The most prominent feature is the twin towers over each end of the footbridge, with decorous bow windows looking down the track. These are splendid, like genteel gatehouses guarding the approach. The interior staircase from the platform up to the bridge is worthy of grand opera. The whole ensemble is vividly painted in what Network Rail tell me are the Caledonian colours of 'burnt umber, cinnamon and cream'.

GLENFINNAN
★

The West Highland line's extension from Fort William to Mallaig was driven through wild country across challenging contours. It was commercially bold, hoping to open up the west-coast fishing industry to Lowland markets. More remarkable is that these lines survived Beeching and other closures and are still running today. Equally impressive is the care shown in the upkeep of stations which cannot have many customers.

Glenfinnan sits high on a hillside looking down Loch Shiel. It is just north of the monument to Bonnie Prince Charlie, who here raised the standard of his abortive rebellion in 1745. The station has acquired celebrity for its careful conservation and its railway museum, which tells the dramatic story of the building of the line at the turn of the 20th century. Its collection includes old posters of Highland railways. A café occupies a disused railway carriage in a siding, with next to it a sleeping car and a ferocious-looking railway snow plough. The old signal-box has been restored.

The station of 1901 is in James Miller's standard chalet style, peculiarly handsome with overhanging eaves, bay windows and glazed wind screens. The surrounding moorland spills gorse and rhododendron onto the platforms, as if determined to overwhelm the intruder and recover the land for nature. Buried in the gorse is a listed water tank, filled from a burn and shared with a local hotel.

Glenfinnan is the base for walks into Glen Shiel, whose spectacular 21-span viaduct features in four Harry Potter films. It is rare in being the first to be built of (unsightly) poured concrete, the local stone being too hard to be easily worked. With the rest of the line, the contractor was Robert 'Concrete Bob' McAlpine, whose family went on to even greater

opposite: Gleneagles goes grand opera
pages 300–301: Glenfinnan's moorland glory

things. To Gordon Biddle, it is the finest viaduct in Scotland. The view from it over Loch Shiel is magnificent.

PERTH
★ ★ ★

This is a glorious mess of a station, much battered by history and not yet back to its old self. For years, Queen Victoria's patronage of Balmoral led to a Highland holiday boom, with Perth as the 'gateway' station, where trains were reconfigured for the climb over the Grampian mountains towards Inverness. From the start, it was a joint station for the Caledonian, North British and Highland railways. One northbound train was recorded as displaying eight different liveries 'of 37 coaches, saloons, horse boxes and luggage vans . . . an irregular caravan'. It was drawn by two engines. The station was even honoured with an 1895 painting by George Earl: *Coming South, Perth Station* (see pp. 288–9). There is a complementary one of *Going North, King's Cross* (1893). The Perth painting depicts wealthy travellers surrounded by a crush of servants, dogs and game, returning from a Highlands holiday. Perth was also the point of departure for the county's overnight strawberry and raspberry crop, famously picked one day and on London dinner tables the next.

The joint nature of the station, opened in 1848, was reflected in a spacious building by the London architect Sir William Tite. He employed a neo-Tudor design (which he called gothic) similar to his contemporary station at Carlisle (see p. 207). This building survives, complete with its octagonal tower, but is surrounded and obscured by major expansion in 1885. The Tite building is now an island enveloped by platforms, canopies and the main shed roof.

Today's entrance is an insipid 1960s building, looking across a forecourt at the former Station Hotel. Opened in 1891, its style might be termed Flemish baronial, splendidly adorned with stepped gables. It was here that Queen Victoria broke her journey to and from Balmoral. Even from the forecourt, we can sense Perth's grandeur. The ridge-and-furrow shed roof rises behind what would have been Tite's rear wall, with the same 'repeated greenhouse' vents as at Carlisle. Below is a charming triple-arched gothic loggia no longer in use.

Inside, the scale of the building is immediately apparent. A grand shed covers the main platforms, with the Tite range facing us across the tracks and a further platform beyond. The building once contained the offices of at least four railway companies. Halfway down the façade is a bay window of what appears to be an office but was the old signal-box within the building, giving staff a view up and down the platform. The bay window is replicated on the platform behind. Both are crowned by spectacular neo-Tudor railway clocks. The woodwork is in Caledonian brown and cream. Over the far platform is a lovely arched canopy, with fan-shaped trusses and lacy valances, like those at Stirling.

There is an element of lost glory to these nowadays under-employed platforms. The most active part of the station is the Dundee branch curving away to the east, conspicuously painted in ScotRail dark blue. The platforms are crossed within the shed by two spacious lattice footbridges, much polluted by pigeons. These have been supplemented by a new 'health and safety' bridge outside the shed, which was nominated for a 'carbuncle award' for ugliness in 2015. As Perth emerges as one of Scotland's liveliest towns, its station badly needs restoration and re-use.

opposite: Signal-box as office as clock

PITLOCHRY

★

Dating from 1863, Pitlochry was rebuilt in 1890 to meet a wave of visitors who arrived after Queen Victoria's doctor declared its air peculiarly healthy. It offers a contrast in Highland Railway architecture. On the up platform is a miniature baronial villa in stone, on the down platform is a painted wooden chalet. Each seems determined to outdo the other in picturesque charm.

The villa is almost a pastiche. A single-storey U-shaped building with two gabled wings encloses a covered veranda facing the platform. One wing has a Venetian window with a drinking fountain in the central panel, the other an outsized bay window. The gables are stepped, with small pyramids on each step. The chimneys are variegated. An extension repeats the stepped-gable theme.

This building houses Pitlochry's justly celebrated second-hand bookshop, not the usual platform booth, but a full-sized store. On the platform outside is a lovely iron fountain with a ferocious heron on top. It is accompanied by a modern statue of a porter and a whisky barrel shaped into a locomotive, filled with some of Pitlochry's conspicuous flowers.

Across a decorative lattice-panelled footbridge is the chalet. It could hardly be more different. It is attributed to William Roberts, designer of Aviemore (see p. 292), which it resembles. Repainted in ScotRail blue, it has a bell-shaped roof and terracotta ridge decoration. The bookshop across the tracks is complemented with an art gallery. This is an admirable community station, beautifully maintained.

RANNOCH

★

Desolate, savage, brooding, rain-swept Rannoch Moor is reputedly the largest uninhabited wilderness in the British Isles, covering some fifty square miles south of the Great Glen. It is certainly a wild place even in the most clement of weathers. When I first visited it, I imagined its only customers were Macbeth's witches, on a trip into Fort William to stock up on eye of newt. Since then, a small car park has appeared, enabling neighbouring Corrour station to the north (of *Trainspotting* fame) to claim Britain's 'most isolated' station status. Rannoch is chiefly a base for exceptionally hardy hill-walkers.

The West Highland Railway was attracted to the moor by local landowners eager to open it up for stalking and shooting, but construction proved desperately hard, the tracks having to be laid on huge bundles of brushwood and imported earth, which kept sinking into the bog. The manager during the building, James Renton, had such faith in the project that he paid the workers out of his own pocket when bankruptcy threatened. A head sculpted in relief at the end of the platform honours his commitment.

The station is in the standard James Miller chalet-style of most of the West Highland's halts. It has a concave roof, boldly hipped, with wood-panelled walls and half-timbered gables. End screens keep out some of the wind, and bay windows brighten the interior. The building now shelters a 'visitor centre' and tea-room, deceptively genteel, given the surroundings. Golden eagles can be seen from outside.

above: Pitlochry's study in styles
opposite: Miller's Rannoch tames the wilds

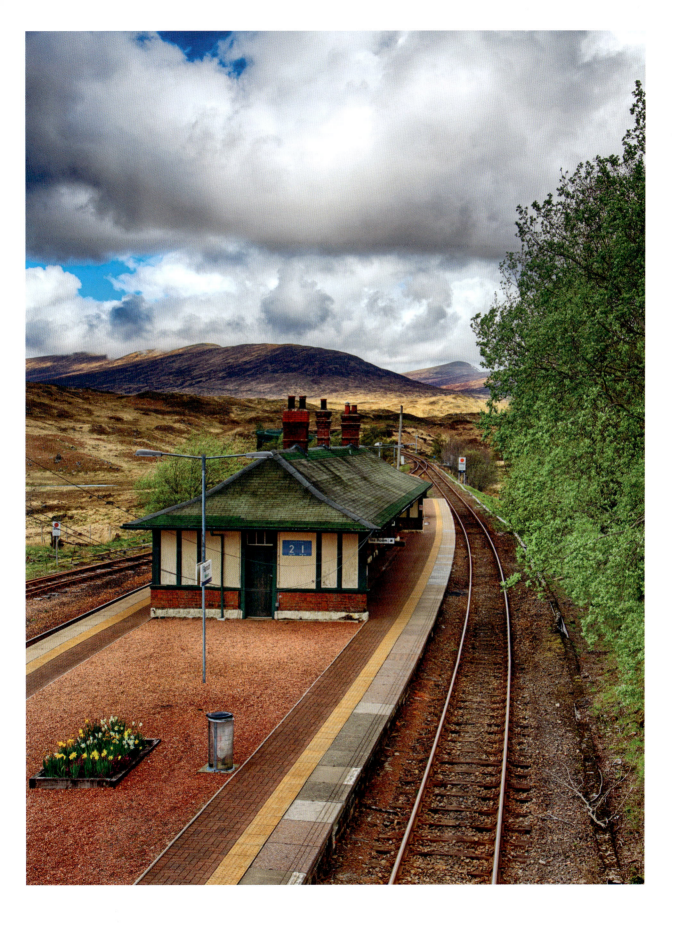

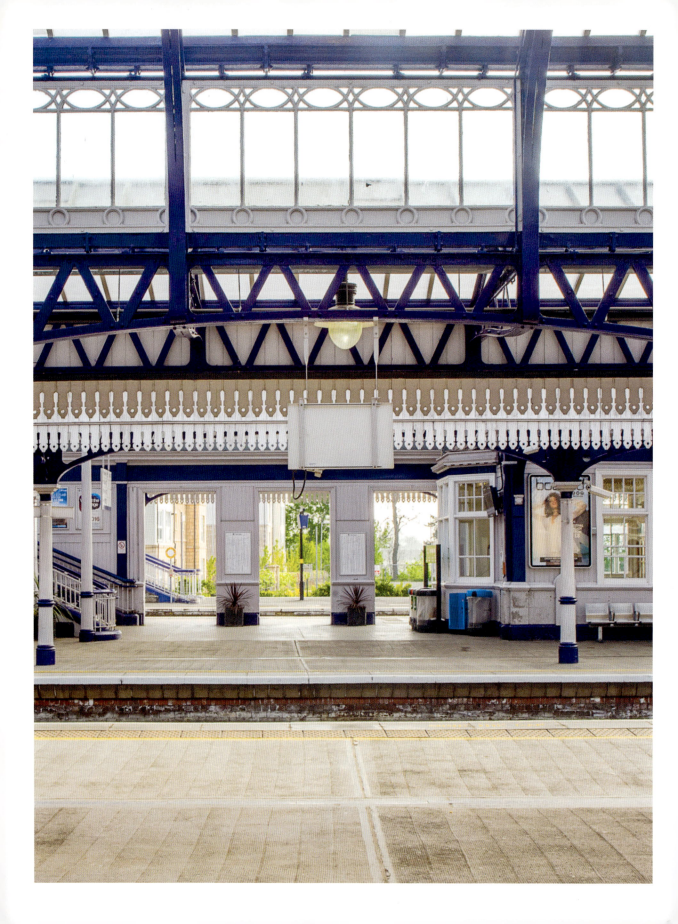

STIRLING

★ ★ ★

Competition is fierce between Perth and Stirling as both the ancient capital of Scotland and gateway to the Highlands. Its commanding rock and castle set above the River Forth made it a prominent seat of Scotland's kings. The station is a more modest affair, overlooking nothing more spectacular than the inner by-pass. At first, it has the appearance of an abandoned hunting lodge, single-storey with three crow-stepped gables and battlements in dark stone. It might be crying out for the castle on the hill to come down and rescue it from the swirling traffic.

The interior is more self-confident. The original was built by the Caledonian Railway in 1848, but this was rebuilt by James Miller in 1915, ten years after Wemyss Bay (see p. 309) and proof that Wemyss was no fluke. He again deploys circular structures and façades to give his interior a sense of flow. Nothing is at rest. A Miller station is a place of transition. As at Wemyss, there is a central, semi-circular ticket office surmounted by radial trusses that spread umbrella-like over the platforms. The bookstall and waiting-room also have curved fronts – a closer parallel to Miller's Glasgow Central (see p. 294) – after which the eye is led easily up the broad staircase to the footbridge.

The station is roofed with three ridge-and-furrow canopies, reglazed in 2016, and illuminating Miller's ironwork and panelled platform buildings. The canopies carry the most decorative of valances, which create a thrilling pattern when seen through to the far platforms. Stirling's paintwork is in ScotRail blue and white, ideally suited to its conservatory atmosphere.

This atmosphere is enhanced by the long-established custodianship of Stirling's flowers by the local Rotary Club. If the cascades of mildly municipal blooms can appear over-eager, there is no complaining about the effect. Greenery and colour spill from every corner, a delight to the eye and an honour to Miller's respect for light and space.

On the footbridge is a memorial to the inter-war film director, John Grierson, a son of Stirling. He was founder of the British documentary film movement, which saw the production of the General Post Office's railway epic, *The Night Mail* (see p. 35). His striking bust is curiously guarded by plastic ducks.

opposite: **Stirling's filigree valances**
page 308: **Wemyss Bay: Clydeside elegiac**

WEMYSS BAY

★ ★ ★ ★ ★

This is one of the few stations that, in my opinion, qualify as a coherent work of art. It is the masterpiece of the dominant personality of Scottish railway architecture, James Miller (see p. 291). At the time of its construction, in 1903, he had left the employ of the Caledonian Railway and was setting up his own business, but he remained close to the company and its engineer, Donald Matheson. The replacement of an earlier utilitarian station was a joint project by both men, engineer and architect.

The resort was at the up-market end of the line from Glasgow, but its importance lay in its position opposite the Isle of Bute, harbour for the highly competitive ferries to Rothesay. Their patronage by Glasgow holiday-makers surged at the turn of the century and the company needed a station designed to minimise the time passengers had to spend exposed to the wind and rain of the Firth of Clyde as they passed from train to ferry. Matheson had just returned from America where he had been fascinated by the attention paid to the movement of large crowds (see p. 296).

Wemyss Bay was thus an exercise in ergonomic architecture. The challenge was to shift a trainload of passengers from train to ferry in just five minutes. They were to pass on foot from the curved platforms down a covered way to the pier and the ferries, while their luggage was taken on trolleys by a separate route, as in a modern airport. Miller's building apparently met this specification, yet it was science encased in art.

The style is impossible to classify, variously called domestic revival, Queen Anne, arts-and-crafts and 'chalet'. To me, it also has a touch of Los Angeles Spanish, perhaps under Matheson's American influence. From the outside we see an L-shaped building, with offices in one wing and, in the other, an entrance façade with a prominent clock tower on its corner. Rising from a red sandstone base, the walls are of cream render with sandstone dressings. The red-tiled roof is punctuated with gables of different sizes, as if to maintain balance. These have black-and-white timbering. The clock tower is white and Italianate, with vertical stone strips and a large bellcote on top, giving it the appearance of a pagoda. The whole composition is sunny, warm and welcoming.

None of this prepares us for the interior, reached through an entrance arch with art nouveau ironwork. Miller united concourse and platforms in a visual whole, on a plan that seems to spin like a Catherine wheel. At the hub is a semi-circular ticket office, its windows separated by pilasters and flower pots. Rising from the pilasters are ribs splaying outwards to an encircling apex ridge, like the chapter house of Wells cathedral. The eye is led onwards to the curving roofs, of the platforms in one direction and the ramp down to the pier in another. Since these all bend out of sight, they create a delicious sense of infinity.

The roof is a maze of steel girders and trusses. As Frank Arneil Walker writes in Pevsner, the effect is of 'sinuous skeletal geometries, effulgent with light filtered through filigree roofs'. The building's 'tentacles coil along the rail tracks as platform canopies, and spill onto the pier in a slow-ramping gallery of light'. The way down to the pier is lined with pilasters and panelled windows. At its foot, the gabled ends are crowned outside with two miniature pagodas.

Round the concourse are arranged offices and shops, all fronted by wide Georgian windows behind which we expect to see genteel Glaswegian ladies taking tea. The windows and doorways have sandstone surrounds and are painted in shades of brown and cream, while the roof members overhead are in soft green. Behind one façade are the gallery and bookshop of the admirable Friends of Wemyss Bay Station, who have championed and presided over the building's recent restoration. After the vistas of the concourse outside, it is a calm place to reflect on the surrounding glory.

Wemyss Bay is no longer busy as of old. Yet if not much patronised, it is clearly much loved, indicated by its fresh paint and effervescence of flowers. They burst from every ledge, bowl and urn. What a wonderful send-off for a holiday.

pages 310–11: **Wemyss nocturne**

ACKNOWLEDGEMENTS

Sir John Betjeman features strongly in this book as it was time spent driving him round London in the 1970s that bred in me an early affection for stations (as for churches). His enthusiasm for these places and his eye for the charm of old buildings were infectious. He was almost in tears wandering through the near-derelict Broad Street. I would love to have known his 'hundred best', except that he would never have stopped at a hundred.

Since I have tended to ask everyone I met to suggest a 'best' station, I cannot thank them all. Those whose help I particularly record are Marcus Binney, Simon Bradley, Ann Glen, Julian Glover, Chris Green, David Lewis, Bill McAlpine, Jeremy Musson, John Prideaux, Andy Savage, Peter Saxton and Tony Travers.

Special thanks go to colleagues at the body I founded in 1984, the Railway Heritage Trust, whose current director, Andy Savage, offered many vital corrections to the text, and whose photographer, Paul Childs, supplied many of the pictures. Paul is among the finest recorders of today's railway, in the tradition of the great John Gay. I also thank many others who have helped make this such an enjoyable book to write. They include the Penguin quartet of editor Daniel Crewe, picture researcher Cecilia Mackay, copy editor Jenny Dereham, and publicist Ruth Killick. Others involved were Keith Taylor, Claire Mason, Catriona Hillerton and Mike Davis.

GLOSSARY

aesthetic movement A late 19th-century movement that championed pure beauty and 'art for art's sake', emphasising the visual and sensual qualities of art and design.

art deco a movement concurrent with international modernism in the 1920s. It drew on tradition while celebrating the modern, mechanised world. The name derives from a 1925 Paris exhibition of decorative and industrial art.

art nouveau an international style of architecture, art and applied art, especially the decorative arts, popular between 1890 and 1910. Art nouveau forms are characterised by the use of undulation, like waves, flames or flower stalks.

arts and crafts movement *c.*1870-1914, initiated by the writings of John Ruskin and William Morris, in response to industrialisation and mass production.

awning *see* canopy.

bargeboards a projecting board, typically an ornamental one, fixed to the gable end of a roof to hide the ends of the roof timbers.

baroque a style of European architecture, music and art of the 17th and 18th centuries, characterised by classical symmetry and ornate detail.

blind arcading pattern of arches attached in relief to a surface but with no depth.

Bradshaw a timetable of (especially) British passenger trains compiled by G. Bradshaw (d.1853) between 1839 and 1961.

brutalism a term coined in England in 1954, inspired principally by Le Corbusier, and characterised by abstract shapes and exposed concrete.

bull's-eye window a small circular window.

canopy a shelter in various materials attached to the exterior of a building. Also an awning.

cartouche an ornamentally, usually oval, panel with curling edges, often bearing an inscription.

chamfer a symmetrical sloping surface at an edge or corner.

clerestory an upper storey of a building pierced by rows of windows to let in light.

concourse a covered area in a station usually placed in front of or above the platforms; usually contains the ticket office, waiting-rooms and food outlets.

corbel stone or wood projection in a wall to support a beam or window sill.

cornice lodge or projecting upper part of a classical entablature. Moulding at the top of a wall concealing a join with the ceiling.

cottage orné late-Georgian/Victorian picturesque style, usually involving thatch and gothic windows.

curtilage an area of land attached to a building and forming one enclosure with it.

cut-and-cover evacuation of a tunnel by creating a cutting and then replacing the ground above.

the Devastation term given in this book to the 'modernisation' period, roughly 1960–80, when Britain's railways were drastically reduced in scale, lines closed and stations demolished.

Dutch gable undulating gable with square and curved edges, sometimes terminating in a pediment. A stepped gable has small steps, sometimes called shoulders, up its side coping.

faience a form of earthenware tile with a tin glaze. Often used on station walls in the 19th century, structurally or as cladding.

gauge width of rails on a track, divided into standard gauge and Brunel's Great Western broad gauge, which survived into the 1890s. A temporary 'shared gauge' involved laying a third rail inside the broad gauge so its tracks could be used by axles of both gauges.

Grouping the consequence of the 1921 Railways Act, which in 1923 grouped some 120 Victorian railway companies into four monopolies, the Southern, the London, Midland & Scottish, the London & North Eastern and the Great Western. They became regions under British Railways in 1948.

halt a small, unstaffed station with few or no buildings. Sometimes, there are request stops.

heritage railways railways revived, usually from previously closed lines, and run by volunteers mostly as charitable enterprises. Typically Victorian in character and specialising in steam traction. They are specifically not part of the national rail network. There are now some 120 such ventures.

island platform station layout where a single platform is positioned between two tracks within a railway station, usually accessed by a footbridge.

Italianate general term applied to 'railway style', echoing the classical architecture of the Regency. Popular to give a sense of dignity to early railway stations.

the Mania term commonly applied to the stock market bubble of 1843–7. This fuelled the second railway-building boom and created the often chaotic pattern of lines and stations that survives to this day.

modern movement architecture that emerged between the two world wars in vigorous reaction to the revivalism of the Victorian/Edwardian eras. Typically functional, rectilinear and stripped of adornment. Variations, some with decorative lapses, were labelled moderne, streamline and art deco.

piano nobile the main floor of an Italian (Renaissance or later) palace, containing the reception rooms.

platforms: up & down up was to London or sometimes the rail company's headquarters. Where there were two tracks/platforms, up was usually but not always on the left.

porte cochère architectural feature attached to the front of a station, big enough for wheeled vehicles to pass through.

Pullman luxury carriages imported from America (thus dubbed cars) in 1874, some including sleeping berths. Never popular, they lived on as the *Brighton Belle* until 1972. There are plans to revive them.

railway time Greenwich mean-time. Since church clocks nationwide were timed to local (sunrise) time, railway time had to be enforced nationwide to avoid the need for time zones. Initially unpopular.

roof: mansard double-pitched roof whose upper slope is more shallow than its lower one. A **hipped roof** is one with the top of the side gable replaced by a triangular sloping plane.

ridge-and-furrow roof usually a concourse or platform canopy, of successive ridges with drainage valleys in between. Usually glazed to admit light.

screen & arch screen elevated end of a shed roof, usually semi-circular or triangular, and glazed; also called a lunette.

semaphore signals a signalling apparatus of a post with a movable arm or arms, lanterns, for use by railways, day or night.

semi-conoid arches a cone-shaped roof laid on its side to form a semi-cone.

shed or **train shed** an overall station roof together with its side walls, once widespread but now generally confined to large stations and usually made from iron and glass. Even the grandest such roofs are referred to as sheds.

siding a short track at the side of, and opening on to, a railway line, used for shunting engines.

spandrel space above the curve of an arch, separating it from an upright or the next arch, roughly triangular.

strapwork strap or ribbon-like decorative scrolls found in Elizabethan or Jacobean design.

terminus station at the end of a railway line.

terrazzo a flooring finish of marble chips with cement and laid *in situ*; the surface is then ground and polished.

tie bar the main horizontal member of a roof to prevent the walls from spreading. Similar to truss and usually supporting ribs.

undercroft space beneath the main floor of a station, used for storage and sometimes shops.

valance decorative vertical border, usually of wood, to platform canopies. Sometimes cut into elaborate fretwork.

BIBLIOGRAPHY

Authors whose books I have used most heavily are listed below. I have not listed innumerable works on individual stations, nor can I list the hundreds of books that deal primarily with railways rather than stations.

Barman, Christian: *An Introduction to Railway Architecture*, 1950

Bennett, David: *The Jubilee Line Extension*, 2004

Betjeman, John, and John Gay: *London's Historic Railway Stations,* 1978, 2001

Biddle, Gordon: *Britain's Historic Railway Buildings*, 2003, rev. 2011

Great Railway Stations of Britain, 1986
Victorian Stations, 1973

with O. S. Nock: *The Railway Heritage of Britain*, 1983

Binney, Marcus: *Great Railway Stations of Europe*, 1984

and David Pearce (eds.): *Railway Architecture*, 1979

Bowers, Michael: *Railway Styles in Building*, 1975

Bowness, David, with Oliver Green and Sam Mullins: *Underground*, 2012

Bradley, Simon: *The Railways*, 2015

Crook, J. Mordaunt: *The Dilemma of Style*, 1987

Dow, Andrew: *Dictionary of Railway Quotations*, 2006

Fawcett, Bill: *Railway Architecture*, 2015

Freeman, Michael: *Railways and the Victorian Imagination*, 1999

Garnett, Andrew: *Steel Wheels*, 2005

Glancey, Jonathan: *John Betjeman on Trains*, 2006

Gourvish, Terry: *British Rail 1974–1997*, 2002

Jackson, Alan: *London's Termini*, 1969

Judt, Tony, 'Glory of the Rails', *New York Review of Books,* 23.12.2010 and 13.1.2011

Kellett, John R.: *The Impact of Railways on Victorian Cities*, 1969

Legg, Stuart, ed: *The Railway Book: An Anthology*, 1988

Lloyd, Roger: *The Fascination of Railways*, 1951

Loudon, John Claudius: *An Encyclopaedia of Cottage, Farm and Villa Architecture*, 1833

Meeks, Carroll L. V.: *The Railroad Station*, 1956

Menear, Laurence: *London's Underground Stations*, 1983

Minnis, John: *Britain's Lost Railways*, 2011

Parissien, Steven: *Station to Station*, 1997
The English Railway Station, 2014

Richards, Jeffrey, and John M. Mackenzie: *The Railway Station: a Social History*, 2012

SAVE (ed. Marcus Binney): *Off the Rails*, 1977

Simmons, Jack: *The Railways of Britain*, 1986
The Victorian Railway, 1991

Wills, Dixe: *Tiny Stations,* 2014

Wolmar, Christian: *The Subterranean Railway*, 2004

PHOTOGRAPHIC CREDITS

x Bridgeman Images (Dennis Gilbert)
4–5 Getty Images (SSPL)
8 Getty Images (SSPL)
13 (a) Getty Images (SSPL)
13 (b) Railway & Canal Historical Society, Jeoffry Spence Collection
13 (c) © Historic England Archive
16–17 Bridgeman Images (Royal Holloway, University of London)
21 Getty Images (SSPL)
24 © Punch Limited
26 David Burrows/Blue Pelican
36 Alamy (Ange)
41 Alamy (Tim Gainey)
45 (a) CRJennings.com
45 (b) Nigel Regden/Re-Format
48–9 Bridgeman Images (Museum of London)
52–3 Alamy (Archimage)
54–5 VIEW Pictures (© Hufton + Crow)
57 Alamy (Jon Ratcliffe)
59 Railway Heritage Trust
60 Bridgeman Images (Mark Fiennes)
61 Wikimedia Commons
63 Getty Images (Alberto Toledano)
65 Getty Images (Simon Dawson)
67 Getty Images (Oli Scarff)
68–9 Alamy (Brian Anthony)
70 Alamy (Johnny Jones)
72–3 Paul Childs/Railway Heritage Trust Construction Photography
74 (© Rail Photo)
76 Alamy (Avpics)
77 Alamy (Brian Anthony)
78 Getty Images (SSPL)
79 Construction Photography (© Rail Photo)
80–81 Alamy (Arcaid)
83 Alamy (Exflow)
84–5 Bridgeman Images (Yale Center for British Art, Paul Mellon Collection)
89 Getty Images (Maico Presente)
91 © Richard D. Allen
92 Paul Childs/Railway Heritage Trust
94–5 © Edwin Jones
96 CRJennings.com
97 CRJennings.com
98 Transport for London/Mike Garnett
99 © Edwin Jones
100 Alamy (Stockimo)
102–3 James Beard
105 VIEW Pictures (© Dennis Gilbert)
106 Paul Childs/ Railway Heritage Trust
108–9 Getty Images (Howard Kingsnorth)
110–11 Getty Images (SSPL)
114–15 Paul Childs/ Railway Heritage Trust
116 Michael Turnbull
118–19 Alamy (Janzig England)
120–21 Railway Heritage Trust
122 Colin Smith
124 Amanda Russell
125 Rex Shutterstock
126 Martin Horne
127 Roger Marks
128–9 Alamy (Greg Balfour Evans)
130 Paul Childs/ Railway Heritage Trust
131 Wikimedia Commons
132–3 Science & Society Picture Library/NRM
136 Alamy (Alex Ramsay)
137 Alamy (MSP Travel)

INDEX

Main entries are in bold
Entries refer to stations unless specified otherwise
London termini are under London

Index

Index

Index

Index